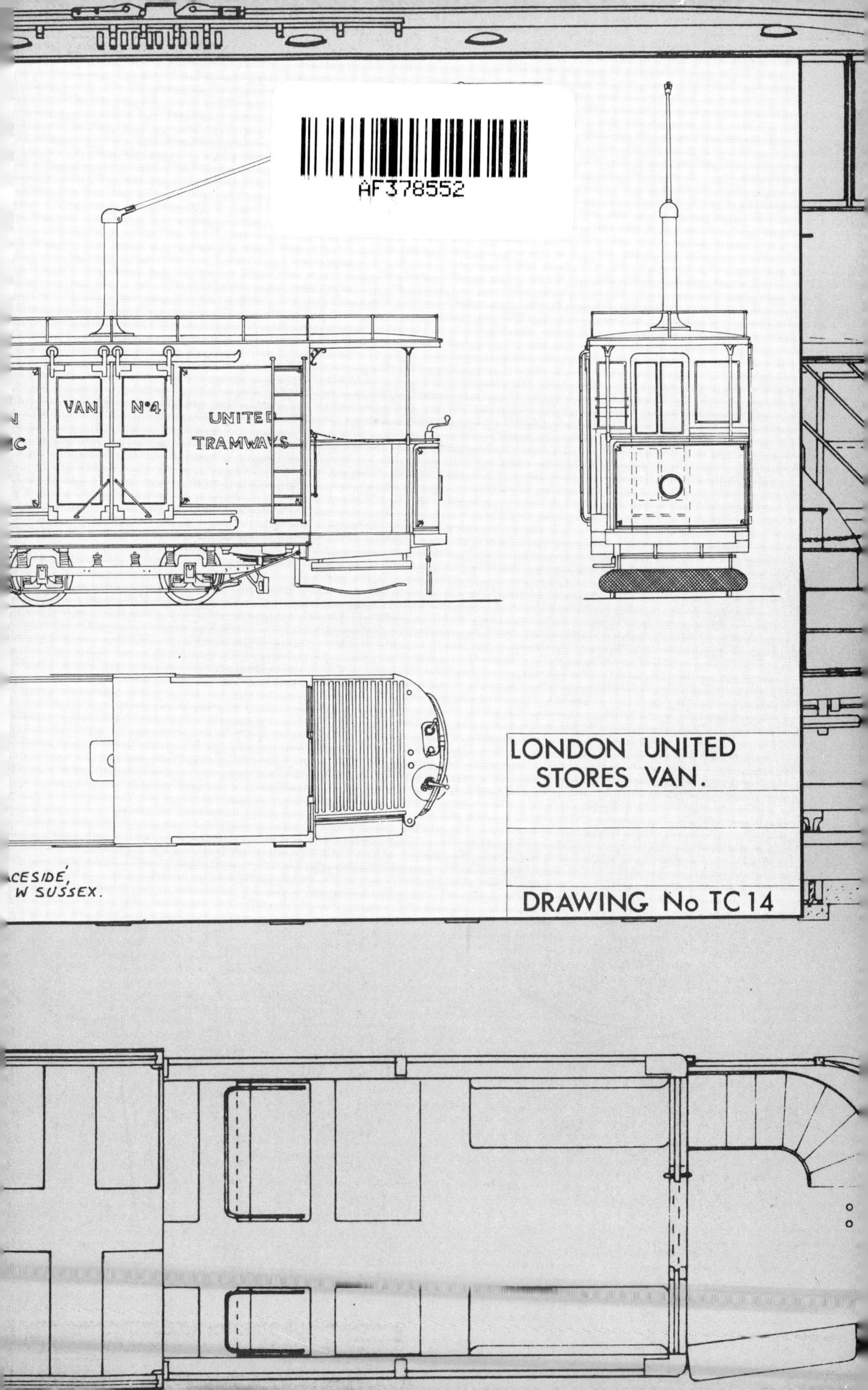

AF378552
VAN N°4
UNITED TRAMWAYS
LONDON UNITED
STORES VAN.
DRAWING No TC 14
ACESIDE,
W SUSSEX.

LONDON'S TRAMWAYS

their history & how to model them

David Voice

Patrick Stephens, Wellingborough

First published in 1985

British Library Cataloguing in Publication Data

Voice, David
    London's tramways: their history and how
    to model them.
    1. Street-railroads—England—London
    I. Title
    625'.66'09421   TF757

    ISBN 0-85059-668-8

*Patrick Stephens Limited is part of the
Thorsons Publishing Group.*

Photoset in 10 on 11pt Times by
MJL Typesetting, Hitchin, Herts.
Printed in Great Britain on 115 gsm Fineblade
coated cartridge, and bound, by
The Garden City Press, Letchworth, Herts,
for the publishers, Patrick Stephens Limited,
Denington Estate, Wellingborough, Northants,
NN8 2QD, England

Contents

Introduction

At the time I wrote *Tram and Tramway Modelling* there had been an ever increasing number of people taking up the hobby of tram modelling. When the book was published it received an encouraging response from critics and readers alike. Since then even more have been prompted to join in the hobby. This has been reflected in the large number of tramway modelling articles that have been appearing in the model railway press and also in the increase in the number of tram kits available. Particularly heartening has been the introduction of kits in moulded plastic by no less than two manufacturers. This has provided an inexpensive method of building very good models. The range of white metal kits has also increased, covering even more prototype tramcars. Indeed there are 34 tramcar kits of British trams now in production and there is promise of yet more.

Perhaps the question that people have most asked has been to enquire about the possibility of a follow-up. Well, I am not sure how serious they were, but it did give me encouragement to develop an idea that had been in my mind for a while. Modelling any prototype must start with some exploration into the real thing. When it comes to tramways the published works seem to fall into two camps. There is the brief résumé, often accompanying a pictorial look at the system(s), giving little information, but with those all important photographs. The other type is the detailed history, usually the culmination of years of research. As important as these books all are, they are not written with the modeller in mind. Those facts that the modeller needs are often tucked away in the midst of quite different material, or most frustratingly of all, omitted. So I thought I would take a system and examine it from the modeller's point of view. Thus the aspects important to modelling have been collected together with suggestions on modelling particular types of car with the various designs in which it ran. I have also given detailed descriptions of tramcars that I have modelled for this book, to show the various techniques and how an unpromising kit can be converted into a scale model of a completely different car.

In picking the system to explore I turned to the trams that I was born and bred with, those of London. Although I can only remember the last years of the system, I have had an interest in the whole development from the inauspicious start with George Train to the current proposals for a modern tramway type system in the Docklands. In writing this book I have covered all of the tramways in the London area, although I must admit I had not completely realised the size of that system, and my task. The book looks at the 24 horse, steam and cable companies, followed by the 16 electric systems which had no less than 3,918 passenger trams with 104 types or classes and each type with a variety of modifications; and also 86 works cars. As if this were not enough there was a multitude of liveries, with changes, variations and experiments. More than enough for any modeller.

Covering so much in one book is an impossible task for one person. I have needed the help of many people, all of whom have been extremely generous in giving their time, information and photographs. There is one who must be singled out. Colin Withey has given incomparable assistance. He has not only given full access to his enormous knowledge of London tramways and tramway modelling, but he has also read through the manuscript correcting errors and adding much invaluable information. Colin had been Hon Secretary for small scale modelling, for the Tramway and Light Railway Society. Indeed he was the driving force behind the development of 4 mm scale tramway modelling in the 1960s and 1970s. I had the honour to take up his post in the Tramway and Light Railway Society when he was obliged to stand down due to work commitments. Indeed it was through this society that I first met him. Certainly without his help this book would have suffered, if indeed it had ever been written.

I would also like to give my most grateful thanks to the many other people who have given me assistance in compiling this book: Bob Appleton, Birmingham Model Tramcar Group, Mike Bragg, Peter Chatham, Stanley Eades, Richard Elliott, Bill Hands, Bill Haynes, Ian Hodgson, Geoff Kelland, Alan Kirkman, Ann Leedham, London County Council Tramways Trust, London Transport and its Museum, Roger Meadowcroft, David Orchard, A. D. Packer, Martin Pamphilon, Chris Perry, John Prentice, Ralph Price, Terry Russell, John Short, Don Sibley, Jonathan Stooke, Adrian Swain, John Tennent, Len Thomson, Chris Thornburn, Malcolm Till, Tramway and Light Railway Society, Tramway Museum Society, Frank Vescoe, Maurice Walker, David Watkins, Peter White, and Alan Williams.

In addition I have relied heavily on the researches carried out by many other people and appearing in the books listed in Appendix Two. I and everyone interested in London's tramways owe them all a debt of gratitude.

Reserved for special mention is my family. My wife Elaine, the boys Aldous and Thomas, and my mother. I would have been thankful for just the love and encouragement, but I also received very practical help. My mother typed the manuscript and Elaine checked it for grammar and untwisted the more tortuous pieces of text.

David Voice
November 1984

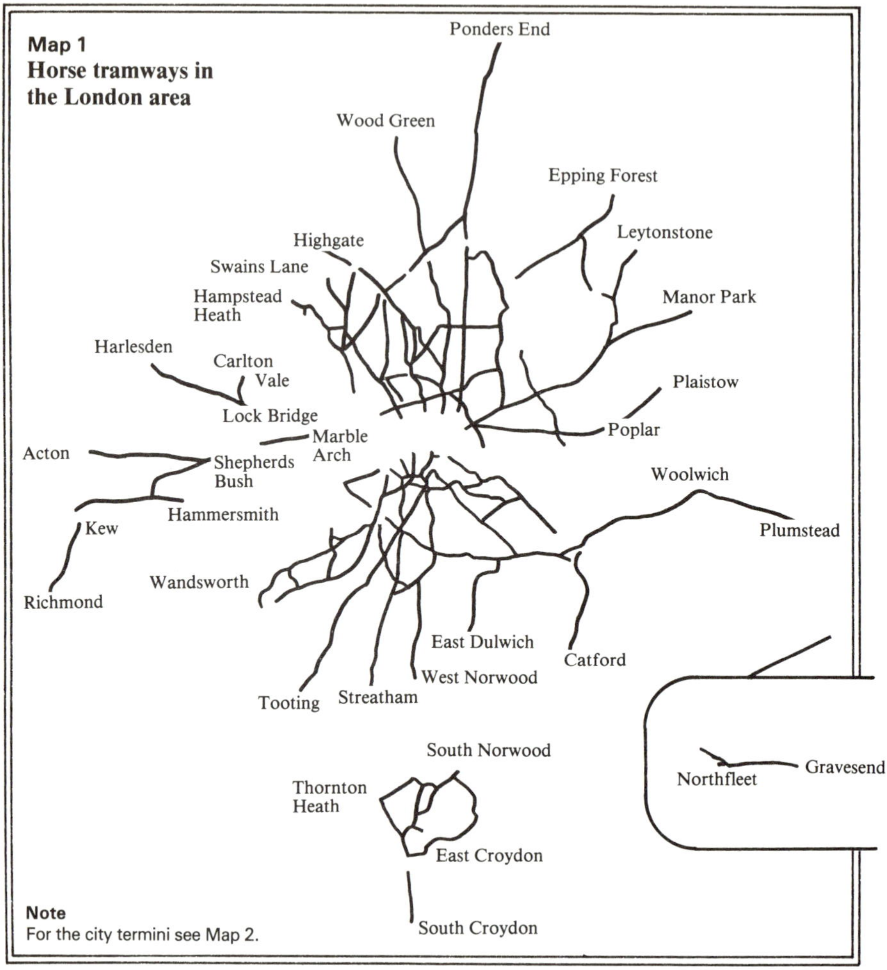
Map 1
Horse tramways in the London area
Ponders End
Wood Green
Epping Forest
Leytonstone
Highgate
Swains Lane
Hampstead Heath
Manor Park
Harlesden
Carlton Vale
Plaistow
Lock Bridge
Poplar
Marble Arch
Acton
Shepherds Bush
Woolwich
Hammersmith
Kew
Plumstead
Wandsworth
Richmond
East Dulwich
Catford
West Norwood
Tooting
Streatham
South Norwood
Thornton Heath
Northfleet
Gravesend
East Croydon
South Croydon
Note
For the city termini see Map 2.

THE PEOPLE.

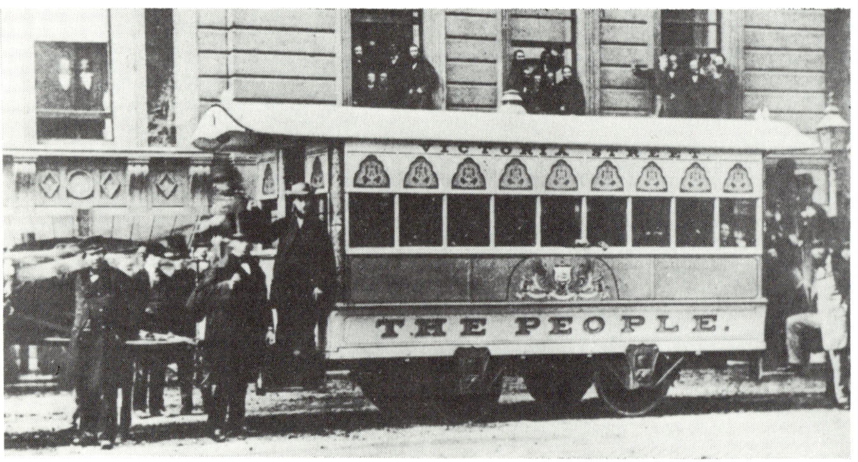

Chapter 1

Horse, steam, cable, battery and gas

The first tramway in London opened on March 23, 1861, and ran from Marble Arch along the Bayswater Road on the north side of Hyde Park and Kensington Gardens to Porchester Terrace. The scheme was developed by George Francis Train, an American who had experience of street tramways in New York, Philadelphia and Paris and who had opened a tramway in Birkenhead in 1860. George Train opened two other London tramways in quick succession. One ran along Victoria Street from Broad Sanctuary, Westminster, to Vauxhall Bridge Road (Victoria Station), whilst the other ran south of the Thames from Westminster Bridge to Kennington Park. Both also began operating in 1861. George Train had seen the tramcar as a means of travel for the wealthy. It is easy for us, with the benefit of over a hundred years of history, to see how wrong this was. In fact the wealthy, with their own carriages, were somewhat displeased to see yet another means of public transport running in their roads. Unfortunately, George Train compounded his error with the choice of a step rail rather than the grooved rail we are so familiar with today. The step rail had a broad running surface with a lip almost one inch high on the inner edge. The tramcar had flat tyre omnibus-type wheels which were guided on the rail by the lip. This type of rail proved to be a nuisance to other road users and it was reported that horse-drawn vehicles crossing the rail at a slight angle had wheels ripped off. The subsequent outcry from very influential people resulted in the Bayswater Road line being closed after a little over six months and the other lines closing in the first half of 1862.

There was a gap of eight years before the horse tram was again seen in the London area. 1870 saw the start of three separate tramways with a total route distance of seven miles. There was evidently a demand for the tramcar for within 25 years there were 15 tram operators working (some having been taken over or amalgamated with other operators). The route distance was 159 miles and there must have been nearly 1,000 tramcars. In looking at this complex period of London tramway history I will group the various undertakings geographically.

Left *George Train's Victoria Street tramcar operated in 1861. Compare this with the photo of the ABS Streetscene model later in the chapter* (D. Voice collection).

North and East

The largest of the horse tram companies was the North Metropolitan Tramways Company. This served the whole of North and East London with just two exceptions. In the most northerly suburbs the North London Tramway Company operated a steam and horse tramway reaching to Wood Green and Edmonton from Finsbury Park and Stamford Hill. In 1891 this operation was taken over by the North Metropolitan Tramways Company who ceased to use steam as a power source in favour of horses. The other tramway was the Lea Bridge, Leyton and Walthamstow Tramway Company. This opened in 1881 and linked the places in its name. It reached north to Epping Forest (The Rising Sun).

As a consequence of the plans to control all the tramways in its jurisdiction the London County Council (LCC) purchased all the lines within its boundary as the option arose. This was the part of the Tramways Act 1870 that gave the right to local authorities to purchase a tramway undertaking in its boundary after a period, usually 21 years. The purchase was made with no compensation for goodwill (sometimes referred to as the scrap price). Thus part of the North Metropolitan and a very small part of the Lea Bridge, Leyton and Walthamstow Tramways were acquired by the LCC in 1896 and 1908 respectively. Between these dates and electrification there were some leasing arrangements. However, by the time the new electric trams were running, all the lines with the LCC boundary were being operated by the council. The remainder of the North Metropolitan Tramways Company became the foundation of the Metropolitan Electric Tramways Company Limited (MET). The Lea Bridge, Leyton and Walthamstow Tramway Company was taken over by Leyton Urban District Council who ran it initially as a horse tramway with the original company cars. Later they electrified the system and the story is taken up in Chapter 5.

Far less well known is the horse tram that plied for a few years (around

Right *Double-deck tramcar from the West Metropolitan Tramways Company* (D. Voice collection).

1870) on the Millwall Extension Railway. It ran from Millwall Junction to the South Dock Station of the West India Docks complex. The tramcar was very similar (if not the actual vehicle) to the one used by George Train on his Victoria Street line. By 1872 the dock companies (and their insurers) were satisfied that steam locomotives could be used provided that spark arresters were fitted. So the horse tram gave way to the steam train.

North-west and West

The North-west, covering the area from Euston to Hampstead Heath and Kentish Town to Kings Cross, was the province of the London Street Tramways. This was the third largest of the horse tram companies. It opened its first line in 1871 and continued expanding its routes until 1889. Since the whole system was within the LCC boundary, the company was acquired by the council in 1896. As the LCC was not ready to operate these lines immediately they were leased to the North Metropolitan Tramways Company until 1906 when the council took over the running. Electrification was carried out between 1909 and 1912.

Just north of this system was the shortest of all the London tramways. The Highgate Hill Cable Tramway was a 3 ft 6 in guage line less than a mile long. It used stationary steam engines to drive a cable which enabled the tramcars to overcome the steep incline of Highgate Hill. The system used was just like the one still used in San Francisco. The company continued cable operations until 1909 when the LCC acquired it and immediately converted it to a 4 ft 8½ in guage electrically operated route. The new electric trams had sufficient power to climb the hill and were able to provide a through service to the City.

Further west was the Harrow Road and Paddington Tramways Company which opened in 1888 with less than three miles of track. This small system remained isolated until incorporated in the MET which extended its tracks from Willesden. Although the other end of the line (to Paddington) was

The Elephant and Castle *in the 1880s with a London Tramways Company tramcar* (London Transport).

inside the LCC boundary, it was isolated from the council system. Therefore, after the council purchased that part of the line, it immediately leased it back to the MET.

The final system in this part of the London area was the West Metropolitan Tramway Company which ran from Shepherds Bush to the north side of Kew Bridge, and from the south side of Kew Bridge to Richmond (trams were not allowed on the bridge itself). The system opened in 1874 and expanded until 1883. The company was taken over by London United Tramways in 1894. They electrified the section north of the Thames in 1901 (thereby being the first to operate electric trams in the London County Council area). The Kew Bridge to Richmond route was the subject of much debate and having had no success at getting permission either to lay lines across the bridge or electrify the route, they closed the horse line completely in 1912.

South and South-west

The largest of the southern systems was the first, other than the third route of George Train's tramways, to start operation south of the Thames. The London Tramways Company opened its first route in 1870 and continued expanding until it reached its full 24 miles by 1892. It laid lines on the major routes from the Thames road bridges. The lines ran to Tooting, Streatham, New Cross and Greenwich. It also had the short cable operated section on Brixton Hill. Since the whole system was inside the council boundary, it was all acquired by the LCC in 1899. The council took over the running of the horse cars while making plans for electrification. Thus, the Westminster to

Tooting route was the first LCC line to be electrified. It was opened in May 1903 by the Prince of Wales (later King George V) who, with his Princess, rode in the special all white tram after paying the ½d fare. Incidentally, the tram covered the entire route of George Train's third line during the first part of its journey.

To the west of the London Tramways was the South London Tramways Company which had lines running from Waterloo and Southwark Bridges to Battersea and Wandsworth. The South London Tramways Company was a relative latecomer to the tramway scene in London. It opened its first line in 1881 and expanded its routes for the next two years. In 1902 the whole system

Above *A London Tramways Company tramcar before entering service. It was photographed in the yard of the factory of John Stephenson Co Ltd, an American tramcar builder from New York (John Stephenson Co Ltd).*

Right *Note the knifeboard seating on the upper deck of this tramcar from the fleet of the Croydon and Norwood Tramways Company (courtesy C. Withey).*

was taken over and run by the LCC. All routes were electrified from 1906 and became part of the integrated LCC operation.

A much smaller system, the London Southern Tramways Company, started operating even later. The first route opened in 1883 and they continued limited expansion until 1887. Both the London Southern and the South London companies give the impression of trying to profit from the tramway boom by laying their lines around the successful London Tramways system. In the case of London Southern, the chosen area was Tulse Hill, Herne Hill and Stockwell to Vauxhall Bridge. Once again the LCC ran the system after acquiring it in 1906.

Much further south and not connected to any other system was the Croydon Tramways Company. The first route opened in 1879 and expansion continued until 1883. In this year the system became the Croydon and Norwood Tramways Company, which was itself acquired by Croydon Corporation in 1900. Electrification began in 1901, two years ahead of the LCC.

South-east

The seven miles of the London, Deptford and Greenwich Tramways Company (originally the Southwark and Deptford Tramways Company) were opened between 1880 and 1882. Again this system was operated by the LCC following a take-over in 1904. Further south was the least fortunate of all the systems. The Peckham and East Dulwich Tramways Company (to become the London, Camberwell and Dulwich Tramways Company) laid its short route in 1885. Arguments prevented any operation until 1895 or 1896. Yet by the time the LCC took it over in 1904 it was almost derelict. Such was the condition that the LCC just closed the system and trams never ran in those roads again.

Another small system, the South Eastern Metropolitan Tramways Company, had just 2½ miles of route, opened in 1890. The purpose seems to have been a means of taking shoppers to and from the shopping centre at Lewisham. The LCC took it over in 1904 and ran the system with horses until electrification.

The next system eastwards was the first 3 ft 6 in gauge horse tramway to be built in the London area. It was the Woolwich and South East London Tramways Company Limited which opened its first line from Plumstead to Woolwich in 1881. In 1882 the line was extended towards London to meet the end of the London Tramway Company line at Greenwich. Of course, direct connection was never possible due to the difference in track gauges. The system was taken over and run by the LCC in 1905. With the introduction of the electric tram, the track was re-laid to 4 ft 8½ in gauge. The first part was re-opened in 1906 with work continuing until 1914 when the LCC completed its link to the eastern boundary at Abbey Wood.

The final system to be considered was the only other 3 ft 6 in gauge horse tramway. It was the Gravesend, Rosherville and Northfleet Tramways Company Limited. This 2¼-mile tramway opened in 1883 with just five tramcars in its fleet. The history of the company was uneventful apart from one interesting interlude in 1889 when conduit experiments were undertaken by the Series Electric Traction Company on a short section at Northfleet. The system was taken over in 1901 by Gravesend and Northfleet Electric

Tramways Limited who ceased the horse tram operation in preparation for electrification.

A summary of the companies and operators in the pre-electric period is shown in Table 1. The livery of the systems and their size in terms of route miles and tramcars is show in Table 2.

Table 1: London's horse, steam and cable tramway companies

Key	Date Opened	Name of system	Date finished	Taken over by
a	1861	George's Train's Tramways	1861-62	Closed
b	1870	North Metropolitan Tramway Co	1896-1912	Various
c	1870	Pimlico, Peckham and Greenwich Tramways Co	1870	e
d	1870	Metropolitan Street Tramways Co	1870	e
e	1870	London Tramways Co Ltd	1899	x
	1871	London Street Tramways	1896	x
f	1874	Southall, Ealing and Shepherds Bush Tram-Rly Co	1881	k
g	1878	Croydon Tramways Co	1883	r
h	1878	North London Suburban Tramways Co	1882	q
i	1879	South London Tramways Co	1902	x
j	1879	Southwark and Deptford Tramways Co	1881	l
k	1881	West Metropolitan Tramways Co Ltd	1894	y
l	1881	London, Deptford and Greenwich Tramway Co	1904	x
m	1881	Woolwich and South East London Tramways Co Ltd	1905	x
n	1881	Lea Bridge, Leyton and Walthamstow Tramways Co	1906	z
o	1882	London Southern Tramways Co	1906	x
p	1882	Peckham and East Dulwich	1884	t
q	1882	North London Tramways Co	1891	b
r	1883	Croydon and Norwood Tramways Co	1900	aa
s	1883	Gravesend, Rosherville and Northfleet Tramways Co Ltd	1902	ab
t	1884	London, Camberwell and Dulwich Tramway Co	1904	x
u	1884	Highgate Hill Tramways Ltd	1909	x
v	1886	Harrow Road and Paddington Tramways Co	1901	ac
w	1888	South Eastern Metropolitan Tramways Co Ltd	1904	x
x	1896	London County Council	1903-15	Electrified

Key continued

y	London United Tramways Co
z	Leyton UDC
aa	Croydon Corporation
ab	Gravesend and Northfleet Electric Tramways Ltd
ac	Metropolitan Electric Tramways Co Ltd

Table 2: London's horse, steam and cable tramways

Tramway	Route mileage	No cars	Livery
North Metropolitan Tramways Co	43(a)	673	White with individual route colours including blue, white, red, brown, yellow, green and light blue
London Tramways Company	24	399 + 40(b)	White with individual route colours including green, chocolate, white and red
London Street Tramways	13	100	White with individual route colours
South London Tramways Company	13	95	White with individual route colours including green, brown and yellow
Croydon Tramways Company	11	18	White with individual route colours including green, blue and red
West Metropolitan Tramways Company	9	49	Yellow and ivory
North London Tramways Company (steam)	8	25(c) + 27	Dark green with white
London, Deptford and Greenwich Tramway Company	7	?	?
London Southern Tramways Company	6	?	?
Woolwich and South East London Tramways Company Limited (3 ft 6 in gauge)	5	33	Blue with primrose
Lea Bridge, Leyton and Walthamstow Tramway Company	5	12	Red with white
George Train's Tramways	3	?	At least one had blue with white (*The People*)
London, Camberwell and Dulwich Tramway Company	3	?	?
Harrow Road and Paddington Tramways Company	3	21	White with red and white with brown
South Eastern Metropolitan Tramways Company	3	?	All white
Gravesend, Rosherville and Northfleet Tramway Company Limited (3 ft 6 in gauge)	2	5	No uniform livery
Highgate Hill Tramway Company (3 ft 6 in gauge, cable)	1	?	?
London County Council	112(d)	(e)	Deep purple lake and primrose, although all white was also used

Notes

Information on these tramways, most of which ceased running around 80 years ago, is rather limited and there are of necessity gaps in the table. In all cases route mileage

(except where noted below) is given as at the greatest extent. Where figures are available over the life of a company for the number of tramcars I have given the largest.
(a) Not including the eight route miles of North London Tramway taken over in 1891.
(b) The extra 40 cars are the cable trams operating on the Kennington Gate to Streatham section.
(c) The 25 vehicles were the steam tram engines and the passenger trailers numbered 27.
(d) Owned but no necessarily operated by the LCC.
(e) The LCC possibly acquired around 650 tramcars for operation, but this is not included in the table as it is an unsubstantiated estimate.

Experiments

The most expensive part of these early tramways was the fleet of horses. Each horse could only work three or four hours a day. Therefore, operators required many more horses than tramcars. For example, in 1875 the London Tramways had 1,200 horses for its 139 tramcars. In contrast the driver and conductor were expected to do a 16-hour day and a seven day week.

In the search for a less expensive form of power, some ideas that seem strange to us were tried out. Perhaps the most unusual was a clockwork tram (it was wound up by a stationary steam engine). Compressed air locomotives were tried on several systems including Woolwich, North Metropolitan and London Street Tramways. Early forms of the internal combustion engine (one called an oil engine and another a gas engine) were given experimental trials on the Croydon and Greenwich Tramways. Various battery and accumulator tramcars were attempted on the North Metropolitan, Croydon and London Tramways. The Croydon company also tried 'fireless' steam locomotives, but with little success.

Preserved tramcars

The body of London Street Tramways tramcar number 39 has survived, despite being withdrawn from service nearly 80 years ago. The Tramway Museum Society has restored one side and is using it at the National Tramway Museum at Crich to form the front of an unusual display case. There is one further horse tramcar that has survived. This is a double-deck car that is owned by the London Transport Collection. It is currently on display in the London Transport Museum awaiting full restoration to its London Tramways Company condition. The car, whose fleet number is not known, ran on the Greenwich to Waterloo route and is believed to have passed into the LCC fleet. It would have been withdrawn in 1904 when the route was electrified.

Modelling the early days

These pre-electric forms of tramcars provide attractive and unusual subjects for the modeller. Attractive not only because the prototypes themselves are so evocative of a century ago but also because it is possible to build a layout using entirely ready-made products. The track can be made with the new Hartel (Conrad) tramway track which has a ready formed road surface with the correct pattern of setts. The remaining road surface can be made from black or dark brown card. With carefully chosen commercial building kits a truly representative scene can be built.

When designing such a layout bear in mind that it is not as easy to turn around the motive power on the model as it was on the real tram. It is recommended that the track design does not use stub termini. Either have turning circles (hidden or open), use a large oval (or double oval) with the rear part hidden or follow the steam tram practise of a reversing triangle at the end of the route (see Diagram 1). Of necessity the electrical supply will be two-rail. This could give problems for a turning circle on a single track system. However, our model railway colleagues have wide experience of these problems and excellent advice can be found in books such as *The Model Railway Guide Number 1, Baseboards, Track and Electrification*, by Michael Andress, published by Patrick Stephens Ltd. If you wish to mix horse, steam and electric on the same layout you will need to arrange for a two-rail supply in addition to any operating overhead system. Diagram 2 shows how one rail can be used as a common return with independently controlled wires to the overhead and the other rail. Note that each controller must have its own independent transformer. This system will allow combined operation of horse, steam and electric, with two tramcars being independently operated on the same track at the same time. The same technique can be used on an all overhead electric layout to get the same operational advantage.

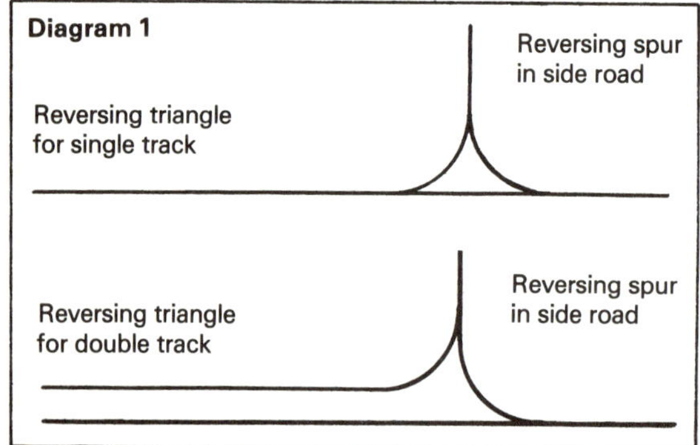

Left Diagram 1: *Reversing triangles for single and double tracks*

Below Diagram 2: *Wiring for independent control of horse or steam tramcars with overhead supply for electric trams.*

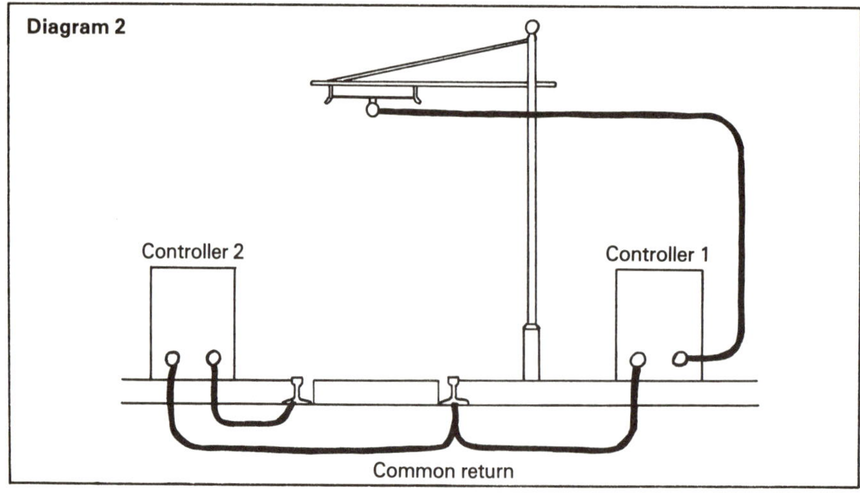

Right *The Lledo die-cast horse tramcar, adapted for operation on a layout by fitting a scratchbuilt chassis (model R. Price, photo D. Voice).*

Below *The ABS Streetscene kit of the George Train 1861 tramcar. This model has been motorised using a scratchbuilt chassis (a 24mm wheelbase chassis from BEC Kits or Tenshodo would do the job equally well) (model and photo D. Voice).*

The modeller of the pre-electric period is far less well served by manufacturers than the electric tramways. There is a die-cast model of a horse tramcar by Lledo under the 'Days Gone' label. It is about 4 mm to the foot scale and is an attractive model. Unfortunately, although it ambitiously carries the word 'Westminster' on the side boarding, it is actually based on the horse tramcar at Disneyland, USA. Very few open sided cross bench tramcars ever ran in London. Indeed I have not come across any photographs of these rare prototypes and so have been unable to see how useful the die-cast model may be. The photographs show a model that has been very successfully motorised.

The only London horse tram model is a kit of the 1861 original George Train tramcar. It is based upon 'The People' which was the tramcar used on the Victoria Street line. Originally produced by Varney the kit is now available under the ABS Streetscene label. When first introduced the kit was sold in two versions; the George Train one, as already mentioned; and as an

'LCC car'. However, the latter was 'manufacturer's licence' as this precise design was not seen in London's streets. As I have noted the tramcar may have seen further service on the Millway railway after the demise of Mr Train's experiments. The kit is sold unmotorised but can be adapted quite simply to run on your layout. The wheel base is 24 mm and, as can been seen from the photograph, I actually built my own chassis using a spare Egger Bahn motor. However, Bec Kits sell a ready to run chassis that is the correct 6 ft wheelbase and it can be obtained direct from the manufacturers. Alternatively the 26 mm wheelbase Tenshodo motor unit can be used. When assembling the kit remove the floor of the saloon to make room for the mechanism to be fitted. The Tenshodo can be fixed as described later for the steam tram. The Bec traction unit can be fitted as described in my previous book *How to Go Tram and Tramway Modelling*. The method described for the Birney tramcar will suit. The only photograph that exists of the original tramcar does not show the dashes. Both ends of the tramcar are obscured by people. It was my view that the dashes were curved rather than straight as provided in the kit. So I adapted my model to suit. Since building it I now feel that it probably had a double curve with the sides sweeping forward as in Diagram 3. Otherwise the kit was assembled following the instructions. There was one additional modification which was to put small skids on two of the leading horses hooves. I discovered that the front nearside legs of the two horses were just about the right distance for the track gauge. I cut pieces of 'N' gauge metal railway wheels and glued them under the two hooves. I used epoxy resin and a small piece of plastic card between the hoof and the piece of wheel. This was to prevent the metal horses shorting out the two-rail supply. The horses were adjusted to ensure that the two skids were at the correct gauge. The function of the skids is twofold. They keep the horses at the correct height above the road surface and they guide the horses into the curves of the track.

When it comes to the other horse tramcars the situation is rather difficult. It may be possible to modify the ABS kit but this has nine windows and the later tramcars had seven or six windows. They were also usually of double deck design to improve the passenger carrying capacity. There is a commerical model that may have potential for modification. This is the

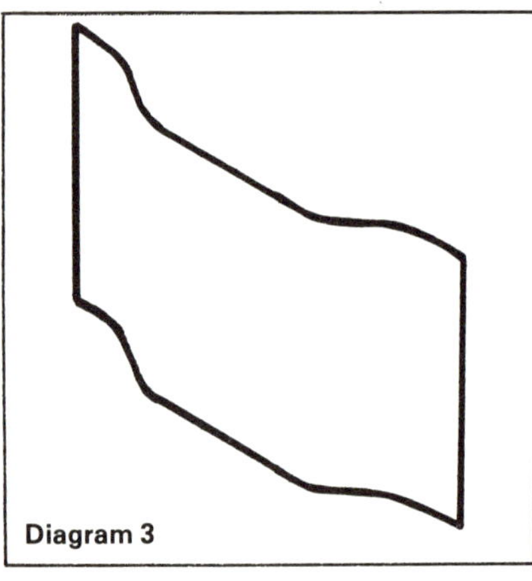

Diagram 3

Left Diagram 3: *Dash panel with double curve that was favoured by some manufacturers of horse tramcars. This style was also used on the London United Tramways Type X trams.*

Right *Merryweather steam tram engine of the North London Tramways Company* (H. A. Whitcombe collection).

Liliput four-wheel HOe narrow gauge Swiss coach (catalogue No 761). As with any model a photograph of the original is essential, particularly as drawings of London horse tramcars are rare (I have yet to see one!).

There is also the problem of the liveries of horse trams. Route numbers had not yet been invented. The general public also had a high degree of illiteracy and so the larger systems used the colour of the tramcars to indicate the routes. They also painted the names of places visited on the side and ends of the car. I have given in Table 2 those liveries that I have been able to determine. In all cases only the major colours can be given. It is not possible to indicate the shade. Indeed, even those restoring the real trams have had problems. A horse tramcar from the Chesterfield systems (No 8) had been restored to what was thought to be its original condition. For many years it was on display at the (alas late) Museum of British Transport at Clapham. It was resplendent in maroon and primrose, the livery of the later electric trams. A few years ago the tramcar was being re-furbished in preparation for the Chesterfield Transport centenary. A sample of original paint was scraped from the body and analysed. It transpired that the correct colour for the tramcar was prussian blue and primrose. The tramcar is now very smartly painted in the correct colours. But it does show how difficult it can be to find the colour, even when you have the original vehicle.

Merryweather steam tram locomotive from the North London Tramways

North London Tramways had twenty-five steam tram locomotives. The first fifteen, Nos 1-15, were built by Merryweather in 1884-86. A futher ten, Nos 16-25, were added in 1886-87 and were manufactured by Dick, Kerr. The Dick, Kerr and Co locomotives have attractive arched windows. However, I found the design of the Merryweather locomotive more appealing and so chose to model one of these. There is no way that any existing kit could be modified. Therefore, scratchbuilding is the only solution. These steam locomotives make a useful first try at scratchbuilding due to their small size and simple design. The description that follows is for a metal model but I am sure that a similar model could be made from plastic card. The main

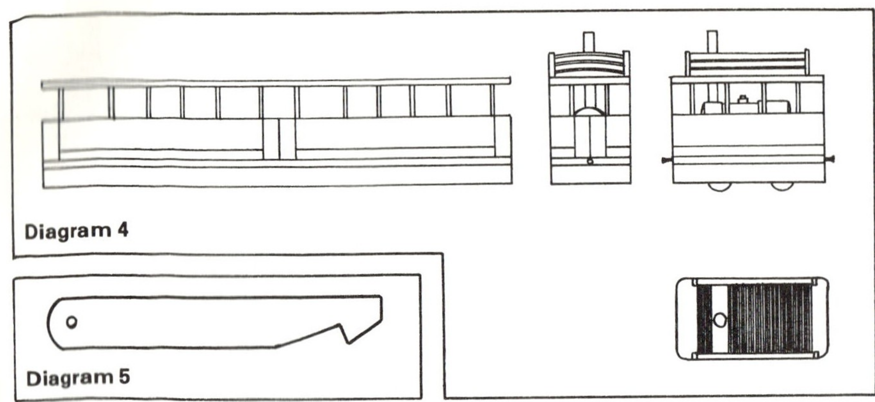

Top Diagram 4: *Merryweather North London Tramways Company Steam Tram Locomotive Series 1-15. Drawing and development of side.*

Above Diagram 5: *Metal cutting tool ground from an old hacksaw blade. It is used by
pulling towards you, cutting a groove in the brass sheet.*

difference would be that where the metal can be bent to shape the plastic card
would need to be bound around a wooden former and dipped in boiling water
to form a permanent shape. In my own model I used my favourite material,
brass sheet and strip.

As usual I started with the drawing. I had a drawing of the Merryweather
locomotive by Peter Hammond. Since Peter Hammond modelled in 1/16th
scale, I needed to re-draw it in 4 mm scale. I also added the development of
the side and these are shown in Diagram 4. Using brass sheet ten thou thick, I
cut two pieces for the side. The larger was 146 mm long and 21 mm wide. The
smaller was 2½ mm wide and the same length. I have now begun using a new
way of cutting thin metal sheets. From a piece of broken hacksaw blade I
have ground a tool shown in Diagram 5. Using a steel rule the tool is pulled
towards me and it cuts a groove in the surface of the metal. This is repeated
three or four times, the metal is turned over and the score mark is reflected in
the light. The tool is then used to cut another groove exactly on this line.
Then it is just a matter of gently bending the metal along the line until it snaps
cleanly off. A quick stroke from a fine file gives a perfect piece of metal that
is absolutely flat. Using the drawing the two main pieces of metal were stuck
down in the appropriate places using double sided adhesive tape. The window
bars were made from 1½ mm brass strip ten thou thick. This was cut into
lengths each about 5 mm longer than shown on the drawing. They were
soldered in place having previously tinned the main pieces in the appropriate
places. It was all checked to make sure nothing had moved and then the
drawing was peeled away from the assembled fret. The part that had been
struck to the drawing formed the outside, leaving all the soldering hidden on
the inside. The whole lot was scrubbed in hot water and detergent with an old
toothbrush. In some places the paper had burnt under the heat of the
soldering iron and had marked the brass. These areas were cleaned up with
fine wet-and-dry abrasive paper (the sort used to rub down paintwork on
cars).

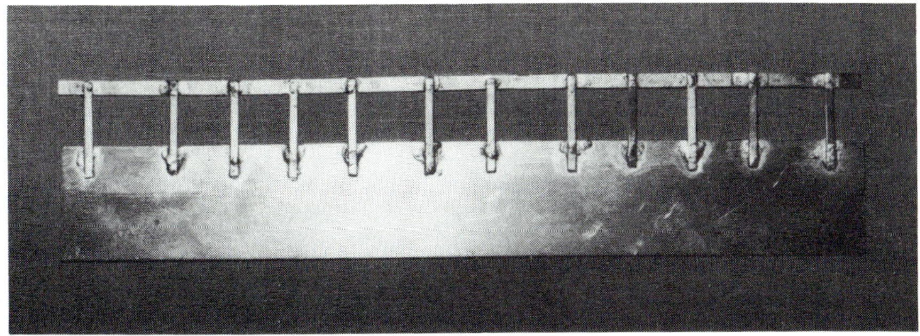

Fabrication of the side of the steam tram engine. This photograph shows the inside where all the soldering is carried out (D. Voice).

At this stage I had the complete side assembly, but in a flat form. So I took the opportunity to mark out the panels. Using a scriber, the dividing line between the skirt and the body of the tram was drawn on the metal. This was repeatedly over-scribed in order to make a deep impression since I intended to use this as a guide to solder on some wire later. The doors in the ends and the other panelling were scribed on.

Now the side was ready for the job I had not been looking forward to. The body needed to be bent to shape. The corners on the tram body are very distinctive, with sharp but smooth curves. I finally decided to try bending the corners over a rod. I used some 6 mm diameter rod. First I cut a piece of self adhesive label and covered the inside of the body below window level. Then I marked on the label lines defining the start and end of each corner (see Diagram 6). The body fret and rod were put in the vice adjusting the rod so that the top was higher than the top of the vice. The body was carefully

Diagram 6: *Lines marked on the back of the fabricated side for bending to shape.*

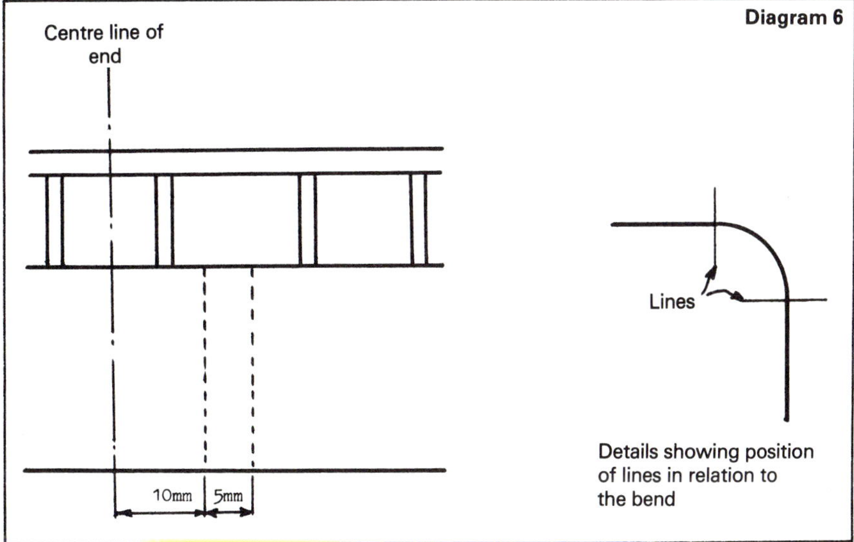

adjusted until the start line of a curve was exactly along the middle of the rod. At this point I found that the crucial line was very effectively hidden by the rod and vice. But I realised, by simple calculation, that the second line (ending the corner) should be 2 mm above the top of the rod. This was easy to measure using a steel rule resting on the rod. I also checked that the line was exactly parallel to the rod by using a set square and getting the bottom of the tram body at right angles to the rod (see illustration).

When all looked right, I tightened the vice and did a final check. Then the body was carefully bent around the rod. I used the pressure of my thumbs keeping them as near to the bend as possible. Due to the spring in the metal I was not able to make a complete right angle. This I left until later while I bent the other three corners. The order in which I did the bending was first to bend the two nearest the end, and then the middle two. At first there was no problem but the final one did give a little trouble since there was not enough room to complete the bend. I overcame this by using an engineer's vice (actually one that I made many years ago). This was small enough to allow the final bend to be made. Then the body was adjusted using a pair of long nosed pliers. To prevent marking the brass I wrapped a piece of thick cloth around the body. The two bends in the middle of the body were completed first. I then checked that the ends met to form the other end of the locomotive. As I expected the bends were very slightly out of place but this was easily rectified with the long nosed pliers. The bends were adjusted until the ends met in the correct place. The body was joined using a seam of solder strengthened behind with a piece of brass strip.

The next part to be made was a floor to hold the boiler assembly and form the main support for the power unit. The latter, I had already decided, was to be Tenshodo chassis with a 26 mm wheelbase. The unit worked out as a 6 ft 6 in wheelbase as against the prototype 5 ft. However, the skirt effectively hides all the working parts (a Board of Trade requirement) and the difference is not noticeable. Purists can build their own chassis to the correct size. I find that the convenience and tested performance of the Tenshodo units are most

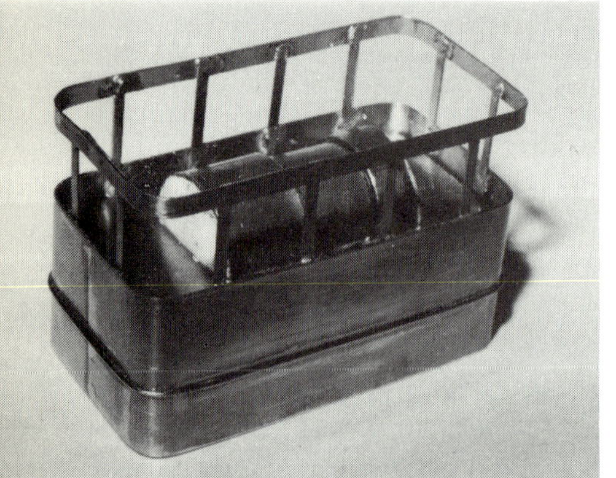

The side is bent to shape and fitted with the floor and boiler assembly (D. Voice).

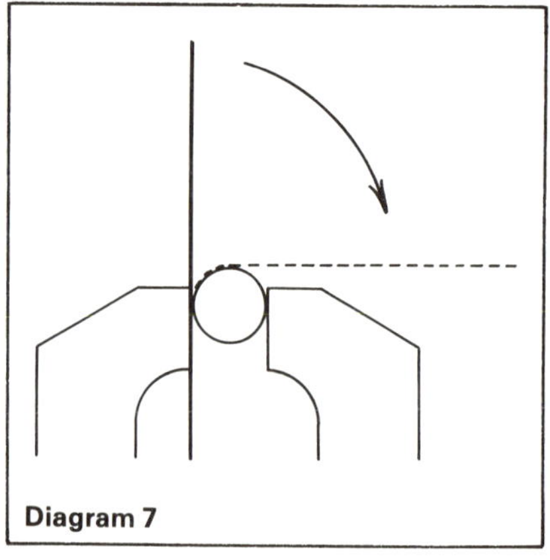

Diagram 7: *Bending the fabricated side to shape using a rod, secure in a vice, as a former.*

attractive. The unit was to be fitted under the floor which was cut from ten thou. brass to fit tightly inside the body. Before fixing in place I decided to mount the boiler assembly. I had some 15 mm outside diameter copper tubing left over from a home plumbing job. I cut three lengths 25 mm, 10 mm and 5 mm respectively. The two shorter pieces were sawn along the length to split them. They were then sprung open and slid over each end of the longer piece to form the fire box and smoke box of the boiler. I smeared the boiler end with flux before sliding the smaller lengths of tube on to it. Then holding it with long nosed pliers, I soldered the parts together by heating the end over the gas stove. This soon made it hot enough to melt solder into the joint. When both the smoke box and fire box had been soldered on, I cut the assembly in half lengthwise making sure that the splits on the outer tubes were on the part to be discarded. I was left with a perfect top half of the boiler which I soldered to the floor plate. The front of the smoke box was set 11 mm from the front edge of the floor. The empty half tube was filled with Milliput shaping the fire box end in a flat curve with a more pronounced curve at the smoke box end. When this had set I fixed the floor in place in the tram. By simple calculation I had worked out that to take the Tenshodo unit the bottom of the floor had to be 16 mm from the bottom of the skirt.

The floor was soldered in place; just two tacks per side and end. I then soldered a length of thin brass wire around the top of the skirt. This is where the heavier of the scribe markings came in useful. It is used as a guide for the wire. In order to do this job I first made sure that there was more than enough wire. I started on one end of the locomotive and at the centre of the wire. I tinned the central part of the length of wire and then tinned a couple of places on the scribe marks. Then I put the wire in place and held the very hot soldering iron on to it until the solder melted. This was repeated at each place that had been tinned on the end of the body. I bent the wire around each corner and tacked it in the same way along the sides and other end. On the other end I cut the wire to length before fixing it down. Then the whole wire was soldered again, running the soldering iron slowly along to form a neat fillet on both sides of the wire. In places the solder ran over part of the tram body. So when this job had been completed I filed and rubbed down to produce a smooth polished surface on the body of the locomotive.

The three main sub-assemblies are ready to be joined to form the model (D. Voice).

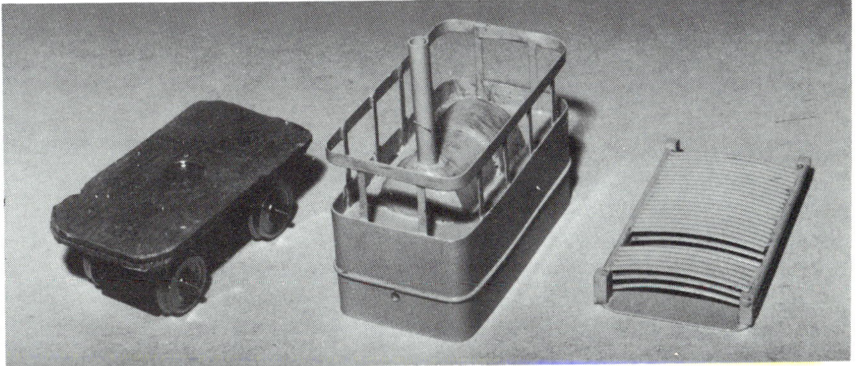

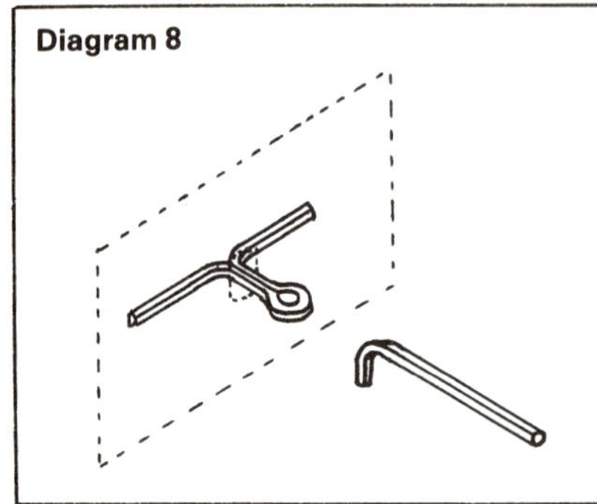

Left Diagram 8: *Using a small split pin and bent wire as the coupling between the steam tram locomotive and the trailer.*

Below right *The finished steam tram engine. It is photographed standing on Conrad (Hartel) ready-to-run track. The lack of overhead follows prototype practice for steam and horse tramways and can be a bonus for modellers* (model and photo D. Voice).

My thoughts now turned to the coupling. Tram locomotives did not use railway type of couplings but had solid rods which were connected to each vehicle by either a patent quick release device or a plain pin fixed through two holes. I decided that this could be most easily represented by fixing a split pin on the locomotive and a stiff wire bent as in Diagram 8. I drilled a 1/16 in diameter hole in each end to take the split pin. However, I left fixing it until after painting the body.

On these small street tram locomotives the roof was nearly always a maze of intricate pipework. This was because legislation required that the locomotive did not emit any smoke or steam. To comply with this the manufacturers used condensing apparatus fitted on the roofs. These Merryweather locomotives had a set of horizontal pipes running along each side of the roof which were connected across the roof by a network of finer tubing. Although attractive in the photograph, the prospect of modelling it seemed a nightmare. I soon realised that it was not practical for a model that had to take the rigours of exhibitions to have such delicate detail. My mind turned to using a corrugated material to represent the pipework. I am lucky enough to have a well stocked specialist model shop who import special section brass from Vienna. This included some corrugated brass sheet which was just what I wanted. If you are modelling in plastic card supplies of corrugated sheet are easier to obtain. The roof itself was flat although the tubes across it were arched. For the roof I cut a piece of ten thou brass 52 mm long and 28 mm wide. The corners were filed to suit the curve of the tram.

The next job was the chimney of the locomotive. I used ⅛ in diameter brass tubing cut 23 mm long. Into the bottom I put a smaller size tube with 5 mm sticking out. This was soldered in place forming a spigot to attach the chimney to the smoke box. In the centre of the smoke box I drilled a hole that was a tight fit for the smaller diameter tube. I then glued the chimney in place. Now it was necessary to drill a clearance hole in the roof plate. A 5/32 in diameter hole was drilled on the centre line of the roof 15 mm from one end. I slipped the roof over the chimney to check that all was well. Now I could add the condensing apparatus to it. I cut six pieces of 1½ mm diameter brass rod 44 mm long. The corrugated sheet was cut to give three pieces 28 mm × 25 mm and three more 8 mm × 25 mm. In each case the corrugations were parallel to the 25 mm sides. I carefully curved the corrugated pieces using long-nosed pliers. The curve was checked against the drawing to ensure that it was correct. If you are using corrugated plastic card then bind it on to a former that has a smaller curved shape and dip it in boiling water for a minute. This will form the permanent curve. On my model I soldered two rods with one large and one small piece of corrugated brass to form a sub-assembly. This was repeated to give a total of three which were mounted on top of each other. This is shown in the photograph. Before making the final soldered joints, I checked that the curves matched each other to give a neat appearance. The whole condenser assembly was soldered to the roof. The ends of the pipes were finished off with a 6 mm long piece of 2 mm square brass set vertically.

The whole lot was given a thorough washing in very hot water with plenty of detergent. This was to remove all the excess flux and grease. Then the tram, inside and out, was given a coat of self etching primer. This is necessary on brass to reduce the risk of chipping the paintwork. The body was now ready for the chassis. I have developed a simple (some may say crude) method of attaching the Tenshodo power unit. It uses the central fixing screw. One of the things I have found about this power unit is that it likes to have a bit of weight on it. This helps to maintain the electrical contact through the wheels even when everything gets a little dirty under heavy exhibition work. I used a piece of 1/16 in thick lead sheet. This is easily cut with a pair of scissors to make a good fit under the floor. A second piece was cut the same shape. In the centre of one I drilled a 9/32 in (or larger) diameter hole to clear the large screw on the power unit. In the other I drilled a 7/32 in diameter hole. This piece was then screwed into place on top of the unit. The other piece of lead was glued over the top. The idea was then to glue the lead to the bottom of the floor (after the tram had been painted). You may be wondering what I do if the power unit needs maintainance or repair. I have found that apart from the casing the whole of the power unit can be dismantled from below. It is only necessary to remove the baseplate. If the worst should happen it would be possible to break the glue joint and remove the chassis without damaging the visible part of the tram.

Once the chassis was made, the only thing left to do was to paint the tram. It had already been given its self etching primer. The boiler and skirt were given a coat of matt black, the roof and ceiling dark grey (Humbrol matt 67). Then the window uprights and top strip both inside and out were painted matt white. The remaining body parts had a coat of matt green (Humbrol matt 76). They were all given a second coat and then the white and black were

given a coat of gloss as was the green (Humbrol gloss 3). The roof and ceiling assembly was given a coat of gloss varnish and when dry was ready to be fixed to the body. This was left to one side as the fitting of the roof was the last job.

The body received detailed attention. The basic colours were already on. As can be seen from the photos of the actual locomotive they have ornate lining out. The first parts I tackled were the large white panels just above the skirt. On my last few models I have been getting very satisfactory results using self adhesive labels. I gave a label two coats of matt white followed by one of gloss. The paper that the labels are made of is a good quality that takes the paint well. When the paint was dry I cut a strip of adhesive tape with a craft knife (I use the snap off blade type and used a new edge for this job). The strip was used to mask off two strips of white on the label that were wider than I required. I then gave it two coats of gloss green. As soon as the second was dry I carefully removed the masking tape to give a clean line between the white and green. I then cut the label to give a white strip with a ½ mm line of green on one edge. The strip was cut to 4½ mm wide. One end was cut square and the backing paper removed. I fixed the strip on to the tram with the trimmed end alongside the end door. It was cut to length alongside the other door. I repeated this on the other side of the tram. I still had some green painted label and cut a 1 mm wide strip which I used to make the vertical lines above the skirt and on the upper strip above the windows. I did find that the green had broken away slightly in a few places in the cutting. So I touched it all up with a fine brush. When I was satisfied and the paint was dry I started on the gold lining. I used the gold self adhesive tape method described in detail in my previous book. Then I painted the black ovals on the upper white strip at the ends. On the prototype these are holes in the strip. As I had not even considered actually cutting these out I thought that a little modeller's deception would be in order.

The finishing touches were added. The number and enclosing garter were represented with dry fix lettering. The garter is actually a letter 'O' from the alphabet laid on its side. The number is from the very small size on sheet BOE 59 from Blick. A little bit of lining on the same sheet was used to represent the buckle and end of the belt. The oval maker's plate was represented by using a pair of etched brass locomotive shed plates from my very helpful model shop. I glued these on face down to show the plain brass back. The whole body was now given a coat of clear varnish to keep everything in place. Two suitable figures were used to represent the driver and fireman. They were cut at about waist height and painted before gluing in place. A small but distinctive feature of this Merryweather tram was a glass screen part the way up the centre three windows in each side. This I cut from glazing material starting with a rectangle 32 mm × 8½ mm and cutting the curves with a pair of scissors (I cut four out before I got a pair I was satisfied with). These I glued in place using the full 4 mm below the window level. Very small split pins (the type sold for fixing handrails to railway locomotives) were inserted into the pre-drilled holes. I spread the pins out at the back of the skirt, cut the excess off and fixed them in place with a dab of epoxy resin. Then the three parts, chassis, body and roof were glued together to produce the finished steam tram locomotive.

The model as it is seen at exhibitions. The trailer is a freelance model quickly made using the Blackpool Dreadnought plastic kit as a basis (model and photo D. Voice).

It can be seen that some of the finer detail lining out, such as on the white panels, has been omitted. This was a conscious decision. I always consider that it is better to leave out small detail than add it in a quality not matching the rest of the model. I felt that I would not be able to complete this detail work without making errors. One's eyes are always immediately drawn to such errors and may detract from the overall impression of the model. I will be interested to see how many people acutally notice that it is omitted when the tram is operated at exhibitions. Sometime after finishing the model I was tempted to enter it in a competition. In view of the prototype it was placed in the model railway category. To my surprise and undoubted pleasure it was selected as the winner.

Chapter 2

London County Council Tramways

In the mid 1890s plans were already being made to serve London with a single, municipally owned, electric tramway system. This was all part of a grander scheme to improve the life of the average Londoner. The close proximity of industry and bad housing led to health risks and disease. The solution was to move the population to the green fields on the outskirts while leaving the industry in its traditional areas. This required a fast, cheap method of transporting the workers. The LCC saw the electric tram as the solution and the lynch pin of its public health policy. To achieve this the LCC purchased the horse tramway companies as the opportunity arose. This was made possible by the compulsory purchase clause in the authorising Acts of Parliament. During the period of acquisition those horse tramways that had already been purchased were either operated directly by the LCC or leased to operating companies.

The LCC Class A bogie tramcar (No 18) in its original form with reversed stairs and an open top. The absence of a trolley pole indicates that this type of tram operated only on the conduit routes (London Transport).

The conversion to electrical operation required the agreement of the London boroughs. One condition that they set was the prohibition of the overhead wire system, which was considered too unsightly. The LCC conducted trials on an experimental stretch of conduit track that was constructed in the yard of Camberwell depot. An open-top bogie car that had been on display at a Tramway Exhibition in London was purchased in 1900 for the trials. These proved successful and the conduit system was selected. However, in the more rural areas of the outskirts the overhead system was acceptable. Since this was considerably cheaper to install and maintain, the LCC adopted it. There was also a short stretch of surface contact stud system over a bridge in East London. This had been laid as there was not enough room to build the conduit. The stud contact system was not a success and was soon replaced by conduit. Where the collection system changed the LCC

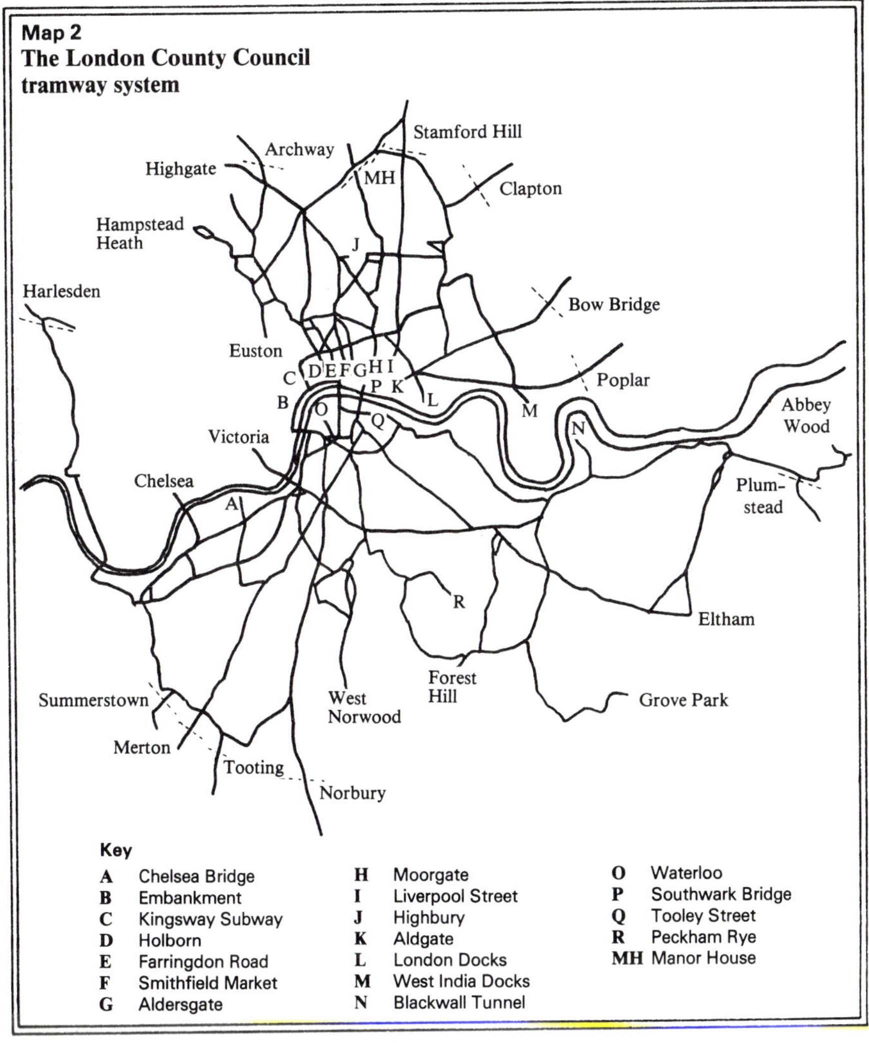

Key

A	Chelsea Bridge	**H**	Moorgate	**O**	Waterloo
B	Embankment	**I**	Liverpool Street	**P**	Southwark Bridge
C	Kingsway Subway	**J**	Highbury	**Q**	Tooley Street
D	Holborn	**K**	Aldgate	**R**	Peckham Rye
E	Farringdon Road	**L**	London Docks	**MH**	Manor House
F	Smithfield Market	**M**	West India Docks		
G	Aldersgate	**N**	Blackwall Tunnel		

installed 'change pits'. These were almost unique to London and will be described in greater detail later.

The first line to open was from Westminster Bridge to Totterdown Road, Tooting, inaugurated by the Prince of Wales on May 15 1903. The tramcars purchased to start the electric services were the open-top bogie cars of the A Class (numbered 1 to 100). These cars are distinguished by reversed stairs and having smaller end windows than middle windows. The modeller can use BEC Kit No 12 (for the E and E/1 Class) with extra items purchased directly from BEC Kits. The following will be required: two early type destination boxes (part 27), a pair of reversed stairs (part 15) with the stair base resistance box (part 14) and the wire mesh for upper-deck sides and ends. The upper-deck windows will need to be removed to produce the open-top condition and the roof set aside for future possibilities. The plastic card floor should be cut to suit the reversed stairs. In the lower saloon extra uprights must be placed in each end window. Purists will want to add the frame of the drop light windows and make the subtle changes of shape needed on the platforms to create the true Class A. The bogie truck-sides should also be modified to the much lighter appearance. Alternatively the correct Brill 22E type side frame castings can be purchased from Meadowcroft Models (address given in Appendix 1).

Like all the early LCC tramcars the Class A were often rebuilt. As well as the open-top version described there was also a balcony top with reversed stairs (classified A1), an enclosed top with reversed stairs (classified A2), and finally an enclosed top with direct stairs (classified A3). Not all the tramcars went through the A1 stage and in the A3 stage there were two distinct types of top cover. The earliest enclosed rebuilds were given the Class E style of top

On the left is a model of the first LCC tramcar, No 101. After rebuilding to this single-deck form it became No 110. The model is easily made from the BEC Kits E Class car with the top deck removed. Note the detail differences between No 110 and the G Class subway car next to it (models A. Swain, C. Withey and D. Voice, photo D. Voice).

cover while the later ones had the later E/1 lower height cover. There were about equal numbers of each type. As a guide, all the cars were in the A3 condition by about 1914. All the various designs A1 to A3 can be modelled using the BEC Kit No 12 of the E Class tramcar as a basis. But in common with modelling all of London trams it is crucial to have at least one good photograph of the actual car you are modelling in the condition that you wish to make. In 1920/21 some of the Class A3 cars were fitted with a single trolley pole and so could work from the overhead as well as the conduit. But the class was not destined to survive much longer and they had all been withdrawn by 1931.

The first car that the LCC purchased was given the number 101. This was the originally unnumbered car used on the Camberwell test track. It was an open-top bogie car which had short canopies and 90° direct staircases. The bogies were of the same design maximum traction type used under the Class A tramcars. About 1920, after a period when it saw little passenger service, it was cut down to a single-deck vehicle. In the single-deck condition the roof was extended over the platforms and the car was re-numbered 110 to enable the Class B tramcar 110 to be re-numbered 101 following an accident when it overturned. It was not unusual at this time for tramway companies to re-number accident victims in order to disassociate the vehicle from the accident. In this final form 110 was outwardly a little like the F and G classes although could easily be recognised as it only had four windows and did not have a clerestory roof.

With the planned expansion of electrification a further 100 tramcars were purchased and designated Class B. They were four-wheel cars and numbered 102 to 201. They were followed a year later by a similar design of tramcars designated Class C (numbers 202 to 301). Both the B and C classes were delivered as open-top cars with reverse stairs. It was planned to use them on routes with smaller numbers of passengers or where the lighter weight of the cars was suited to steep gradients. Although outwardly similar in design the B and C Classes were made by different manufacturers. There were small differences, for example the Class C had chamfered lower saloon corner pillars and screw down track brakes operated by a wheel beneath the hand brake handle. It is thought that some of the B Class were cut down to single deck in 1905-1906. Certainly number 118 was converted. They were used as sand cars and were able to travel between the north and south parts of the system using the then low height Kingsway Subway. One was used as a trainer car to teach crews at Telford Avenue depot.

Increasing patronage and the introduction of the E/1 Class caused the B Class to become redundant. By 1918, 59 had been sold to other operators. The remainder were used only for peak hour services. By 1927 the survivors were either designated as, or actually converted for, works use. Ironically it is a B Class tramcar that is the sole surviving four-wheel LCC tramcar. Withdrawn by London Transport in 1952 as a single-deck snowbroom (No 022) the tram has been superbly restored and is now running at the National Tramway Museum Crich. It is now the only example of a tramcar in the original LCC purple lake and primrose livery. In order to allow this open-top car to use the overhead wire it has been restored in the condition of one of the eight B Class cars which were given direct stairs and trolley poles in order to

Above *The superbly restored B4 Class tramcar No 106. It was photographed in the summer of 1983 in service at the National Tramway Museum, Crich (D. Voice).*

Below right *A busy scene on the layout, showing three versions of the B and C Class cars. On the left is a model of a B4, with normal stairs and open top. In the centre is the original B, while the snowplough shows the final form of some Class C cars, as cut down works vehicles (models A. Swain and C. Withey, photo D. Voice).*

Below *The B Class car in its B2 version with the enclosed upper-deck and retaining the reversed stairs (courtesy C. Withey).*

work in the Woolwich area, with the classification B4. The restored number 106 differs from the 1908 modification as it has kept its plough carrier. Perhaps it should be regarded as being in its own classification of B5.

In a similar manner to the Class A cars the B and C classes were much modified. In addition to the B4 cars, there was a balcony top version with reversed stairs (B1 and C1), an enclosed top version with reversed stairs (B2 and C2) and finally an enclosed top version with direct stairs (B3 and C3). In 1915 six cars were fitted with trolley poles and loaned to Bexley. This number was increased to 23 by 1917. I have seen photographs of them at Bexley in the B3 condition. Whether any were originally transferred in the B2 style I have no information. During the years 1917 and 1918 42 of the B Class tramcars were sold to systems outside London. In the mid 1920s M Class cars were replacing C Class cars. About this time number 118 was given a top cover. Twenty-one of the B Class were converted to single-deck snowbrooms in 1927 (numbers 016 to 036) and 18 of the C Class to single-deck snowploughs in 1931 (numbers 037 to 044 and 046 to 054) with a further one becoming stores van number 015 in the same year. Two further cars were fitted with snowploughs although they remained in the double-deck condition. These were numbers 131 and 215 (the later renumbered 045).

The tramway modeller is particularly well supplied for the B and C Class tramcars. The B and C original condition is a straight construction of BEC Kit No 3 (with reversed stairs) whilst the B4 (there were no C4 versions) is the same kit with normal stairs, destination box (part No 26) and a trolley pole. The B1 and C1 conditions can be made from BEC Kit No 4 with reversed stairs (part 15) and stair base resistance box (part 14) replacing the direct stairs. Since in this condition the cars were conduit only, the trolley base and pole should be omitted. BEC Kit No 2 makes the B2, C2, B3, C3 conditions

More models of the B Class tramcars in different versions. On the left is the open top B4 Class, next to it is an enclosed top B2 with reversed stairs and no trolley pole. Second from the right is another B2 with a trolley pole (there is no conclusive evidence that any B Class car ran in this form, but it may have happened at the time of the Dartford crisis when cars were loaned to Bexley). On the right is the end of the original version of the B Class car (models A. Swain, C. Withey and D. Voice, photo D. Voice).

and works cars 131 and 045. The difference being that for the B2 and C2 the direct stairs need to be replaced by reversed stairs and stairbase resistance boxes. In all cases the deep purple lake and primrose livery is appropriate. As always, ensure that you have a photograph of the car you wish to model. This helps to get such detail work as lining out, destination boxes, and handrails correct.

Kits are also available for the B and C Class works trams in their single-deck condition. BEC Kits No 1 contains all the parts to construct the snowbroom or the snowplough or the stores van. Indeed if you have no experience in building white metal kits this is the ideal one on which to start.

The next type of tramcar to enter service was the D Class with 100 cars (Nos 302 to 401). These open-top bogie cars were very similar to the A Class and they followed the same pattern of rebuilding; the balcony top condition with reversed stairs being designated D1, the enclosed top with reversed stairs conditions known as D2, and the enclosed top with direct stairs designated D3. In addition some cars appeared in an open top condition with direct stairs and a trolley pole. These were designated D4. The similarity in appearance of the Class D and the Class A allows the modeller to treat them in the same way, except that the D Class cars had chamfered corner pillars to the lower saloon (their manufacturers mark of distinction and also seen on the C Class). The earlier observations on the kit modifications for the Class A apply equally well to the Class D. Those modellers using the overhead system can run Class D tramcars in either the D4 condition or the D3 with trolley poles. However, it should be noted that not all the cars in the D3 state were equipped for dual conduit and trolley operation. The majority remained conduit only. The top covers on Nos 377 to 401 were of the later E/1 type whilst the other cars in this Class had the original A Class design. Like all the tramcars before them the D Class always carried the deep purple lake and primrose livery (none were painted red and cream).

In 1906 came 300 tramcars of the E Class. This design was the immediate forerunner to the LCC's standard tramcar — the Class E/1. The Class E, when bought, were intended for conduit only operation and arrived in two batches numbered 402 to 551 and 602 to 751. In 1922-26 single trolley poles were fitted to numbers 402 to 511. All the Class E cars were painted in the new red and cream livery between 1928 and 1930. This coincided with the 'Pullmanisation' programme where the cars were fitted with cushioned seats and refurbished interiors. In the early 1930s the bogie mounted plough carrier was replaced by one fitted to the underframe in the centre of the car. For the modeller BEC Kits No 12 provides the necessary parts to construct a model of the Class E in most of its major variations. These cars did vary in detail towards the end of their life and the usual advice is given to have at least one photograph of the actual tramcar you wish to model. Note that cars numbers 420 and 454 were later rebuilt with E/3 type top covers, making them completely different.

It was decided that there should be a direct link between the Northern and Southern Areas of the LCC system. Advantage was taken during the rebuilding of the Holborn district to construct a subway link under the new Kingsway. In order to avoid the large Fleet sewer the subway was restricted in height allowing operation only by single-deck tramcars. The Board of Trade, who at that time were responsible for tramway matters, were most concerned about fire risk in the tunnel. So all-metal cars were a requirement and two classes were built, the F and G. In general design the two classes were very similar, although there were detail differences such as the bulkhead windows.

Built as a smaller version of the Class E, the four-wheel M Class tramcar had a unique type of truck. This particular car is looking resplendent in the later LCC livery (London Transport).

The two classes were not given any major changes during their lifetime. In 1912 two cars were coupled in multiple unit night trials but the project was soon abandoned. They were never fitted with trolley poles (although they were fitted with a trolley plank). As delivered, they carried the three light code route indicator, later replaced by a route number stencil holder. There is a body kit available for the modeller produced by Meadowcroft Models and the construction is described later in this chapter. All the Class F and G cars were scrapped by 1930, except number 600 whose body was used as a store in Holloway depot. The bogies of all the cars were used under the third series of E/1 class cars.

1917 saw the first of what became the most numerous of all the London tramcar designs, the Class E/1. In total there were 1,050 of these purchased by the LCC in three series. The numbers carried by this class were 752 to 1426 and 1477 to 1676 (first series), 1727 to 1851 (second series) and 552 to 601 (third series). As delivered, the first series had a single trolley pole except numbers 1350 to 1353 which were fitted with double trolley poles. In 1920 numbers 1366 to 1400 were fitted with double trolley poles to work the double overhead wire section Woolwich to Lee Green (a requirement set by Greenwich Observatory). The second series tramcars were delivered with double trolley poles for this route in 1922. The third series were all fitted with double trolley poles to prevent conductors having to turn the poles at stub termini. They were officially known as reconstructed subway cars but in fact the double-deck bodies were new with E/3 style top covers and were mounted on the bogies of the withdrawn classes F and G. All the E/1 Class were given the new red and cream livery along with cushioned seats and refurbished interiors between 1926 and 1930. Some were fitted with vestibules before being taken over by London Transport. Indeed number

The G Class subway car, another conduit only tramcar. All the F and G Class cars were without trolley poles, but were fitted with a trolley plank (London Transport).

Top *A trailer car in service behind an E/1 Class car. The trailer car is from the T9-T158 series* (London Transport).

Above *Model of a trailer car set. This shows how attractive the scratchbuilt trailer looks with the BEC Kits Class E car. It is a real eye-catcher at exhibitions* (models C. Withey and D. Voice, photo D. Voice).

1506 was the first LCC tramcar to be fitted with windscreens (in 1930). These were wooden and other cars received experimental ones or Alpex 'domed' metal frames. The BEC Kits No 12 can be used to make most of the E/1 variations, but not the third series cars. London Transport put aside an E/1 tramcar for preservation and number 1025 can be seen in The London Transport Museum at Covent Garden. The London County Council Tramways Trust have the lower half of tramcar number 1622 which is under restoration, detailed in Chapter 9.

In order to service those routes with steep hills or where traffic was light, the LCC developed a four-wheel equivalent of the E/1. This was the Class M delivered in two batches, numbers 1427 to 1476 and 1677 to 1726. The four-wheel truck on these cars was one of the most unusual on any tramcar. It had

Above *E/1 Class No 581. This was one of the batch of cars known officially as the rebuilt subway cars. In fact only the trucks, electrical equipment and numbers were transferred to the new bodies* (courtesy C. Withey).

Below *A model of the Class E car constructed from the BEC Kit* (model D. Watkins, photo D. Voice).

what appeared to be enormous, pressed steel side frames. The truck was attached to the body by swing bolsters at each end (rather in the manner of a bogie car). For the ordinary passenger there appeared to be no physical connection between the impressive side frame and the body. The plough carriers were fitted each end of the truck rather than the middle. This was because the track brake was attached to the mid-point of the truck. The first car number 1427 was originally a conduit only open-top car but was soon given the E/1 style top cover. Numbers 1428 to 1437 were not initially fitted with plough carriers but carried two trolley poles for the Woolwich section, replacing the trolley fitted open-top B Class cars. These M Class cars were later fitted with plough carriers around 1914. The remainder of the first batch were conduit only and worked on the Highgate Hill line. The second batch had plough carriers and a single trolley for operation on the Dog Kennel Hill route. The M Class tramcars took part in the trailer experiments, and eventual service, between 1913 and 1919. Between 1928 and 1930 the whole class was refurbished inside and repainted in the red and ivory livery. In 1931 numbers 1715, 1723 and 1726 were given new trucks (each from a different manufacturer) and fitted with wood framed vestibules. Three cars (Nos 1441, 1444 and 1446) were lengthened and given bogies in 1932 making them similar to the E/1 Class. When reconstructed number 1446 was renumbered 1370. These upgraded tramcars were designated ME/1 (later reclassified by London Transport to ME/3).

This latter conversion by the LCC gives the modeller an idea for the construction of a model of the class M four-wheel tramcar. By starting with the BEC Kit No 12 of the E/1 an M Class car can be made by removing one window from each side. The body will need to be spliced back together as a

This layout was obviously seen during the rush hour. Of particular interest is the centre E Class car which shows the experimental orange livery that was part of the project leading to the new LCC red and cream livery (models A. Swain, C. Withey and D. Voice, photo D. Voice).

centre window must be removed. The wide corner pillars of the E/1 kit must be made even wider and the pillar on the upper-deck between the wide windows and the small windows on the vestibule must be made about three times as wide. It is recommended that a drawing and photographs are used during this conversion. But beware of some of the drawings as they are not always accurate. The best is the scale drawing by Terry Russell (see Appendix 1). The very distinctive truck sides will need to be scratchbuilt using your favourite material, either plastic, card or metal.

In 1929 and 1930 tramcars Nos 1852 (designated Class HR/1, the only tram of its class) and 1853 (HR/2) were the experimental tramcars leading to a new class of four motor equal-wheel bogie tramcars. These had the characteristics of the third series E/1 Class with straight flush panelled sides and other details. The four motors gave the power for the hilly routes combined with a greater passenger carrying capacity than the C and M Class tramcars. Numbers 1854 to 1903 of the HR/2 Class entered service with double trolley poles and without vestibules whilst the later numbers 101 to 160 were built with Alpex vestibules and were not fitted with trolley poles. Actually the equal-wheel trucks destined for No 160 were used under the experimental car LCC No 1. So No 160 was given maximum traction trucks and designated E/3 (the only E/3 not to have a trolley pole). There are differences in the truck sides so always check the photographs.

At the same time as the first of the HR/2 Class was being built, the LCC ordered another new class, the E/3. These had the same design body as the HR/2 but were two-motor tramcars with maximum traction bogies. The first batch (Nos 1904-2003) was delivered unvestibuled but within two years they were all fitted with windscreens. In 1930 the Leyton Council ordered 50 tramcars to the E/3 design. LCC specifications were used in order to reduce the costs. The LCC were used as agents for the purchase as they were at this time operating the Leyton services. In consequence the tramcars, whilst the property of Leyton Council, were numbered in the LCC series 161 to 210. Alpex windscreens and double trolley poles were fitted. The HR/2 and E/3 Classes were all fitted with plough carriers and delivered in the new red and cream livery. Those cars owned by Leyton carried that council's coat of arms instead of the LCC crest. One of the HR/2 Class tramcars was preserved by Peter Davies when the London Tramways ceased running. After spending some years behind wire fences in Chessington Zoo, No 1858 was moved to Carlton Colville to form part of the East Anglia Transport Museum, where it can now be seen.

Despite the fact that these two classes ran until the closing of the London system and three cars went on to give further service in Leeds, the modeller has not been well served. A kit was developed by Varney, however only one production run was achieved before manufacturing ceased. A small number of kits were made up to fulfil orders for ready to run models. The remainder were sold to modellers either directly or through a retailer. Unfortunately, the kit itself is not completely true to scale and the completed model looks rather small against true scale replicas. The masters have been acquired by ABS Models and it is understood that there are plans to rebuild the kit to the correct scale before re-issuing it.

In 1932 an experimental tramcar appeared in public. This was to be the

The tramcar that could have been the start of a modern fleet for the London County Council, No 1. This shows the car repainted in London Transport livery and on display at the National Tramway Museum, Crich (D. Voice).

beginnings of a new and modern class of tram. Given the fleet number '1', the tramcar was painted in a distinctive blue livery and soon earned the nickname 'Bluebird'. Development of further tramcars from this design was halted when London Transport took over on July 1 1933. Number 1 retained this number in the London Transport fleet although it was later repainted in the red and cream livery. As the car used the equipment originally destined for number 160 it too was given the classification HR/2. Under London Transport control the designation of number 1 was HR/2 Special. It was sold to Leeds in 1951. In fact Leeds had not intended to purchase this tram but accepted it as a replacement for two Feltham bodies that had been purchased by them and badly damaged before delivery. At the end of the Leeds tramway, No 1 (or rather Leeds No 301), was presented to the British Transport Commission for preservation. The tram can now be seen at the National Tramway Museum, Crich, where it has been returned to its London Transport red and cream livery. The flush sided design of this tramcar lends itself to scratch building using the techniques described in the last chapter or in my previous book for the Mumbles car.

The use of trailers by the LCC has already been mentioned. For the initial experiments in 1910 a modified double-deck horse car number 585 was used. By 1913 trailers were in regular service, using converted North Metropolitan horse tramcars renumbered T1 to T8. This development was such a success that 150 new trailer cars (numbers T9 to T158) were purchased in 1915-1916. The towing tramcars were converted E, E/1 and M Class cars and they were in operation until the use of trailers ceased in 1924. The LCC Tramways Trust is hoping, in the long term, to restore a trailer using the body of T86 on the chassis of T131.

Trailer car sets make an attractive subject to model. Colin Withey built such a set and has kindly described the construction. He used two Roche drawings of the trailer car (originals as photocopies reduce the scale). He cut out the saloon sides including the window frames from the drawings. The paper was then glued to stiff card and the windows cut out, leaving the frames recessed. The matchwood lines on the waist panels were scored and thin strips of balsa cut to form the rubbing strips and beadings. The saloon ends were next to be cut from the drawings. After cutting out the doors, panels and windows they were glued to card. The card was cut to give the windows. The saloon doors were made in the same way. All parts were painted, the end panels lined out and the windows glazed. In positioning the saloon doors one end could be left open (or both could be made to slide open like prototype). The saloon was assembled and strengthened with balsa strips. The platforms and saloon floor were cut in one piece seats added from BEC seating strip or Tramalan castings and glued to the body. The dashes and steps were cut from card to match the drawing and fitted to the platforms. Slots were cut in the saloon floor to clear the flanges of the wheels. Balsa strips were fitted to the platforms and upper deck floor to represent the slatting. BEC seats were cut, painted and added (the Tramalan cast seats with movable backs could be used, but the lower deck will need to be similarly fitted to compensate and stop the model tipping over). Model railway wheels were fitted to a balsa sub-frame using balsa boxes set the correct distance apart. This was joined to the floor using balsa blocks at the saloon ends across the width of the floor less 1 mm each side (these blocks

Works car No 05. This model uses BEC Kits trucks, chassis and undergear. Use could also be made of BEC platforms, dashes and roof. The body used thin wood which was scribed to represent planking (model I. Hodgson, photo D. Voice).

were also used to fit the truck sides). The trucksides and complete lifeguards were made by gluing the drawings of them on card and cutting the whole out like a fret. The fret was carefully bent to fit the model with the trucksides being glued to the saloon floor and balsa strips. Detail work was added using balsa and card. All the unpainted parts were painted.

This left the stairs. Colin also made these from card, cutting the treads and risers from the drawings. The stringers were cut by trial and error. Assembly was tricky but rewarding. No doubt modellers like myself will resort to using the ready made stairs available from BEC Kits. They were painted and fitted. The upper-deck, stair and platform rails were added using broom bristles, although wire may be easier to use. The finishing touching-up was carried out and BEC transfers used to add the LCC fleet name and numbers.

Although the more accurate Terry Russell 4 mm scale drawings may be better, the Roche drawings give the full livery details, and further information can be found in the book *The LCC Trailers*. Expert modellers will also wish to construct working replicas of the lattice safety gates. Colin came to the same decision as I had and opted for a single wire coupling to join the trailer to a BEC Kits Class E.

One of the lesser known classes of LCC tramcar was the Petrol Electric Class nos P1, P2 & P3. These were developed to overcome the expense of electrifying the remaining horse car lines which were lightly loaded. The London boroughs had refused to defray the costs and so trials with the three petrol electric cars began in 1913. Like the early trailers they were converted from double-deck horse cars and had the distinction of being the only London tramcars to have radiators and starting handles! But they were not successful and were soon withdrawn. The bodies were removed and the chassis were used for shunting trailer cars at Marius Road depot. This lasted until 1922 when they were scrapped.

The LCC also had a whole fleet of works cars. I have previously discussed modelling the cars converted from B and C Class trams. There are no kits available for modelling the other 14 cars that formed the remainder of the works fleet. However, many parts such as truck sides, platforms, dashes, roofs, ready to run chassis and controllers can be obtained as individual items from BEC Kits. These are an enormous help when scratch-building such unusual tramcars. The bodies of the stores vans can be built from plank embossed plastic card or even from thin modellers plywood. Because of the fairly simple design of most of these work cars, they can form an ideal introduction to scratch-building techniques for those wishing to develop their modelling skills beyond that of kit building.

I cannot leave this look at the LCC system without examining that unique feature, the change pit. As mentioned previously the conduit electrical supply was not used in the outer suburbs, nor did any of the other systems surrounding the LCC use conduit. Therefore, many of the LCC fleet were fitted with both trolley pole and plough carrier. There was a switch on the car to allow either overhead or conduit to be used. If running on the conduit, when approaching such a change pit the driver stopped the tram just short of it. The conductor would raise the trolley pole while the driver changed the switch. Then the tramcar would be driven slowly forward under power from the overhead until it reached the place where the conduit slot moved from

The unique feature of the LCC tramways was the change pit. Here Class E/1 car No 1602 takes up the plough as it moves from the overhead to the conduit. Note also the detail of the bogies and plough carrier (W. J. Haynes).

between the running rails across the inner rail to form a siding. The plough then slid out of the plough carrier under its own momentum and the tram, now free of the plough, continued without stopping. On the return trip the plough would be taken on at the change pit. The fitting of the plough was helped by the 'plough man' guiding it onto the plough carrier bars using a special tool called a fork. Where there were through running arrangements with other systems they had their own cars fitted with plough carriers to allow running over LCC lines.

It is an attractive thought to build a layout incorporating a working change pit, but seems somewhat impractical. Although in 1939 the late Frank Roche had built a London tramway layout in 3.5 mm scale (HO gauge) using working ploughs. Actually the miniature plough only picked up the electrical feed (the real thing had both feed and return). In the model the return was through the rails. However, the modern modeller would use the two-rail form of current supply, the conduit being for visual effect only. This, of course, fits nicely with the ready-to-run chassis such as those provided in BEC Kits or the Tenshodo unit. The easiest way of representing the conduit is to use Peco code 100 rail upside down. The base has a groove formed in it along the centre which looks just like the plough slot. Check first that the rail is of this type as there seems to be some variety in the rail now used by Peco. One cheap way of doing this would be to used second-hand track taking out the rails from the sleeper base.

The LCC can offer a variety complete enough to satisfy any modeller. An attractive scene for either a static diorama or an operating exhibition layout could be a city terminus like Aldgate with queues of trams from the LCC and through running cars from other systems. Indeed the feature of through running giving a mixture of liveries can be enhanced if the late 1920s is chosen with the old and new LCC liveries running together. Further variety could be added with some of the short-lived experimental liveries such as the orange E Class tramcar or E/1 number 795 left in unpainted beaten aluminium. Any layout could be enhanced by the addition of a depot and the LCC had a whole variety with greatly differing designs and sizes. Most were conduit only and had internal traversers in lieu of an external track fan. The entrances tended to be small and even the very large Clapham depot had a main entrance that was just a narrow archway in a row of shops. This would make an ideal subject for a low relief layout with a short length of track behind the facia. Just enough for the operator to remove and replace cars. Of course if you are more ambitious then a working traverser, like the type used in the storage sidings of model railway layouts, could be built.

Table 3: London County Council Tramways 1903-33

Number	Class/ type	Year built	Body type	Trucks/Bogies	LT Nos	Scrapped, sold or changed
1-100	A	1903	OT then ET	MT Bogie Brill 22E	—	by 1931
101	—	1900	OT then SD	MT Bogie Brill 22E	—	1931
102-201	B	1903	OT then BT and ET	4 W 6 ft 6 in Brill 21E	—	1917-29
202-301	C	1904	OT then BT and ET	4 W 6 ft 6 in 21E	—	1931
302-401	D	1904	OT then BT and ET	MT Bogie McGuire	—	by 1931
402-551& 602-751	E	1906	ET	MT Bogie M&G	402-551& 602-751	1936-38
552-567	F	1906	SD	MT Bogie M&G	—	1930
568-601	G	1906	SD	MT Bogie M&G	—	1930
752-1426 1477-1676	E/1	1907-12	ET	MT Bogie M&G/HN/ H&F	2; 752-1369 1371-1426 1477-1676	1938-52
1427-1476 1677-1726	M	1910	ET	4 W 7 ft 6 in H&F	1370; 1427-1445 1447-1476 1677-1726	1938-51
1727-1851	E/1	1922	ET	MT Bogie HN	1727-1851	1938-52
552-601	E/1	1930	ET	MT Bogie M&G	552-601	1938-52
1852	HR/1	1929	ET	EW Bogie EMB	1852	1940
1853	HR/2	1929	ET	EW Bogie EMB	1853	1940
1854-1903 101-160	HR/2	1930	ET later TE	EW Bogie EMB	1854-1903 101-160	1940-52
1904-2003 161-210	E/3	1930-31	ET later TE	MT Bogie EMB	1904-2003 161-210	1940-52
1	Bluebird	1932	TE	EW Bogie EMB	1	1951
T1-T8	Trailer	1913	OT	4 W LCC	—	1919

Number	Class/ type	Year built	Body type	Trucks/Bogies	LT Nos	Scrapped, sold or changed
T9-T158	Trailer	1915	OT	4 W 6 ft 9 in Brush(?)	—	1924
P1-P3	Petrol-Elec	1913	OT	4 W LCC	—	1922 (see text)
01-04	H	1904	Water car and rail-grinder	4 W M&G	01-04	?
05-06	J	1905	Stores van	MT Bogie Brill 22E	05-06	1951
07-010	K	1908	Stores van	4 W M&G	07-010	1936-52
011-012	L	1909-10	Wheel van	4 W M&G	011-012	1952
013-014	L/1	1918	Stores van later staff car then rail-grinder	4 W Brill 21E	013-014	1938-48
015	C	1927	Sand car	4 W 6 ft 6 in Brill 21E	015	1952
016-036	B	1927-28	Snowbrooms	4 W 6 ft 6 in Brill 21E	016-036	1938-52
037-054	C	1928-30	Snowplough	4 W 6 ft 6 in Brill 21E	037-054	1935-38

Notes
BT Balcony top; **EMB** Electro-Magnetic Brake Co; **ET** Enclosed top; **EW** Equal wheel; **H&F** Heenan and Froude; **HN** Hurst, Nelson; **M&G** Mountain and Gibson; **MT** Maximum traction; **OT** Open-top; **SD** Single-deck; **TE** Totally enclosed; **4 W** Four-wheel.

Livery
1903-31 Deep purple lake and primrose. Gold lining on the purple lake with burnt sienna lining on the primrose. Lettering and numbers gold, edged red and shaded black. Trucks, lifeguards etc red oxide, fenders and controllers black.
1926 Various experimental liveries including deep crimson and cream; crimson and primrose; 'Midland' red and cream; all orange; and all aluminium.
1926-33 As cars were refurbished they were given a livery of vermillion and rich cream, other colours as before; except for cars painted in 1932/33 where the trucks and lifeguards were grey.

Single-deck subway G Class car

For this unusual tramcar I used the etched brass kit produced by Meadowcroft Models. At the time I constructed it, only the body kit was available and this is how I have described the construction. It is the intention of Meadowcroft Models to extend the kit to include the roof (in cast white metal) and a motorised chassis.

On my kit the sides and false roof were separate. On future kits these will be etched in one piece and the construction details that follow may not be needed. However, I include them as such techniques are often required for etched brass tram kits. The sides and ends were removed from the fret. An old heavy duty craft knife was used to cut through the retaining lugs. The fret

Right *The etched brass fret of the F and G Class subway car manufactured by Meadowcroft Models* (D. Voice).

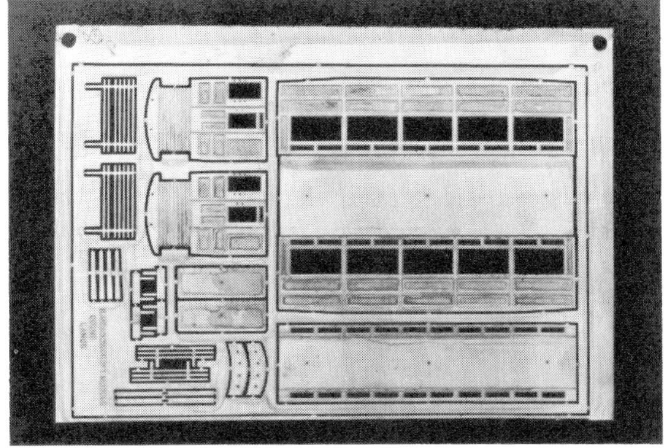

was laid on a piece of scrap plywood and the lugs cut through, taking care not to distort the piece required. Then with a fine file the remaining parts of the lugs were filed off. Each side was fixed between two substantial strips of metal (I used a 2 ft steel rule of the hinged type) and the side was bent along the top of the rubbing strip to form the tumblehome. I know that many people may not have tried soldering before so I will go into detail on the method I use. It may seem laborious when first read but it is the easiest method I have been able to find that always ensures good results. The techniques is to 'tin', that is apply a thin layer of solder to each part to be joined, then assemble and finally solder them together. Thus the ends and sides were tinned first. I used a paste type of flux and smeared it along the edges of one end. Then with the soldering iron nice and hot I melted a small blob of solder onto the tip and smeared it along the edge of the end. Under the heat the flux on the part melted and burnt off and a shiny, thin layer of solder flowed on to the part as the metal got hot. This I repeated for the other end and the sides, tinning the inside at the end. This allowed the ends to be fixed inside the side. A square cut piece of wood was used to position one side and one end. They were placed upside down against the piece of wood to ensure that the joint would be at right angles and that the top edges lined up. A lightly tinned soldering iron was touched top and bottom of the corner just to tack the side and end in place. They were removed and checked for squareness and correct positioning. Then I returned them to the wooden block and gradually completed the joint by running the soldering iron along the outside of the corner. I again checked it for positioning and to make sure that the solder had taken all along the joint. Any gaps were filled using a little more solder. The other side and end were joined in the same way.

It was then possible to bring together the two sub assemblies and complete the saloon. Note that the platform had not been bent at this stage. Once I was satisfied that the saloon looked right I removed excess solder with a file and wet and dry paper. The inside of the top edge was tinned as were the edges of the false roof. This was positioned to check that it fitted nicely. There were no problems so the saloon was placed upside down on some scrap plywood. The false roof was dropped into place and soldered. I found that the easiest way to do this was to position the upside down saloon and roof so that it over-hung the plywood allowing me to solder the end from below. When I had checked that both ends were soldered correctly, I held the saloon in one hand whilst soldering the side seam with the other (taking great care not to burn myself). The platforms were bent into position and the plaform bearing frames soldered underneath. These ran from the inside edge of the platform to the front, protruding 2 mm over the end (they support the fender). The dash was separated from the fret and drilled out to take the headlamp (a component I had purchase from Meadowcroft Models). The headlamp was fixed in place, soldering from the inside of the dash in order to conceal it. I curved the dash to shape and soldered the bottom edge to the platform. The platform frames helped to keep the dash in the correct position for this job. The fender was removed from the fret and curved to shape. It was joined to the tramcar at the ends and by the platform bearing frames. This method of construction gave a fender that would stand up to the rigours of exhibition work where they often become functional pieces of equipment. As regrettable as it is, the sight of model trams running into each other is not unknown especially during hectic exhibition working, particularly when the operator is trying to talk to the public whilst driving the tramcars. So I tend to ensure that the fenders will take the force of the impact rather than damage being caused to the rest of the model.

Now that the main body parts had been assembled my thoughts turned to the chassis. I decided to use the well established BEC Kits maximum traction motorised bogie units. I ordered two bogies from the manufacturer. To mount the bogies in the model I opted to use the press stud method that had been used in the Green Goddess described in my previous book. On each bogie I soldered a 9 mm male press stud and used an 11 mm female stud for the mounting. By using a larger female size than male the necessary amount of free play is obtained. I always choose the silver type of press stud as this solders easily. The female studs were soldered between two 100 mm lengths of code 70 rail, keeping the centres of the studs 48 mm apart. The method I used was to draw the pattern on a scrap of paper and use it as a guide for soldering. Note that the little clip wires inside the female stud must be parallel to the rails, that is parallel to the length of the tram. This allows the bogies to swing and take up any irregularities in the track, whilst restricting the rolling of the tram body. I then soldered two pieces of 10 thou brass 100 mm long and 8 mm wide to the outer edges of the mounting frame. These were to form a combined mount for the passengers and supporting plates for the chassis. I mounted the bogies in place and checked that they ran freely. I soldered a short piece of very flexible wire between the insulated brushes on each bogie. This gave electrical connection between each bogie thus preventing one bogie

Left *The chassis unit for the single-deck car uses the BEC Kits bogies. Passengers, the top part of plastic figures, will be fitted to the flat plates* (D. Voice).

Right *The component parts of the subway car ready for final assembly* (D. Voice).

from stalling on dirty track whilst the other bogie tries to push against it. This means that if one bogie gets electrical supply then they both get it and all eight wheels are used as pick-ups. I took care and did several checks to ensure that the connecting wire did not interfere with the movement of the bogies.

At this stage the body of the model was still in its unpainted brass condition. I took advantage of this to solder a strip of 1½ mm wide thin brass along the inside of the saloon sides. This was positioned ½ mm below the window line. I found it impossible to actually measure and solder the strip in place. So I decided to tack solder it temporarily. Holding the strip roughly in place I put the first tack on. I adjusted the strip by eye and gave it a second tack. Then I went back to the first one to re-position it. When all looked well I gave it two further joints. It was quite easy to line it up using the bottom of the windows as a guide. The reason for these strips is twofold. They act as a stiffener reducing the tendency of the sides to bow inwards through handling, and they also form the locating ledge on which the chassis rests. When the two strips were in place I dropped the body over the chassis and checked for any faults. It all looked in proportion but when I touched the top of the body there was an unacceptable amount of rocking. This I traced to the female studs on the chassis being slightly out of alignment with the male studs of the bogies. I carefully twisted the chassis until the rocking was cured. The whole lot was assembled and checked again and all seemed well. The next thing was a quick test run on the layout. This was satisfactory and so the bogies and chassis were removed. I then soldered the lifetrays and steps in place. The lifetrays were in fact placed nearer the end than on the prototype, this was to leave sufficient swing for the bogies. I found it easiest to solder the top of the lifetray to the inside of the bulkhead. The compromise is worth it for the extra strength given to this delicate item. The lifeguards were left until later. I tend to find that these get damaged during assembly and painting and so I always leave them until the very end. The chassis and body were washed in very hot water with plenty of detergent and scrubbed with an old toothbrush. I then gave them a coat of self-etching primer inside and out.

I painted inside the saloon a dark brown with a white ceiling (Humbrol matt HR142 and matt 34). The outside of the car was given three coats of lining cream (Humbrol matt HR103). Using self adhesive tape I masked off the edges for the LCC purple lake. This I did in my usual way by first sticking the tape to a piece of flat sheet metal. I then cut strips about ¼ in wide with a new edge on my craft knife. These strips were peeled off and stuck on the body in the appropriate place. I have gone over this in detail because I have had a number of comments from people who tell me they are not able to get

good results using this method. It is most important to do this cutting as it achieves two crucial points. The edge is cut clean (the edge of the usual roll of tape gets ragged and sticky and is not suitable for masking). It also takes away some of the sticking power of the tape making it less likely to peel off the existing paint. This is very important on brass models as the paint bond is very weak. When the painting was complete (the purple lake is a mixture of equal parts of HR102 and HR144) and the top coat had been allowed to dry for about two hours, the tape was peeled away. This was done with the adhesive tape folded back on itself and drawn back very slowly checking that there was no sign of the painted surface lifting. In places it did look as if it was starting to lift and I worked the tape very carefully to try to get around the lifted section. On one occasion this failed and I then started from the other end of the tape. I was lucky as the paint did not actually break, it just left a bubble. This I was able to press down with a cocktail stick and it kept in place when the varnish was applied. But it is a pointer that care is needed in operation on the layout as even slight knocks can give nasty paint chips.

As can be seen in the photographs I chose an early version of the livery. I left the bulkheads primrose with just a strip of purple lake along the bottom, and the door dark brown. The platforms were painted dark grey and the insides of the dashes, steps and under gear red oxide (matt 67 and HR110 respectively). The truck sides (BEC castings of the E and E/1 maximum traction bogies parts 107A and 107B) were low melt soldered to the bogie unit. One bogie was fitted with the plough carriers. The truck sides and plough carriers were painted red oxide.

My attention now turned to the roof. To make this item with its double curvature ends I always use balsa wood. A strip of 5 mm thick balsa was chosen for its close grain and stiff feel. I cut it to the length over the dashes and 2 mm wider than the top of the saloon. I sanded it to shape using one of the foam rubber blocks covered with emery cloth. I used the Medium/Fine block. When I was satisfied I gave the roof a good coat of sander sealer. A good tip is to add ordinary talcum powder to the sander sealer, mixing it well in prior to painting. This makes it very thick and it covers the grain very easily. If necessary add further coats until all the grain is concealed. I sanded my roof down to a smooth finish (the added talcum powder allows a glass like finish to be obtained ready for painting). Such is the finish that can be obtained that it is not possible to tell whether balsa wood or metal was used for the roof. A smaller piece of 2½ mm thick balsa was used for the clerestory roof and given the same treatment. It was fitted with a trolley plank just as the prototypes were (although, of course, they were never fitted with trolley poles). The roof surface was painted white all over whilst the clerestory fret was bent to shape and painted purple lake. I used small pieces of balsa for the ends of the clerestory. When the painting had been completed the three sub-assemblies forming the roof were glued together.

I lined out the body using gold self adhesive tape on the purple lake panels. This was done by cutting strips and laying them carefully in the correct position. I chose a suitable number from the Class G and applied it using Blick gold rub-on numbers. The LCC transfer was one that had been left over from a previous BEC Kit (it is available as a separate part). On the prototype the primrose colour was lined out with a fine black or brown line. I felt that

Looking well patronised, the G Class car No 568 is ready for exhibition duty (model and photo, D. Voice).

anything I tried would be grossly over-sized and decided it was better to leave it off. So I next gave the body a coat of gloss varnish, fresh from a new tin. The windows were glazed using acetate sheet. The roof was glued on and the handrails and bars on the bulkhead windows were cut from brass wire and glued in place. Model shops have started keeping 'Metal Centres' and these often have fine diameter brass wire available in straight lengths. They are ideal for handrails. I also use it, appropriately bent, to make the handbrake. The controller was a BEC spare, part No 8, which was painted black with a gold top and glued in place.

BEC also provided the two line route box. This was painted dark brown and the destination chosen from the range of Mabex transfers. Unfortunately, the exact termini were not available and so I used the Westminster destination on the basis that my car was to be turned short at Westminster to be returned through the subway. In actual fact there was a suitable crossover at Westminster but whether such things actually happened I do not know. In keeping with the early style of livery I fitted colour light route indicators. These I made from a small piece of balsa with pin heads glued in place to represent the lenses. I used the colour combination red, green, red which was one of the subway routes. In the case of the model it was, of course, painted on.

The chassis was fitted with passengers, these being the top half of suitable scale figures. These were painted and then the chassis was glued in place using the ledges inside the saloon to locate it in place. Finally the lifeguards were fixed using epoxy resin and painted red oxide. An opportune exhibition allowed me to give the model a good testing. The idea was to determine which direction of travel the model favoured. In actual fact there was very little to choose. However, I did glue the driver at the end which was running slightly better. The usual protective carrying box was made and the model was ready for plenty more exhibition work.

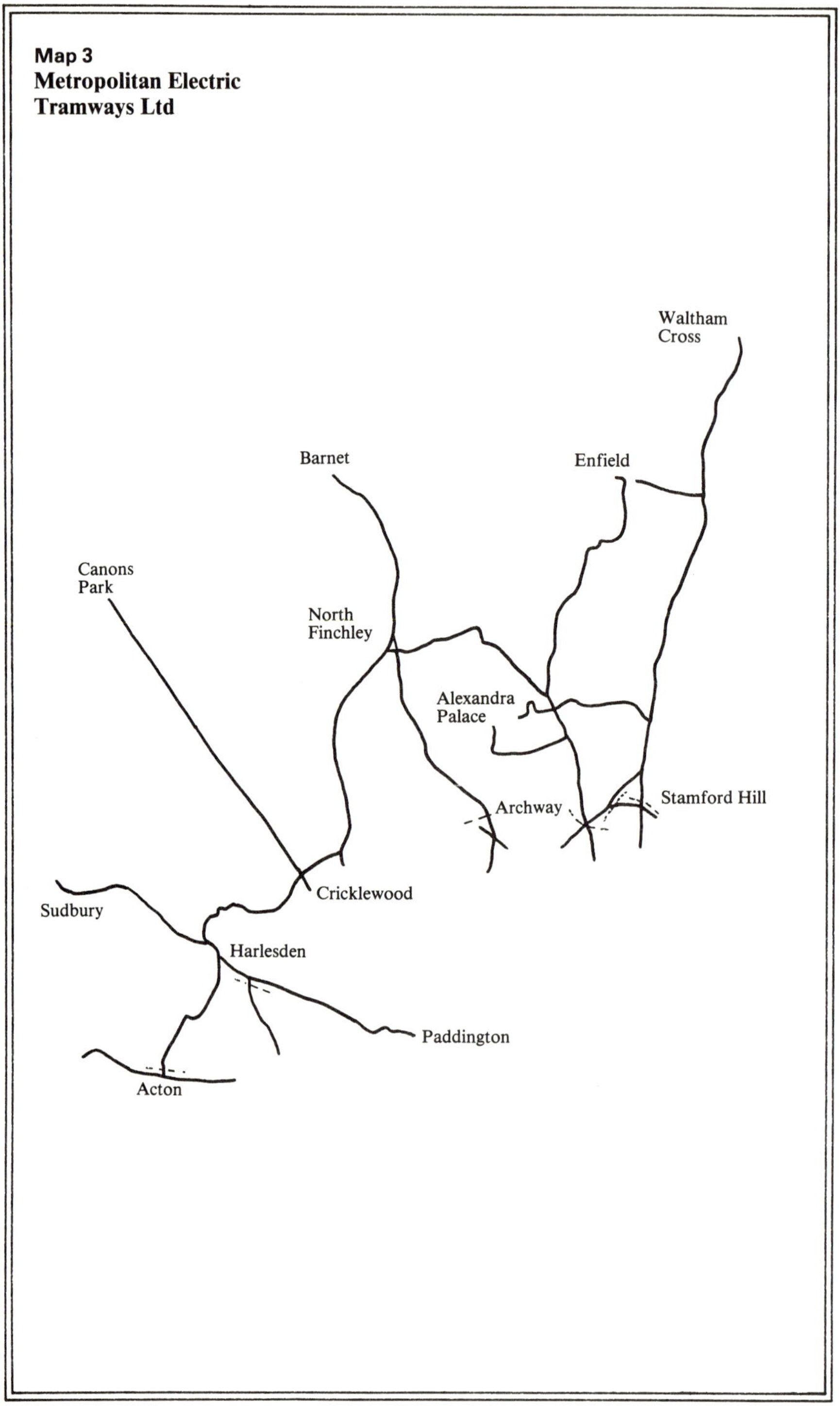
Map 3
Metropolitan Electric
Tramways Ltd
Waltham
Cross
Barnet
Enfield
Canons
Park
North
Finchley
Alexandra
Palace
Archway
Stamford Hill
Cricklewood
Sudbury
Harlesden
Paddington
Acton

Chapter 3

Metropolitan Electric Tramways

North London and its outskirts were served by the North Metropolitan Tramway Company. As we have seen this was the largest of London's horse tramway systems. The LCC took over that part of the company within their jurisdiction. The remainder was acquired in 1901 by the Metropolitan Electric Tramways Ltd (MET), a member of the British Electric Traction Group (BET). The aim of the new owners was to electrify and expand the system. Agreements were soon reached with Middlesex and Hertfordshire county councils whereby the company would operate the services over all their lines. The necessary powers were obtained and construction of the electrified lines began. The first routes served by electric trams opened in 1904 from Wood Green to Finsbury Park, the last part of this route being inside the London County boundary. Expansion was rapid over the next few years, including a short length at Highgate from the Archway to the *Archway Tavern*. This was also inside the LCC boundary and was actually constructed by the LCC and leased to the MET. There were also two routes in the grounds of Alexandra Palace which were some of the very few miles of reserved track in the London area and the only open-sleepered track in the whole of the London systems. Extensions continued to be made although up until 1909 there were two quite separate parts of these electrified tramways. One was centred around Wood Green and the other around Willesden. They were finally joined when extensions from North Finchley and Cricklewood met at Child's Hill. There was a further thrust into LCC territory with the electrification of the line from Willesden to Paddington. However, these lines were only leased to the MET. By 1911 all the route mileage was complete. There were some proposals to extend further north and east but they were never started.

In 1912 that part of the original Wood Green to Finsbury Park route that was inside the LCC boundary was taken over by the London County Council. This section was unusual as it was equipped for both conduit and overhead operation. Thus LCC tramcars could run on the conduit to Manor House whilst those MET cars with only trolley poles could still reach Finsbury Park. The controlling interest of the MET changed hands in 1913 to join with the LUT and Southmet under the management of the London and Suburban Traction Company. The Underground Electric Railways had a large interest in the London and Suburban and thus the MET became part of the 'Underground' group. This was an attempt to counter the increasing bus competition which was eating into tramway profits. The decline had begun and by 1920s there was a deficit of costs over income for two years in every three. In the early 1930s, however, there was a large investment in new modern tramway cars of the Feltham design. This occurred while the first moves were being made towards the unification of public road transport under London Transport.

In discussing the early days of the fleet, mention must be made of the Brush Electrical Engineering Company Limited. Like the MET, it was a member of the British Electric Traction Group and naturally supplied the tramcars needed. In fact the co-operation was such that finished component parts were supplied by Brush for assembly by the MET. However, on the opening of the system when 150 tramcars were needed, and at times when overhaul and repair work prevented the MET building tramcars, they were delivered ready assembled from Brush. Orders were placed for the first three designs in 1903 for delivery in 1904/5. The classification of the tramcars into types defined by letters was carried out by the Underground Group in 1912. This seemed to complicate matters, so for our purposes I will describe the trams in their numeric grouping (roughly in the order of delivery) whilst noting the Underground classification.

The first cars to be ordered were Nos 1 to 70 and they were delivered in 1904/5 in their open top condition (designated B Type). In outward design they resembled the LCC Class A in original condition. The MET tramcars

MET Type B tramcar No 9 in its B/2 condition with balcony-top cover. Note the reversed (pony wheel leading) maximum traction bogies (London Transport).

had Brush BB maximum traction bogies which were fitted with the pony wheels outermost (or reversed). One car, No 25, did have its bogies turned so that the larger, driving wheels led. This followed an accident where a Type A car ran away down Archway Road colliding with another tram, a bus and a hearse. The experiment was inconclusive but the bogies on No 25 were never restored to their original state, nor were any other trams so modified. There were two distinct batches of the B Type delivered, the difference being in the bulkhead windows. On one batch they were 6 in shorter than the other batch. In 1914/15 sixteen of the Type B cars were given top covers with open balconies. The numbers were 3, 4, 5, 7, 9, 10, 11, 13, 15, 16, 19, 24, 26, 27, 30 and 34, and when so altered were given the classification B/2 (B/1 had been used for a short while to define the difference in the batches, mentioned earlier).

It is worth noting that when delivered the trams were known as the 'MET' cars as they were painted with the MET name on the lower rocker panel and did not carry the Middlesex County Council title. In modelling terms the BEC Kits No 12 can be used to construct this type of tramcar. The changes required are similar to those described for the LCC Class A. The major difference is in the bogies. The bogie carrier will need to be re-positioned in the body to ensure that the reversed bogies are positioned correctly. The stairs should be 90° direct (unlike the reversed stairs on the LCC cars). For the B/2 balcony top covered version the same kit can be used as a basis. However, the top will need considerable modification. The balcony ends of some of these cars were very pronounced as they had a continuation of the dash plates in place of the more usual wire mesh. This gave the ends a very heavy look and one can imagine that small children would be on tip toe trying to peer over it. The upper-deck side windows will also need modification. The two middle windows will be as the kit but the windows at each end will need to have the inner half panelled in. The upper-deck bulkheads can be made of plastic card or fabricated from brass in the way described in Chapter 1 for the body of the steam locomotive.

Five of the B Type tramcars, all of which had been damaged in accidents (Nos 2, 12, 22, 31 and 46), were completely rebuilt in 1924/25. When they came out of the Hendon Works they were identical to the H Type but retained their original numbers. Under the classification scheme they were re-designated H Type. In 1927 No 56 was cut down to single deck and fitted with a four-wheel truck for experiments in twin-car operation. It ran with a Type H car and this episode is discussed in more detail in that section. All the B/2s, the five Type H and twelve of the remaining 49 B Types in original condition survived to be re-numbered in the London Transport fleet.

The second design of cars, Nos 71 to 130, were also built in 1904/5 for the opening of the electric routes. Designated Type A these were also bogie open-top tramcars. But there the similarity stopped. Although originating from the Brush works alongside the Type B these cars had six equal sized windows in each saloon side. The windows had the tudor-arch style of top and had three louvres in place of the usual quarter light. The upper-decks were not canopied but stopped square just protruding beyond the bulkhead. The stairs were in two straight flights with a small landing half-way up (sometimes referred to as 'Exhibition' or 'Robinson' type). The headlamps were fitted on the ends of the upper decks. As with all the early MET open-top trams there was ornate scrollwork where lesser companies would have used wire mesh. When delivered these tramcars were known as the 'MCC' cars as they carried the title 'County Council of Middlesex' and the County coat of arms on the upper rocker panel as well as 'Metropolitan Electric Tramways Limited' on the lower rocker panel. This, with the ornate scrollwork, makes a modellers' nightmare.

All of the A Type vehicles had maximum-traction bogies with the pony wheels outermost. Like the Type B, BEC bogies can be used when modelling these cars. However, there are no tramcar kits that can be modified to represent the A Type. The modeller must scratchbuild. This can be done either in brass (my favourite material) or plastic card. The smaller parts such as controllers, lifeguards and trays, bulkheads and destination boxes are all available as spares direct from BEC Kits (parts Nos 7, 12, 113, 4 and 29 respectively).

Six Type A tramcars were fitted with plough carriers in 1919 for through running on to the LCC conduit. Like the remainder of the class, they remained in the open top condition until all 60 were rebuilt with top covers in 1928/29. The first 20 cars were given top covers with open balcony ends. However, this made the tramcars rather tall and there were worries that they may have been prone to overturning. On the remainder the lower saloon was reduced in height and as a result the upper flight of stairs shortened and turned to give a 90° angle instead of 180°. The three vents above each tudor-arched window were removed. This was the area where the reduction in height was achieved. The upper-deck was totally enclosed but only to the length of the original open-top design. The roof had a short extension over the stairs which were otherwise left open to the elements. The headlights were moved to the dash. Fifty-five of the Type A tramcars survived to be re-numbered in the London Transport fleet. Like many other of the MET cars the modeller will need to scratchbuild to produce either of the variations of this type. There was one of the Type A that would be most attractive to model. No 77 was given a totally enclosed top deck that extended over the platforms and that had a domed silver-painted roof which gave it a much more modern appearance and gained it the name 'Silver Queen'.

The final design of tramcar that was ordered for the opening period was the single-deck four-wheel car designated Type E. The 20 in the batch were numbered 131 to 150 and they were delivered in 1905, all with the MCC title. They were purchased to work the Alexandra Palace route (site of electric tramway experiments in 1898/99) which had a low bridge in Station Road, Wood Green and were also used from the Edmonton depot. They were delivered with the headlamps fitted on the roofs and mechanical track brakes applied by the turning of a wheel behind the handbrake. This was for working the steep hill to the Palace. Tramcars were not permitted to stop on the hill. There was a dance hall half-way down the hill. In order to provide a service for patrons four cars were fitted with air-oil brakes. These were the only cars allowed to stop on the hill. By 1908 double-deck cars had taken over all the workings from Edmonton, so being surplus to requirements four of them (Nos 135, 136, 143 and 144) were sold to New Zealand systems. Two (Nos 145 and 150) were loaned to the Southmet in 1921. As will be seen in a later chapter they were returned to the MET by 1926. No 132 was converted in 1922 into a one man operated car. This followed damage caused by an accident. The body was shortened to five windows while the platforms were extended and fitted with vestibules. The completed car was given experimental runs on the MET but was transferred to the London United Tramways (LUT) where it became No 341. Around 1924 the headlamps were re-positioned to the more usual dash mounting although some cars did run for a while without headlamps.

Apart from those previously noted, the remainder were re-numbered in the London Transport fleet and continued running on the Alexandra Palace routes until 1938. This tramcar design was the one chosen to become the first white metal kit of a British tramcar. In 1957 the model railway kit manufacturer Keyser (K's) introduced this model. When first sold the drive between the motor and the driven axle was a rubber band, but later the kit was modified to the more usual worm and pinion drive. Production of these kits ceased about 1977, but they are occasionally seen in the second-hand market. The kit, unfortunately, had a design fault and the chassis was rather weak. In use it tended to gradually disappear into the body until the tram ground to a halt as the under-gear slid along the road surface. For this reason, and the fact that the body was unstiffened over its length and tended to bow in the middle, they are usually fairly reasonably priced. Do be prepared to put the model on a new chassis and to spend time on the detail work that was lacking in the original kit. For example, there were no trolley poles, controllers, lifeguards or lifetrays. With a little bit of work this kit can be made into a most attractive model.

Numbers 151 to 165 formed the next batch of tramcars which were built in 1907 and designated Type C. The design was similar to the Type A except that the upper-deck was extended to cover the platforms and the staircase was a 90° direct type. The headlamps were placed on the upper-deck dash panel. When delivered, five of the cars carried the title 'County Council of Hertfordshire' on the upper rocker panel (probably numbers 159-163). The

Single-deck Type E tramcar seen outside the Alexandra Palace. Modellers will be relieved to know that the fleet and county titles were removed in later years giving a much more simple livery (D. Voice collection).

Left *The Keyser (K's) kit modelled as No 145 Type E car, in the condition at the time it was hired to the Southmet (model and photo, D. Voice).*

Right *Number 201, a Type C/1 tramcar at Manor House, showing the original open top condition. Behind is a four-wheel Type D (Lens of Sutton).*

Below right *Originally an open-top car, No 233 shows the later version of the Type G, with enclosed top cover. This photo shows clearly the plough carrier, fitted for through running on LCC routes (courtesy C. Withey).*

bogies were again reversed for maximum traction. The 15 cars were all given balcony-top covers in 1914/15. In the upgraded condition they were re-classified C/2. In the mid 1920s numbers 151 and 153 were the subject of twin-car experiments. However, the brakes were found inadequate and the tests brought to a close. The comments on modelling the A Type apply equally to these cars.

Next came 25 open-top, four-window, four-wheel tramcars designated Type D and numbered 166 to 190. The order for these was placed following tests with a three-window, reversed stair, four-wheel car built by Brush and originally sent to Leicester for testing. When the MET had tested the car they ordered the Type D. The test car itself was also kept after the stairs had been altered to 90° direct. It was numbered 191 and classified D/1. The Type D looked like a shorter, four-wheel, version of the Type C. The four windows were tudor-arched and the open top was extended over the platforms with a direct 90° staircase. The trucks were 6 ft 6 in Brush 'A' type and the head-lamps were fitted to the upper end decency panels. During the year 1922/23 the cars (including 191) were fitted with 7 ft 5 in radial type trucks and plough carriers (at the same time No 191 was re-built with four windows). This type of tram can be modelled using BEC Kits No 8 and altering the windows to suit. For conduit operation a longer 7 ft 6 in truck side and matching chassis will need to be fitted. You will also have to add the plough carrier. Unless you are skilled in bending fine wire I would recommend compromising with the scrollwork and using the etched brass mesh supplied with the kit. All the Type D remained open-top until being withdrawn in 1931. When equipped with plough carriers they ran on routes 39 and 51. They also held the dubious distinction of being the last open-top tramcars to run into central London. Some Type D cars were used as works vehicles, although they remained in their passenger carrying condition.

A further batch of Type C tramcars were the next vehicles to be delivered. These 20 cars (Nos 192 to 211) were slightly longer than the first 15 as they were given stronger corner pillars. This is probably why the cars were given the designation C/1. But otherwise the design was the same as the Type C. Numbers 207 and 208 carried the Hertfordshire title at a later date. The C/1 type were all top covered in 1928/29 with totally enclosed upper-decks. All the cars in this batch survived to be taken over by London Transport and re-

numbered in their fleet. The modelling comments of the Type C apply to the C/1.

The MET departed from their open-top design in 1908 by ordering five totally enclosed top bogie cars, Type F, Nos 212 to 216. The lower saloons were made from parts intended for C/1 cars but were reduced in height to accommodate the top cover. The reason for building this batch of cars was for the proposed through running with the LCC. So the maximum-traction bogies were fitted with plough carriers. In appearance they were like the first batch of C/2 cars. Three of the Type F were fitted with vestibules although the work was not completed until after the London Transport took over the fleet. The modelling comments of the C/2 apply to the Type F.

In 1909 the policy reverted to open-top cars when a batch of 20 tramcars (Nos 217 to 236) were bought, known as Type G, and all with the Middlesex title. Again the lower saloon had six tudor-arched windows and the trams were generally similar to the C/1 type but with glazed quarter lights in place of the louvres. The trucks were maximum traction type fitted with the pony wheels inside (as was normal). The whole batch were given totally enclosed top covers in 1928/29, but for reasons beyond my comprehension, kept the designation G. Cars of the Type G were used in through running on the LCC conduit and were fitted with plough carriers. All of this class were fitted with vestibules in the early 1930s. Again the modeller has to scratchbuild the body work for this type of tramcar.

These were followed by the Type H, which were delivered between 1909 and 1912. There were 80 cars in this class and they were numbered 237 to 316.

Below *Number 240 was a Type H car, seen here at the Waltham Cross terminus* (D. Voice collection).

Below right *'Bluebell', the first experimental car, No 318. Seen here at Wood Green depot in its rebuilt form following an accident. The roof was originally flat and the upper-deck windows taller* (London Transport).

They entered service with totally enclosed top decks, carrying the headlamp on the upper dash plate. Numbers 237-241 and 297-316 carried the Middlesex title. Apart from some small detail differences they were like the final condition of the Type G. Again these cars were destined for through running services on LCC conduit and were fitted with plough carriers. Although when the first through route began in 1912 (route 29) the MET had insufficient conduit equipped trams and had to borrow 14 LCC Class E/1 cars. They were the recently delivered tramcars Nos 1590 to 1604 which continued to carry their crimson lake and primrose livery. The letters LCC on the upper rocker panel were replaced with MCC and the name 'Metropolitan Electric Tramways' appeared in small letters on the lower rocker panel. One of the Type H cars, No 316, was selected for further twin-car experiments in 1927. It was paired with Type B number 56 which had been cut down to single-deck, fitted on a four wheel truck and made single-ended by totally enclosing the non-driving end (but fitting an emergency exit). The earlier braking problems encountered with the Type C/2 twin set was overcome by fitting air brakes to each car. However, the trials could not have been very successful as they were abandoned after a short period. No 316 returned to normal service while No 56 was scrapped.

Number 315 was also the subject of an experiment which was, to say the least, unusual. It was felt that by providing a front exit passenger flow could be speeded up. So the end platforms were lengthened and fitted with steps both sides. Loading at the rear of the car was no problem. However, the staircase would interfere with passengers wishing to dismount on the near-

side front. So the MET solution was a revolving staircase! The front end of the car had its stairs rotated 180° to allow passengers to exit. At the stub end terminal the conductor would not only turn the trolley pole, tip over the seats but would also turn both staircases. These modifications reduced the seating capacity on the top deck. However, they did not prove popular and so the car was returned to its original condition except for the lengthened platforms which it kept until scrapped. The earlier comments about modelling the Type G apply equally well to the Type H.

By the late 1920s the fleet was showing its age. The last batch of Type H tramcars were fifteen years old and the rest of the fleet over twenty years old. The MET decided to design an experimental car as a preparation for a more modern type. This was No 318 which entered service in 1927. It was totally enclosed with front exit, rear entrance passenger flow, and an upper-deck with plenty of glass giving a light and airy atmosphere. Most striking to the public was it blue livery which soon earned it the nickname 'Bluebell'. It was involved in a serious collision in 1928 and soon after rebuilt. Its flat roof was replaced by a deeply domed type which reduced the height of the upper deck windows. At the same time the passenger flow experiment was discontinued and the rear entrance widened. Again the modeller will find that there are no kits available for this most attractive tramcar. However, the design of the car does lend itself very well to the techniques of scratchbuilding described in this book.

Around this time the MET's now sister company, the London General Omnibus Company, was building an experimental tramcar using their bus technology. In fact it looked like two NS buses that had been joined back to back (history has repeated itself recently with the new single-deck tramcar delivered to Blackpool and built by East Lancs bus builders). Originally destined to join the MET fleet it wore the number 139. This was an error at Chiswick Works as it should have been 319! However, before it could enter MET service the tram, known as 'Poppy', was transferred to the LUT where it became number 350. Its history will be further explored in the following chapter.

The first experimental tramcar of what was to become the Feltham type entered service in 1929. Number 320 known as 'Blossom', was built by the Union Construction and Finance Company (UCC). It was very similar in appearance to the final design of the standard Feltham except that its cabs were lower and it was mounted on equal-wheel bogies. It had an enormous impact on the travelling public with its sleek, streamlined appearance. However, its non-standard equipment meant that it had a limited life and it was scrapped by London Transport in 1936.

The same external body design was used on the next experimental car No 330. This, however, had maximum traction trucks and other standard equipment. Originally intended for 'Pay As You Enter' service, it had staircases sloping the other way from all the other front exit Felthams. Service use showed the impracticality of that system at the time. No 330 continued to give service after being acquired by London Transport and it moved to South London along with the standard Felthams. In modelling terms Nos 320 and 330 can be considered together. They are easily modified from BEC Kits No 14 and the method is described in detail later in this chapter.

Above *The London General Omnibus Company experimental tram 'Poppy'. It was number 319 in the fleet, but the painters put the wrong number on! This was never corrected as the car went to the LUT as No 350 without giving any service for the MET* (courtesy C. Withey).

Below *The second experimental Feltham car, No 330. This is the car I have modelled in the latter part of this chapter* (MET official).

Above *'Cissie', the experimental centre entrance Feltham in model form with a standard Feltham. The car on the left is a straightforward construction of a BEC Kit. The modifications required for No 331 have been described in detail in* Tram and Tramway Modelling (models and photo, D. Voice).

Below right *Number 321, the standard MET version of the Feltham car with a plough carrier* (MET official).

The final experimental Feltham was No 331 known as 'Cissie'. This was a further trial of 'Pay As You Enter' using a single central entrance and exit. The conductor was to have been in the central well collecting fares as passengers mounted the car. This was once more unsuccessful. Number 331 was the first of the Felthams to have the high cab so that the eye level of the driver was the same as that of a standing driver on an ordinary tram. It was fitted with equal-wheel bogies. Again its non-standard equipment meant it was not suitable for the London Transport fleet. It was sold to Sunderland in 1937 where it ran as number 100 until the end of that system. It was saved by the late Mr W.J. Fowler, a founding member of the present-day Light Rail Transit Association, and can be seen at the National Tramway Museum at Crich. The modelling of this prototype is described in my previous book *How to Go Tram and Tramway Modelling*.

The standard design of Feltham car arrived in 1931, and 54 cars were delivered to the MET (others were delivered to the LUT) the MET numbers were 319, 321 to 329 and 332 to 375. This modern design car was not restricted to North London as those south of the Thames became familiar with the Felthams when London Transport moved them to Telford Avenue Depot in Streatham. Ninety of the Felthams were sold to Leeds (50 of them being MET cars). Two have been saved. MET No 355 can be seen restored to its original MET livery in the London Transport Collection, Covent Garden. Further afield MET No 341 went to the United States of America. The modeller is well served for this delightful tramcar. BEC Kits No 14 allows the tram to be modelled in its standard form and it can also be easily modified to accommodate the small variations that there were during the life of these cars.

The works fleet of the MET is quite a different proposition for the modeller. Information on some of the earlier vehicles is very sparse. The first three works cars were probably bought at the opening of the system and were identical water cars (numbers 01 to 03). They were probably built by BET. The next two cars, numbers 04 to 05 were a box van and sand van respectively. These five works cars were all four-wheel vehicles whose life is a mystery. There is no record of when they were scrapped, except 05 which lasted until 1938. What is known is that 02 was replaced by a bogie stores van-cum-wagon equipped with cranes which lasted into London Transport days. 03 was rebuilt as a four-wheel concrete breaker (operated like a pile driver). The winch was steam driven using a boiler towed on a four-wheel trailer. However, this was replaced by an all electric version mounted on a bogie chassis with a driving platform at one end only. There is still some uncertainty about 04 as this number was later carried by an ex-D type, which lasted to 1935. Number 05 was the longest lasting of these first works cars. It was vestibuled (the only London freight car to have windscreens) and remained in London Transport service until the closure of the old MET tracks.

Car 06 remains a complete mystery, but perhaps Mr C.S. Smeeton will discover some detail, and if so, it will be published in the new series of books on the MET. It may have been sister to 07, which was possibly a stores van. It is known that the second 07 was a converted ex-Croydon four-wheel double-

MET works car No 02 in London Transport livery. This scratchbuilt model uses a load of 'sand' to hide the motorised bogie (model C. Withey, photo, D. Voice).

deck car used as a rail-scrubber. 08 was a breakdown car, cut down from a B type bogie passenger vehicle. Ex-Croydon and Southmet cars were used as works cars 09 and 010, probably rail-scrubbers or stores vans. It is interesting to note that the companies preferred to use the title 'rail-scrubber' against the municipal use of 'rail-grinder' for the same job. This was the necessity to remove corrugations worn on the rails. This phenomenon was a natural result of operation. The rails were smoothed by driving a tramcar, that had carborundum blocks pressed hard against the top surface of the rails, backwards and forwards over the offending section of track. This could only be done outside normal passenger hours, much to the annoyance of local residents. Finally, D type cars were used as breakdown cars, although they were left in their passenger condition. Four were renumbered in the works fleet to 011 to 014 while a fifth (Type D/1) retained its original number of 191.

There are no kits of the works cars available so modellers are left to their own devices. Of course, kits of other prototypes may help, as would the spares lists of manufacturers. Easiest to model are the final 07, 09 and 010 which are best made from BEC Kit number 1, using the stores van version but omitting the central doors. The trolley and plank should be replaced with a trolley on a mast (the type used on open-top cars). These were converted from Types M and W/1 described in Chapter 7. Note that the windows should be boarded up. The remainder of the works fleet will need to be scratchbuilt. The final 02 was modelled by Colin Withey using the underframe and traction unit of a BEC Kits original E/1 kit. The bogies were end pivoted to an outside frame from which the platforms were cantilevered. The dashes, wagon and van bodywork were cut from card with the planking scored and the girder post cranes made from balsa and card. A false load of sand (sandpaper folded and allowed to naturally spring out against the sides of one wagon section) hid the traction unit, which then used the Triang 'Rocket' motor. Now that this type of mechanism is no longer used by BEC (the latest bogie units use a smaller motor and a central mounting) it is probably best to consider the central motor type of mechanism produced by Meadowcroft Models. The livery of cars 08 and 011 to 014 were red and broken white, the remainder were all brown.

Table 4: Metropolitan Electric Tramways 1904-33

Number	Class/ type	Year built	Body type	Trucks/Bogies	LT Nos	Scrapped, sold or changed
1-70	B	1904-05	OT later 16 were BT as Type B/2	MT rev Bogie Brush BB	2467-2482 (B/2) 2498-2521 (B)	1931-36
71-130	A	1904-05	OT later ET	MT rev Bogie Brush BB	2412-2466	1931-36
131-150	E	1905	SD	4 W 9 ft 6 in Brush	2302-2316	1908-38
151-165	C	1907	OT later BT as Type C/2	MT rev Bogie Brush BB	2483-2497	1936-37
166-190	D	1906	OT	4 W 6 ft 6 in Brush later 7 ft 5 in	—	1931
191	D/1	1905	OT	4 W 6 ft 6 in Brush later 7 ft 5 in	—	1931
192-211	C/1	1908	OT later ET	MT rev Bogie M&G	2282-2301	1936-37
212-216	F	1908	BT	MT Bogie Brush	2256-2260	1937-38
217-236	G	1909	OT later ET	MT Bogie Brush	2262-2281	1937-38
237-316	H	1921	ET	MT Bogie Brush	2169-2254 (inc. conv. Bs)	by 1938
317	G	1921	OT later ET	MT Bogie Brush	2261	1938
318	Bluebell	1926	TE	MT Bogie Brush	2255	1936
320	Blossom	1929	TE	EW Bogie MET	2166	1936
330	Exp.	1929	TE	MT Bogie Brush	2167	1949
331	Cissie	1930	TE	EW Bogie UCC	2168	1937
319; 321-329; 332-375	Feltham	1931	TE	MT Bogie EMB	2066-2119	1940-51
01-03	Works	?	Water car 03 rebuilt as a concrete breaker	4 W	—	?

Number	Class/ type	Year built	Body type	Trucks/Bogies	LT Nos	Scrapped, sold or changed
02(ii)	Works	?	Van and wagon crane	MT Bogie M&G	02	1936
03(ii)	Works	?	Pile-driving car	MT Bogie Brill 22E	—	?
04	Works	?	Box van	4 W	—	?
04(ii)	Works	?	Rail-grinder ex-D Type	4 W	04	1935
05	Works	?	Sand car	4 W	05	1938
06	Works	?	?	?	—	?
07	Works	?	Stores van(?)	?	—	?
07(ii)	Works	1927	Breakdown car ex-Croydon	4 W	07	1934
08	Works	1928	Stores van ex-B Type	MT rev Bogie Brush	08	1934
09-010	Works	1928	Stores van(?) ex-Croydon (09) and Southmet	4 W	09-010	1934
011-014	Works	1928	Breakdown car ex-D Type	4 W 7 ft 5 in	011-014	1934-37

Notes

BT Balcony top; **EMB** Electro-Magnetic Brake Co; **ET** Enclosed top; **EW** Equal wheel; **M&G** Mountain and Gibson; **MT** Maximum traction; **OT** Open-top; **SD** Single-deck; **TE** Totally enclosed; **UCC** Union Construction Company; **4 W** Four-wheel.

Livery

Post Office red and broken white, under-gear red oxide, fenders black, roofs dark grey.

Experimental Feltham No 330

This model is a simple conversion of a standard BEC Kits Feltham No 14. Since No 330 was the design upon which the production Felthams was mainly based there are only a few modifications to be made to the kit. Most distinctive of all are the ends since the cabs were noticeably lower than the standard Feltham. However, I will start the description with the modifications needed on the sides. The first job was to remove the advertisement mouldings on the panel below the upper-deck windows. The raised strip was carefully filed away, finishing with wet and dry paper to give a really smooth finish. This process was repeated on the vertical mouldings on the lower saloon panelling. The little mouldings on the outer uprights of the doorways were also taken off. The second window on the left on the lower saloon was enlarged to give a 5 mm wide pillar between it and the larger window on its right. The corners of all the lower saloon and drivers cab windows were filed to give a clean square outline. Then the skirt by the left door was shortened by sawing and filing to shape. The outer uprights of the upper windows needed to be removed but this was left until the ends had been assembled in order to prevent accidental damage to the upper horizontal strip. Diagram 9 shows the modifications necessary to the side castings.

Right *The first steps in making No 330 are the modifications (lower) to the sides and ends of the standard (upper) BEC Kits parts* (D. Voice).

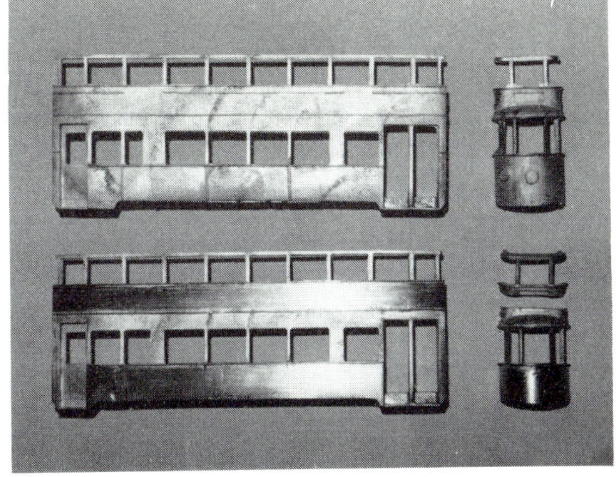

Below Diagram 9: *Modifications required to the standard Feltham side casting, from BEC Kit number 14.*

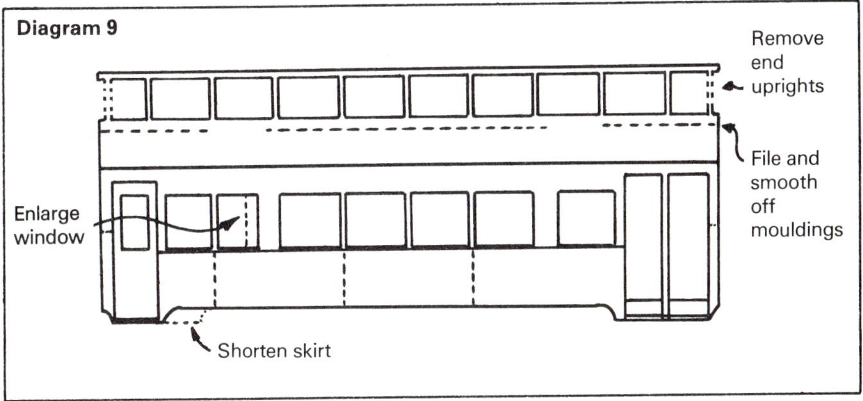

The ends needed a little more drastic action. First the two lights on the dash were filed off to give a smooth panel. Then the bottom of the dash panel was cut with a razor saw so that the new edge was level with the bottom of the floor casting. Finally the end was cut into two across the centre of the destination box. The photograph shows these modifications. The sides and ends were then assembled. Because the ends were in two parts I decided to use the extra strength of low-melt soldering to fix them together. If you are not sure about this technique then epoxy resin would do an adequate job. Actually when I described my method of low-melt soldering before, I was taken to task by Keith Thompson. He, quite rightly, pointed out the danger of the switching on and off method as the soldering iron could easily get too hot and start melting the white metal castings. So on his advice I bought a 14 volt soldering iron. This is connected through my resistance mat controller (actually an H and M Clipper). By adjusting the control knob the soldering iron can be held at the right temperature to melt the solder but not the white metal. In the full knowledge that the component parts of the kit are quite safe, soldering can be carried out with the same technique. An appropriate flux should be used (my favourite is Eames 40) and all the surfaces tinned before soldering together. It is also quite easy to low-melt solder other metals. However, you must first tin them with a layer or ordinary solder and then give a second tinning with the low-melt solder. This is worthwhile remembering, since complex brass assemblies can be made simpler by fitting the final parts with low-melt solder, thus eliminating the risk of seeing the whole lot disintegrate before your eyes. Since acquiring my 14 volt soldering iron I have had excellent results. I have also seen that one manufacturer is selling a soldering iron that can be temperature set by the user. This is specifically for such use a low-melt soldering.

However, back to No 330. The ends and sides were joined and the bogie bolsters fitted. I was left with a large hole in the ends of the upper-deck. I cut a piece of thin plastic card and glued it behind the hole which was then filled with Milliput. When set, the whole end was carefully filed and sanded to shape. Rather than risk damaging the ends I decided not to recess the destination or route number boxes. I felt that the water slide transfers I had decided to use would give an acceptable finish. The whole body inside and out was painted with two coats of matt white and one of gloss ivory (Humbrol No 41). The interior colour is not stricly correct, but in this small scale model the difference is difficult to detect, provided the window frames are painted the right colour. Whilst waiting for the various coats of paint to dry I painted the bulkheads (the screens behind the driver) brown (Matt number 70), the controllers black, the conductor and driver matt black with flesh colour for the hands and faces (No MC15). I low-melt soldered the bogie side frames to the bogie power unit and painted the visible parts red oxide (No HR110). The twin doors were painted red (gloss 19) and the seating strip was cut to give 14 seats 9 mm long. These were painted dark blue (gloss No 15). The stairs on MET No 330 were in the opposite direction to all the other Felthams and so new ones needed to be fabricated from balsa and plastic card, see Diagram 10. These were deliberately cut short in order to avoid interfering with the motor units.

Using the method of masking with self adhesive tape, the lower panelling was painted red (matt No 60) followed by gloss (No 19). The whole of the single door on each side was also painted red. The cab roof was painted grey (matt No 64). The distinctive five broad black bands were added using black

Scotch 3M plastic tape. This is the thinnest plastic tape I have come across. A length was laid on my metal cutting board and, with a new edge to the craft knife, I cut strips of the appropriate width. This was done by previously cutting a small piece of paper to the correct width, gauged by eye against the model. The paper was then used as a measure to set the steel rule when cutting the tape. The strips were then positioned on the tramcar. The number and 'Metropolitan' lettering were added using Blick dry press transfers. The larger 'M' and 'N' being made up from two of each letter. I combined the top three-quarters of one letter with the bottom three-quarters of another to give a single letter about 1½ times the original height. See Diagram 11. Destination blinds were chosen from the Mabex range of transfers. There is one specifically for Feltham cars with the route number 21 and the destination 'Wood Green'. This I cut to the exact size needed and applied in the usual manner. I took the route numbers from a different transfer that I had in my spares box as they were smaller on No 330 than on the standard Felthams. The outside of the model was now ready for a coat of gloss varnish which fixes the tape and transfers in position as well as giving the model a

Left *The sides and end are assembled and the bogies temporarily in place. The next job is filling the gaps above the driver's cabs* (D. Voice).

Above *Applying the black strips using self adhesive tape cut to the right width and stuck in place. A coat of varnish applied later will hold them in place* (D. Voice).

Right Diagram 10: *New stairs for Feltham 330. Leave the stairs smooth as they will not be seen when fitted. Paint the sides and underneath blue and the stair 'treads' dark grey.*

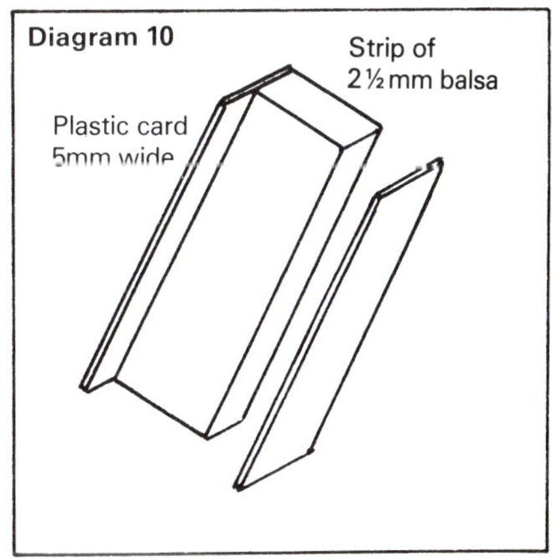

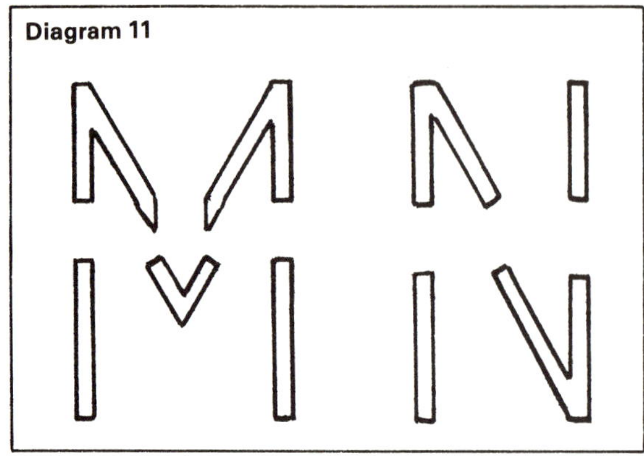

Diagram 11

Left Diagram 11: *Enlarging dry transfer letters by combining parts of two letters.*

Below *Making the doors from plastic card. These were painted red and glued over the kit doors (D. Voice).*

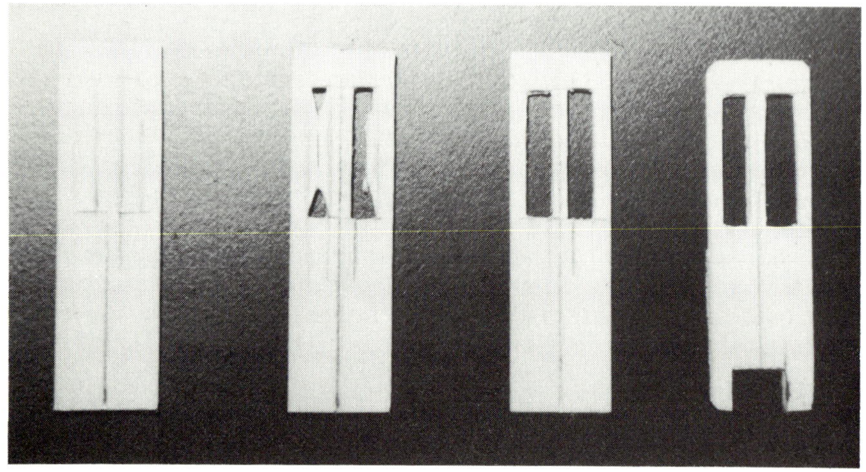

pleasing sheen. Do not foget to use a fresh tin of gloss varnish. The still separate double doors were also varnished to match the rest of the car.

The upper saloon floor was cut from plastic card and glued in place. I left the underside white to represent the ceiling while the floor surface was painted grey. Seats for the curved ends were fabricated from balsa and plastic card and were painted dark blue. Before the seats could be fitted in place it was necessary to glaze the windows. Past experience on modelling the Feltham tram has taught me that the driver's cab must be glazed first. This was not difficult. A strip of clear acetate was cut 15 mm wide and pushed into position. I firmly held the edge against the ridge formed by the open door frame and curved the acetate around the windows. By poking the craft knife through the door I marked the length against the other ridge. I removed the acetate and cut it to size. It now fitted firmly between the two ridges. To make sure that it did not slip out of place I removed it, smeared below the window frames with contact adhesive and re-fitted the window. Then I glued the controllers in place and fitted the bulkheads. The driver was glued to a bulkhead at one end (lower than indicated on the kit to compensate for the lower cab). The kit is not designed to be assembled in this way and it was necessary to file the sides of the bulkheads to squeeze them past the door ridges. But once glued in place these adjustments could not be seen. Now the double doors could be fitted in place and the rest of the tramcar glazed in the usual way. The upper-deck seats were then glued in place. The panels around the stairwell were cut from plastic card, painted blue and fitted. As is my preference some seated passengers were painted and added to the upper-deck. The lower-deck interior was finished by adding a piece of card that just filled the area between the bogie bolsters. This was painted to represent seating and the tops of plastic passengers cut off and glued in place. When painted, and the card mounted in the saloon, the traction units were very effectively hidden. The stairs were fitted in place by sticking double sided self-adhesive tape to the outside and then sticking the stairs to the glazing in the appropriate position.

In order to minimise erratic running on dirty track it has always been my policy to electrically connect the motors of both traction units. The common return was connected through the body of the tramcar. It was only necessary to solder a piece of thin, very flexible, wire between the insulated brushes on each motor. The wire was looped to allow complete freedom of movement for each bogie. At the same time, I made sure that the wire did not protrude under the tramcar or touch the road surface. The bogies were clipped into place and the model tested. By now it really began to look like a tramcar. The fenders were painted black and the undergear red oxide and fitted in accordance with the kit instructions. Now all that was left was the roof. The catwalks were glued in place and the upper surface of the roof painted grey (matt 64). The lower surface which was to be the ceiling of the upper saloon

The finished model. This can be compared with the earlier photo of the prototype car. The cut-away parts of the lower panels of the doors was a later modification (model and photo, D. Voice).

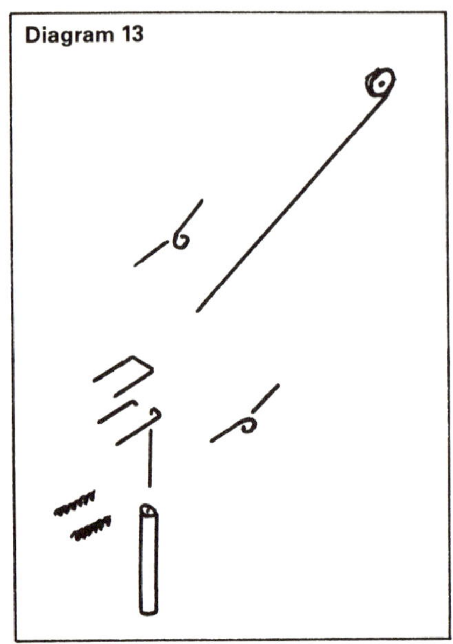

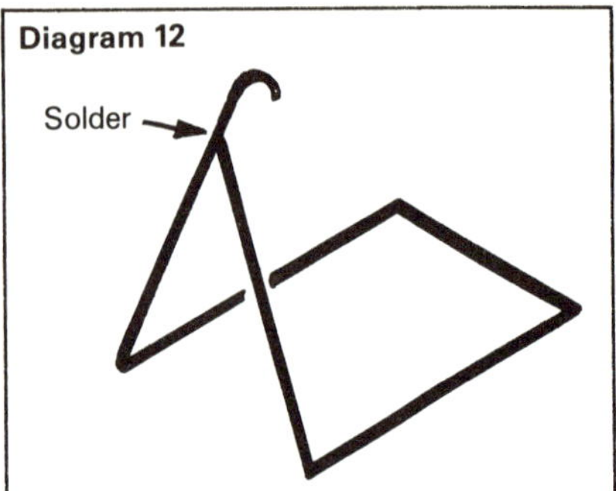

Above Diagram 12: *New trolley hooks for the Feltham car, fabricated from nickel silver wire.*

Left Diagram 13: *Exploded diagram of trolley pole construction, note the use of a Meadowcroft Models trolley wheel, which I have found gives the most reliable operation on overhead frogs.*

was painted white. The holes for the trolleys were drilled out to take a short length of fine bore tubing. Having had some problems with stray currents through the overhead I now insulate the tubing by wrapping it with self adhesive tape before gluing it in place. The trolley hooks supplied in the kit were discarded (they are too weak for exhibition use). New ones were fabricated from nickel silver wire and glued in place, (see Diagram 12). I made my own trolley poles as in Diagram 13. Those who read my previous book will notice that I now use Meadowcroft trolley wheels. I have found that the fixed head works better than my swivelling head, particularly through overhead frogs. These trolley wheels are available as separate items direct from Meadowcroft Models. The ends of the upper-deck were filed to accommodate the stronger trolley hooks and the roof was glued in place. The trolley poles were fitted after being painted black. Finally the box that the kit came in was modified using strips of corrugated cardboard to make it into a protective storage and carrying box.

One of the things that I find most enjoyable about my hobby is the challenge of rectifying mistakes when I make them. This came to mind when I thought I had finished car number 330. I took it along to one of my meetings with Colin Withey. A few days later Colin contacted me to say that something had been nagging him about the model and he had only just worked out what it was. The main doors were incorrect. I had used the doors as supplied in the kit and had not noticed that those on 330 had a quite different design. How to modify the complete model set me a problem. I decided to try an overlay of plastic card. As can be seen in the photos I cut the doors from 15 thou plastic card and made sure they fitted exactly. Then they were painted red and glued in place and luckily the last minute addition did not look out of place. I am now keeping my fingers crossed that there are no other mistakes!

Chapter 4

London United Tramways Limited

The west of London and the outer suburbs of Acton, Chiswick, Kew and Richmond were served by the West Metropolitan Tramways Company Limited. This horse tramway had been in decline and the Receiver was appointed in 1893 to control it. In the following year the London United Tramways Company Limited (LUT) purchased the company. Although they appear to have gained a dubious asset the LUT had ambitious plans. Electrification was very much in their minds. After much compromising, permission was granted for the running of electric tramways. Thus the new electric cars began public operation in April 1901. The Shepherds Bush part of the line was inside the London County boundary and this gave the LUT the distinction of being the first electric tramway system to run in London's streets.

The ambitions of the LUT were clearly announced by their purchase of 150 tramcars in 1901 to open their lines. The first 100 (numbered 1 to 100, they were later designated Type Z) were open-top tramcars on maximum traction bogies and with six tudor-arched windows in each side of the saloon. The ends of the upper-deck did not extend over the whole of the platform, but just protruded enough to allow access by means of the 'Robinson' double flight straight staircases (named after the General Manager). The dash panel behind the stairs was replaced with an ornate scroll-work screen. This scroll-work was repeated around the upper-deck decency panels. They originally had no pilot gate (lifeguard) for their lifetrays. The latter were constructed from wire-mesh and had a pointed end extending to the front of the platform. These were later replaced with the more normal style of lifeguard and lifetrays, once again using wire-mesh. The cars were fitted with mesh dog-gates each side at a later date. The cars were all delivered in a scarlet and white livery and they had a most attractive period appearance.

Number 52 became the subject of an experiment in 1909 when it was fitted with a Barber six-wheel radial truck. This was presumably not a success since the car was re-mounted on bogies. In 1910/11 65 of the batch were fitted with top covers and re-designated Type Y. The cars seemed to have been chosen at random and a full list can be found in the Autumn 1981 issue of *Tramway Review* (volume 14 No 107). These top covers never did suit the tramcars and they gave the vehicle a quaint and slightly ugly look.

As originally fitted the work seems to have been performed as cheaply as possible. The first car so modified (No 18) had just upper-deck bulkheads, a

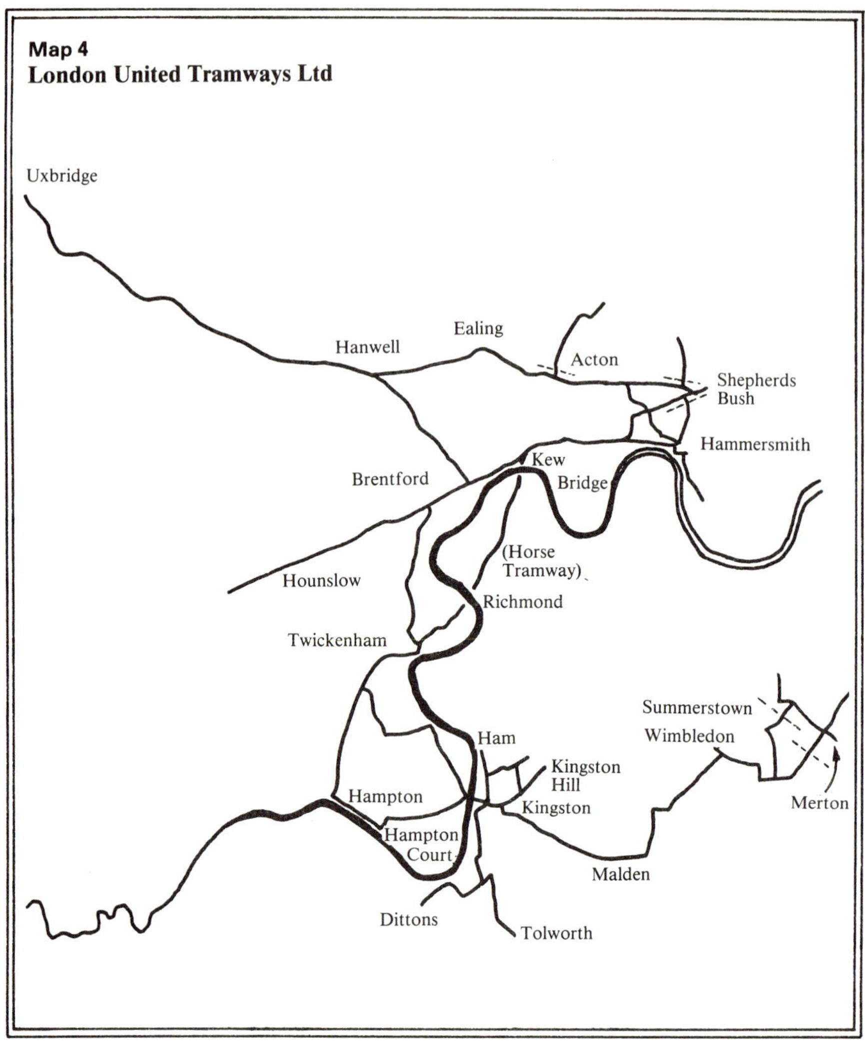

roof and a few side uprights. The trolley standard was left in place and the trolley pole poked through a hole in the roof. A further experiment with number 27 led to six-window sides being fitted to the top deck. On this car the window corners were square, but the remaining 63 cars and number 18 were adapted with curved tops to the windows. Again the trolley standards were left in place, poking through the roof. Around the hole created, a sort of guttering resembling an inverted umbrella was fitted to catch the rain (without much success). In the early days the scroll-work around the top of the decency panels was left in place, indicating the low budget basis of these modifications. To further add to the inconvenience of passengers only the four end windows on each side were glazed; the two central windows remaining open to the elements. Canvas blinds were fitted to allow the unfortunate passengers to gain some protection when it was raining. However, even these were removed later due to the springs being broken by children playing with them. It was not until the mid 1920s that these central windows were glazed. Following a fatality the remaining open-top cars were slightly modified in 1918 by the fitting of a handrail structure that resembled an extensive scaffolding project for a major block of flats! The purpose of all this ironwork was to protect the passengers. If a trolley spring broke, the pole would be held above their heads by the framework.

In the early 1920s some of both types were withdrawn and 15 of the Type Y top covers were saved and fitted to Type W cars. In the late 1920s the LUT were developing proposals to replace some tram routes with trolleybuses. When it had become evident that this was definitely the way forward, there was a policy of minimum maintenance on the track and trams in those areas where conversions were anticipated. Such was the state of the cars that opportunity was taken in 1931, when the Felthams were delivered, to swap tramcars around and scrap the most defective. With the start of trolleybus operation in the same year more tramcars were withdrawn and scrapped.

Type X cars lined up ready for service. This view shows the all white livery carried by the X Type in the early days of the LUT (P.J. Davis).

Around this period car No 58 was used as the breakdown car at Fulwell depot. But the end for the Z and Y types was close and they had all been withdrawn by 1933 when London Transport took over.

Modelling these types of tramcars presents a problem. There are no kits currently made of this design. I understand that one manufacturer is planning to introduce a range of kits to cover the arched window LUT cars, but in the meantime, the modeller must look to his own resources. The saloon sides must be either scratchbuilt in your favourite material or perhaps converted from the BEC Glasgow Standard kit. However, it would be necessary to use three sides to produce one tramcar. The upper-deck windows will need to be removed as will the end extensions. Then an extra window needs to be spliced into two sides to give a six window lower saloon 80 mm long. This would be 8 mm short of the true scale prototype dimension. These sides are *not* carried on the usual BEC Kits spares list, but they are obtainable by special order direct from the manufacturers. The bulkheads, stairs, controllers and other fittings are listed. The bogies can be represented by Meadowcroft Models Brill 22E type. Strictly speaking the Type Z and Y cars had Peckham 14D.2 bogies, but with slight modifications the Meadowcroft castings can be adapted to suit.

The second type of car delivered for the opening of the system was the

Type X cars Nos 141 and 142 working as the special 'flood cars'. This photograph also shows clearly the high railing to protect the upper-deck passengers in case the trolley spring failed and the pole fell (courtesy C. Withey).

Type X, numbered 101 to 150 and delivered in a striking all white livery. A parade of nine of these cars performed the inauguration ceremony, albeit three months after passenger service began. At first glance these cars appeared to be the same design as the Type Z. But in fact there were detail differences. For example the Type X decency panels were not as deep and this meant there was more of the upper-deck ornate scroll-work. Also the Type X cars had different style dashes. They had reversed curves at the end which were reminiscent of some horse tramcars. Despite the similarities in design to the Type Z tramcars, the Type X did not prove so successful. One problem was the extra projection of the bogie sides which were prone to colliding with other road users. These cars were little used from about 1910 and none were given top covers. In 1919 six (Nos 108, 118, 125, 137, 149 and 150) were sold to Blackpool. As part of a paper exercise, 40 cars of Type X were sold to the LCC in 1917 and later purchased back, never having left the LUT system. Numbers 141 and 142 were subject of an unusual conversion in 1917. The motors were removed from No 141 while those on No 142 were tilted upright and protruded through the lower-deck floor. The cars were coupled together and the trailer car only used for passenger carrying. The 'Flood Cars' were restricted to a section of road in New Malden which frequently became flooded. The set ran a shuttle service across the water between crossovers where service cars reversed. In 1921 No 107 was transferred, as a financial adjustment, to the MET who completely rebuilt the body to their Type G design, as number 317. In 1931 car No 148 was relegated to work duties in Hanwell depot. To maintain a high standard of cleanliness on the new Feltham tramcars this X Type was used as an aid to clean the upper-decks. It was classified as a Vacuum Cleaner car. Type X cars had been gradually withdrawn and 148 was the only car of this class that remained to pass into London Transport hands in its original state. The transfer of the Felthams cars to South London in 1936 made this car redundant. It too went south, but in this case for scrap. It was a great pity that London Transport were so disinterested in tramways that no move was made to preserve their last open-top tramcar.

The modelling comments of the Type Z apply equally well to the Type X. The modeller must, of course, note the differences between the two types of design. The Type X was originally given an all white livery, but this was found to be costly to maintain and was dropped in 1905. Although in the usual way, the cars would have been given their new liveries as they required repainting and some would have been seen in the old livery for many years. It has been suggested that a yellow and white livery replaced the all white. However, it is possible that cars were also given other colours; one source reports them re-painted in red and white. They would have received the red and white livery in due course as this became the standard LUT (or rather 'Underground') livery from around 1920.

The 150 tramcars purchased in 1901 were followed by a further 150 in the following year. Numbered 151 to 300, these became designated as the Type W. With the exception of one car the basic design was the same as the Type Z and X. There were detail differences and in many ways they were more like the Type Z, but the Type W had Brill 22E maximum traction bogies. They were delivered in a blue and white livery. Two of these cars, numbers 175 and

275, were 'Special Saloons'. Number 275 had been delivered in single-deck condition and fitted with luxurious extras including armchairs, carpets and curtains. Originally this car was intended as a directors' saloon particularly for the use of the manager, Sir James Clifton Robinson. It was often kept on a special siding at his house in Hampton. It was also hired for private parties and such was the interest that in 1907 car Number 175 was converted to single-deck as a matching 'Special Saloon'. They lasted in this form until 1924 when they were re-classified Type 52 and the story of numbers 175 and 275 will be taken up later. The rest of the class were open-top, double-deck tramcars until 1911 when 35 of them were given top covers similar in style to the Type Y. The cars so converted were numbers 265 to 274 and 276 to 300. The top covers went through the same design changes as the Type Y. In the same way those Type W cars that were so converted were re-designated, this time to Type U. In 1919, Walthamstow Council approached the LUT to purchase numbers 226 to 230 and 232 while Erith bought numbers 187, 192, 221 and 252 all of which had been on hire to them since 1915.

In common with the other trams they were repainted in the standard red and white livery from 1920. Some indication of how long a process this could be is given by number 218 which was reported to still be in its blue and white livery in 1931. In 1924 number 178 joined numbers 175 and 275 to become the S2 Type, described later. 1928 was a year of much modification with numbers 157, 161, 211, 243 and 261 rebuilt with T Type top covers and they were thus designated Type WT; their canopies now extending the full length of the platforms. The end panels of the balcony were very high, giving the cars a much heavier appearance than the more elegant Type Ts. Numbers 155, 199 and 288 were given top covers of the old type and designated Type U2. Several of the open-top cars (including 163, 194, 200 and 203) had their upper-deck scroll-work replaced with plain metal sheets. Number 247 was given a major reconstruction with a Type X lower-deck and a Type U upper and, not surprisingly, was designated Type XU. The Southmet came to an arrangement with the LUT for the exchange of ten Type U cars for a similar number of the Southmet open-top cars. The numbers involved are detailed in the chapter on the Southmet system. If these ten cars are included then 62 of the original 150 tramcars were still in existence when London Transport was formed. They all received new LT numbers and livery. However, they were withdrawn as the trolleybus programme was extended and all were out of service by 1936.

Modelling the Types W and U is not quite as much of a problem as the previous types since they had Brill 22E bogies. The Meadowcroft Models motorised units can be used either as a separate motor bogie with unpowered trailing bogie, or as a complete chassis using a centrally mounted motor with a flexible drive to each bogie. The latter form of mechanism is shown in the description of constructing the Type T tramcar at the end of this chapter. Otherwise, unless the previously mentioned commercial kit has been produced, the Type W will need to be scratchbuilt. Use can be made of commercially available parts as previously described.

Between 1901 and 1906 the LUT continued to expand their system and the network was completed with the exception of the extension from Kingston to the London boundary at Summerstown and Merton. Thus by 1906 further

Number 168 shows the original condition of the Type W cars, while No 296 has been converted from a Type W to a Type U by the addition of the enclosed covered top. Both cars are seen at Merton terminus. The lack of through running with the LCC meant that passengers had to walk between the two systems. The LCC terminus can be seen in the background (London Transport).

additions to the fleet were required. A further 40 tramcars (numbers 301 to 340, designated Type T) were purchased. These tramcars were delivered in top covered, balcony ended condition. They were mounted on Brill 22E maximum traction bogies and had the standard LUT straight half flight stairs. They retained the six window style of saloon, but the windows were square topped and those in the lower saloon had top lights. These tramcars had a most elegant design and soon gained the name 'The Palace Cars'. They were delivered in a red and white livery that they retained all their working life, although the style varied during the years. The features of these cars were little changed during their working life. In the 1920s the lower saloons were modified from longitudinal to transverse seating. However, this did not affect the external appearance. All the cars were fitted with magnetic track brakes. Number 301 was given high upper-deck dash panels around 1928 but the others were not altered. An external change to all cars was the addition of a route number box to the single line destination indicator and, at the same time, it was moved from just above the balcony mesh to a position on the mesh itself. 307 was the exception where the boxes were placed in a gap in the balcony panel. In 1932 between 13 and 20 cars were fitted with vestibules (including numbers 307, 310, 318, 319, 333-7 and 339) for working with the Felthams.

All 40 tramcars of the Type T were merged into the London Transport fleet in 1933, re-numbered, and eventually given the new livery. However, their

further life was short. Trolleybus development meant that they were no longer required and all had been withdrawn and scrapped by the end of 1936. The modelling of these outstanding tramcars is discussed in detail in the later part of this chapter.

The year 1907 saw the opening of the final line to complete the system. This was the link from Kingston, through Wimbledon to the London boundary. Unlike the MET, the LUT never entered into agreements with the LCC to enable the company cars to run through to the inner London termini, despite many attempts at reaching such arrangements. Hence there was never the need to equip LUT tramcars with plough carrying equipment. Indeed it was only after London Transport took over the system that some ex-LUT cars were so fitted, to allow them to give further service in other parts of the city.

As has been described in the previous chapter the MET Type E tramcar number 132 was re-constructed in 1922 into a one-man operated car. It had a shorter saloon (one window section was removed), a fully vestibuled platform and a front entrance. After a short period of experimental running on the MET it was transferred to the LUT. It was re-numbered 341 in the LUT fleet and designated Type S. The car worked on the lightly used branches of the Kingston network and the development was a success. Three more tramcars were modified in 1924 to become numbers 342-344 (Type S2). These were the 'Special Saloons' number 175 and 275 and the double-deck car number 178. At the same time the original car number 341 was given an extensive re-building as Type S1. At the end of this exercise all four cars were similar in design, with six window saloons mounted on maximum traction bogies. They provided the complete service on the Boston Road, route 55. This they did until 1928 when they were withdrawn from service and stored but not scrapped until 1931.

Number 341 can be modelled using a second hand Keyser MET Type E kit

Left *The advertisements take away some of the elegance of this Type T Palace car* (courtesy C. Withey).

Right *Some of the Type W cars were rebuilt with top covers similar to the Palace cars. They were designated Type WT and No 161 shows the high balcony ends given to these cars* (M.J. O'Connor).

Below *This view of a Type U car shows how the enclosed top was fitted to the short canopy cars. The stairs and driver were left to the elements* (M.N.A. Walker).

and then carrying out the same modifications as were done on the prototype. The re-built version of number 341 and the three Type S2 cars are more of a problem. These are single-deck versions of the six arched window Type W. Again if the proposed kit is produced then the conversion would be quite straightforward. A full vestibule would need to be added, as would the wooden structure on the roof numbers 342 to 344. The lining out on the one-man operated tramcars was very elaborate in the early days, but became

a little simplified later. As for the Type W cars the bogies would be best obtained from Meadowcroft Models and this would much simplify the construction of these models.

In 1928 the MET had ordered an experimental tramcar from the London General Omnibus Company (LGOC) and this was delivered in 1929. As has been discussed in the previous chapter it was to have been number 319. By error it arrived carrying the number 139 but this did not matter as it was delivered directly to the LUT depot at Hounslow and became number 350 in their fleet. Because it was built by a bus manufacturer it incorporated much of the then current bus technology. In design it was much influenced by the LGOC 'NS' type bus. The outcome was somewhat clumsy, although the beginnings of the Feltham design could be seen. It worked on the Shepherds Bush to Hounslow route and always remained the only one of its design. From the early days it was nicknamed 'Poppy' and survived to be absorbed into the London Transport fleet in 1933. It was given the new number, but retained the old livery, and continued in service until 1935 when the route was replaced by trolleybuses. 'Poppy' was not considered suitable for further work and the body was scrapped. The electrical and running equipment were saved for re-use.

This unique tramcar provides a nice prototype to model. However, once again there is little to help the modeller. 'Poppy' could be scratchbuilt using the technique described in other chapters. I have not explored the possibility but it might be practical to use the Pirate Models white metal bus kit of the LGOC 'NS' type. A kit (or possibly two kits) might well be modified into a replica of 'Poppy'. Motorising the vehicle is probably the best done with BEC motor bogies and a chassis similar to that described in Chapter 2.

'Poppy' was one of the experiments that preceded the Feltham type

Type S2 one man operated car No 342. This was originally one of the Type W special saloons (courtesy C. Withey).

tramcar. The others of that period are described in the previous chapter. When the 100 standard Felthams were produced, 46 were built for the LUT. These became numbers 351 to 396 and entered service in 1931. All except number 396 were standard Felthams with maximum-traction bogies. Number 396 was used as a test bed for experimental inside bearing equal-wheel bogies driven through a Carden flexible shaft fitted with worm gears. The undergear was given protective lifeguards the length of each side. The Felthams were set to work on the busy route 7, Shepherds Bush to Uxbridge. They were all taken over in 1933 and re-painted in the London Transport livery. They did not have plough carriers but continued to work over LUT routes until replaced by trolleybuses in 1936. In order to enable them to give further service the LPTB fitted them with plough carriers and number 396 was given a different set of bogies (from 'Poppy'). They were transferred to Telford Avenue depot to give many more years service south of the Thames. In 1950/51, 40 of the ex-LUT Felthams formed part of the 92 that were sold to Leeds. However, of these 40, seven never actually entered service in Leeds. One ex-LUT Feltham was saved for preservation. This was LUT number 369 (LT 2138, Leeds 544, later 517) and it was acquired by the Middleton Railway Preservation Society. When that society was no longer able to store their tramcars a further home was sought. Unfortunately, they were not successful and the only remaining LUT Feltham was destroyed.

Modelling the Felthams is simple. BEC Kits No 14 provides all the parts to make numbers 351 to 395. Even number 396 in its early form can be made from this kit. This tram had an unusual series of slats covering the bogies and the gap between them. This effectively hid from view the bogie design. So the modellers could use the maximum traction bogies in the kit and by adding scratchbuilt slatting nobody would be able to tell the difference. One thing to note about the Felthams is the window by the stairwell. In the kit it is small, showing the conversion that was carried out in order to provide extra ventilation for the resistance boxes under the stairs. The original condition of the tramcar had a larger window. The conversion required is described in the construction of MET number 330 in Chapter 3.

At the same time as the Feltham tramcars were being delivered the LUT was receiving it first trolleybuses. These were affectionately known as the 'Diddlers'. This was the beginning of the extensive trolleybus conversion that was happening in the LUT area. In 1931 all the Kingston routes were converted. This programme was continued by London Transport, with the result that people in South London were given the opportunity to travel on the ex-LUT Felthams.

The story of the LUT may be concluded with a look at the Works fleet. The first works cars came early in the life of the system, probably between 1901 and 1903. Number 1 was a four-wheel sand van, used to take dry sand to the depots. This was an essential service since all tramcars were equipped with sand boxes to enable the driver to spray the rails and prevent skidding when braking and wheelspin on greasy or icy rails. At some time this van was adapted to a rail-scrubber. With the merging of LUT and MET works cars in a common pool the LUT numbers were prefixed by '00'. Thus number 1 became 001. There is a distant view of this car on the MET and another photograph in its final condition awaiting scrapping in 1938, but they are not

Left *The LUT version of the standard Feltham car is demonstrated by No 370, without plough carriers* (courtesy C. Withey).

Below right *One of the two small motor water cars built at the beginning of LUT operations. This would make a good project for a first scratchbuilt model* (photo, probably makers official).

readily available. Works cars number 2 and 3 were small water vehicles on short four-wheel trucks. The trolleys were mounted on trolley standards fixed to the roof. A good photograph of this type of car is available and they would prove easy vehicles to scratchbuild. The short wheelbase might be a problem, but there is plenty of room in the body for a mechanism. These two cars were also converted to rail-grinder operation and also re-numbered to 002 and 003. Number 002 was scrapped in 1931 but number 003 lasted to London Transport days, fitted with a new longer wheelbase truck by now. It was scrapped in 1936 and again a good photo exists of it in this condition.

Works car number 4 was a ticket van (see front endpaper). In these days of tickets being printed by the issuing machine we tend to forget the vast numbers of tickets that were needed for the different values and routes of a large system. Thus a ticket van was a useful addition to a works fleet as it could also be used as a general stores van. In line with the others it was probably re-numbered at some stage to 004. There is no record that it lasted to London Transport days. Much later came the first bogie works vehicle which was stores van number 005. This was rebuilt from a passenger car (Type W) with flat wagon-like ends and a small van in the centre. Mounted on the roof of the van and extending each side, was a gantry with two block and tackle hoists. These were hinged to swing to either side for loading and unloading heavy equipment. The trolley pole was mounted on top of the gantry. This would make a most interesting model and with the Brill 22E chassis from Meadowcroft Models would prove an easy modelling project. The car lasted until 1936, eventually carrying the London Transport fleet name and livery. Number 006 arrived in 1931. This car has a complicated history. It started life in 1901 as Number 13 in the Croydon Corporation fleet. In 1927 it was one of a batch of 12 tramcars sold to the Southmet only to be sold to the LUT who converted it to a rail-scrubber. It is thought to have been scrapped in 1936. A model would be similar to the Croydon Searchlight car shown in Chapter 7. The upper-deck should be devoid of seats, just the floor and decency panels. The stairs were removed, but otherwise the boarding and all over brown livery are appropriate.

The final car in the works fleet was the old Type X car number 148. The history of it becoming a Vacuum Cleaner car in 1931 has already been told. It was never re-numbered and was taken over by London Transport in 1933 where it continued as number 148, finally being scrapped in 1936. Although that was the last of the official works cars, you will recall that mention has been made earlier of car numbr 58 being the breakdown car for Fulwell depot. In fact the LUT, unlike the MET, did not have designated breakdown cars as part of the works fleet. In emergency the repair crew would take any available car from the depot. However, I am sure that they would earmark a particular tramcar for their needs, just as number 58 seemed to have become. One can imagine that during the period of running down those routes to be converted to trolleybus operation the breakdown crews would have had many call-outs. It would be natural to keep all the equipment on a vehicle that was known to be reliable itself. I am sure that this would have been rotated around a number of such cars depending upon the fancy of the particular crew working at the depot.

Table 5: London United Tramways 1901-33

Number	Class/ type	Year built	Body type	Trucks/Bogies	LT Nos	Scrapped, sold or changed
1-100	Z	1901	OT later 65 were ET and designated Y Type	MT Bogie Peckham 14D2	—	by 1932
101-150	X	1901	OT	MT Bogie McGuire	148	1919-36
151-300	W	1902	OT later 35 were ET and designated U U.2 and XU. Some BT as WT Type	MT Bogie Brill 22E	2358-2411 2522-2529	1919-36
301-340	T	1906	BT	MT Bogie Brill 22E	2318-2357	by 1936

Number	Class/ type	Year built	Body type	Trucks/Bogies	LT Nos	Scrapped, sold or changed
341	S	1922	SD ex-MET Type E built 1905, later Type S1 when rebuilt	4 W 9 ft 6 in Brush later MT Bogie Brill 22E	—	1928
342-344	S2	1924	SD ex-Type W built 1902	MT Bogie Brill 22E	—	1928
350	Poppy	1928	ET	MT Bogie Brush	2317	1935
351-395	Feltham	1931	ET	MT Bogie EE	2120-2164	1940-51
396	Feltham	1931	ET	EW Bogie EE later MT	2165	1948
1 later 001	Works	?	Sand van, later rail-scrubber	4 W Brill 21E	001	1938
2-3 later 002-003	Works	?	Water tank, later rail-scrubber	4 W Brill 21E	002-003	1931-36
4 later 004	Works	1903	Ticket van	4 W Brill 21E	—	?
005	Works	?	Stores van ex-Type W	MT Bogie Brill 22E	005	1936
006	Works	1931	Rail-scrubber ex-Croydon	4 W Brill 21E	006	1936

Notes
BT Balcony top; **EE** English Electric; **ET** Enclosed top; **EW** Equal-wheel; **MT** Maximum traction; **OT** Open-top; **SD** Single-deck; **TE** Totally enclosed; **4 W** Four-wheel.

Livery
1901-20 Originally all Z Type were scarlet and broken white; all X Type white overall; most W Type royal blue and white; and all T Type scarlet and broken white. In 1905 some cars were painted yellow and white.
1920-33 Red and broken white, the areas painted red or white varying according to the different styles. In the early 1930s number 268 was given an all-over red livery. Undergear and trucks red oxide, fenders black, and roof mid-grey.

LUT Type T 'Palace' tramcar

When I was deliberating on the tramcar to model for this chapter I happened to find out about the Brill 22E motorised bogie unit produced by Meadowcroft Models. I wrote off to enquire and explained why I wished to obtain one (at that time I had in mind the Type W). In the reply was a reminder that they could offer a Type T from their range of stamped brass parts. I leapt at this opportunity and sent the appropriate payment. After a while the chassis and parts arrived. It transpired that my chassis was the first central motor Brill 22E type produced by Meadowcroft Models and I must say that it was very nice. At the same time I had ordered a pair of headlights, appropriate stairs and destination boxes. I could also have obtained lifeguards and lifetrays but in this instance I had decided to make my own. Meadowcroft

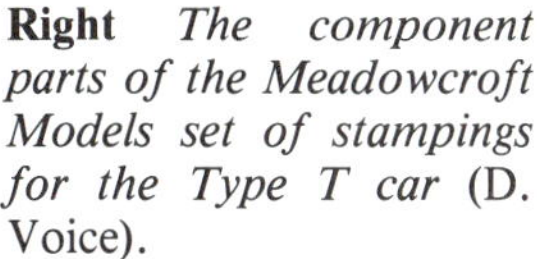

Above *Model of the Palace car built from the Meadowcroft Models brass stampings* (model and photo, Meadowcroft Models).

Right *The component parts of the Meadowcroft Models set of stampings for the Type T car* (D. Voice).

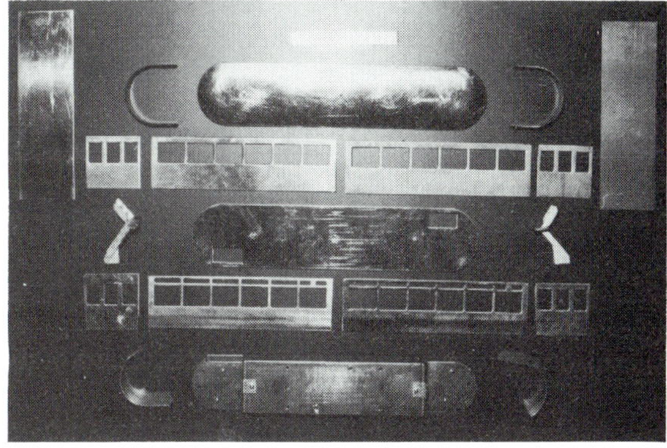

Models had sketched out the assembly in a letter to me so I was ready to make a start.

I decided to use my big soldering iron (a 65 Watt monster). This was chosen to allow plenty of heat to solder together the stamped brass parts. These are considerably thicker than etched brass and can really soak up the heat. If you are not happy about using such techniques then I am sure that modern glues will prove effective. I took the lower saloon sides and bulkheads and tinned the inside ends of the sides and the edges of the bulkheads. They were soldered together. I used a piece of wood to hold one side and one end in place first, and then soldered a pair of these sub-assemblies together to form the complete lower saloon. The bulkheads fitted just inside the saloon sides. I then made the sides 2½ mm deeper by soldering a brass strip on the lower edge to form a solebar. I checked that it fitted over the floor pressing and then I decided to fit the floor retaining brackets. These I screwed to the floor and offered up to the body. There was a gap between the brackets and bulkheads. So, putting the body to one side, I tinned both sides of a couple of small pieces of brass strip and soldered one each to the outside of the brackets. Then I tinned the appropriate area inside the bulkheads. Finally the floor was assembled to the body and the brackets soldered in place. I unscrewed the floor and refitted it to check that all was well. Then I turned to the false roof of the lower saloon. Turning the saloon upside-down on a piece of scrap wood, I slipped the false roof in place, then soldered it securely from the inside. It all got very hot and I found it useful to have pliers, tweezers and bits of wood handy to hold and move parts to the right position. Although inevitably I burnt my fingers several times.

Next I tackled the dashes. With the floor assembled in the saloon I tinned the edges of the platforms and inside the bottom of the dashes. These were soldered in place to the platforms, but not to the saloon. I had not come across this form of assembly before and wondered how it would work. When the floor was removed the platforms and dashes were also taken out as they were an integral part of that sub-assembly. I had feared that there would be an unsightly gap between the edge of the dash and the bulkhead. I should not have worried as it all looked very neat. I soldered the headlamps in place. Now that it was beginning to look like a tram, I started on the upper saloon. The sides and bulkheads were assembled in the same way as the lower saloon. Then the upper sides of the bulkheads were tinned as were the edges of the roof retaining strips. These strips were screwed to the inside of the roof. The upper saloon was offered up and the retaining strips soldered in the correct place at the top of the bulkheads. Again I checked the assembly by removing and replacing the roof. Then it was taken off again and put to one side. The balcony dashes were soldered to the bulkheads and the whole upper-deck assembly tinned on the bottom edges. I took the upper-deck floor and opened up the stairwell to suit the shape required by the Type T (see Diagram 15). Then the upper saloon assembly was soldered to the upper-deck floor. This really did soak up the heat and in the end I used a Ronson blow-torch to put it together. A word of warning here. The blow-torch produces a lot of heat quickly and must be used with care. I ended up with some of my earlier joints springing apart and had to solve the problem of getting everything back in to the right position. In hindsight it would have been better if I had just warmed it all up using the blow-torch and then actually soldered using the iron.

Now the big soldering iron was put away as I had the five main sub-assemblies forming the model. Firstly the lower saloon was positioned under

Below left *The Meadowcraft Models Brill 22E bogie power unit with a central motor driving each bogie through flexible shafts* (D. Voice).

Below right Diagram 15: *Stairwell opening required in the upper-deck floor to suit the Type T tramcar.*

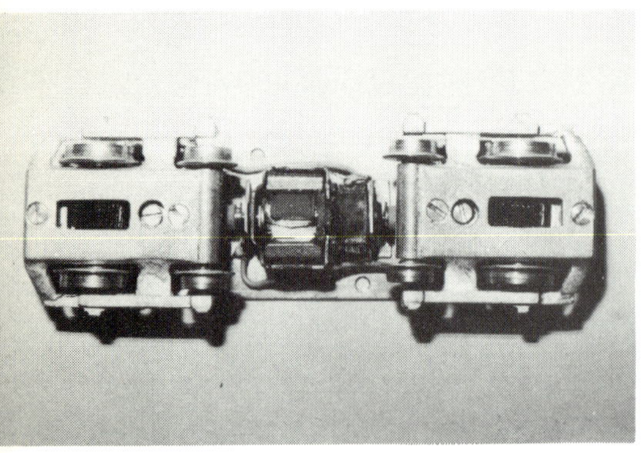

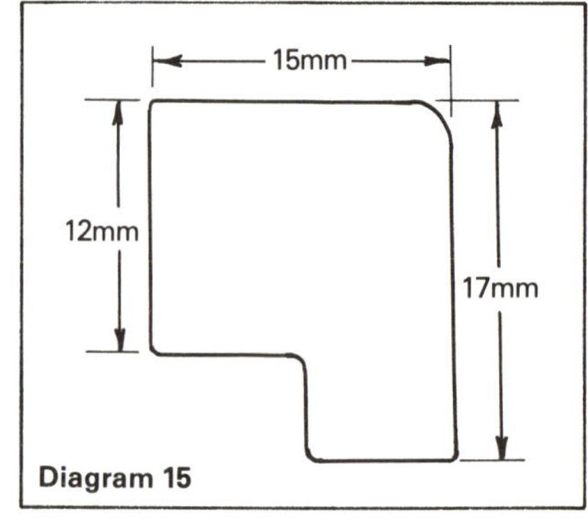

the upper saloon and marked through the tapped holes in the floor. Then the false roof was drilled out to allow clearance for the fixing screws. I was then able to screw these two parts together. The roof could be screwed to the upper saloon and the floor to the lower saloon. Finally the ready-to-run bogie unit could be screwed in place. I did all this to check the assembly and then took it all apart again. The bogie unit was put in a safe place and the rest washed in very hot water with detergent added. I used an old toothbrush to scrub all the flux from every part. All the parts were thoroughly dried and given an overall coat of self-etching primer. When this was dry I screwed the lower saloon to the upper saloon and for the remainder of the construction treated them as one unit. Straight brass wire was glued along the lower saloon using very thin wire to represent the beading under the windows and thicker wire for the waist rail. It should be noted here that I decided not to use the second curved false roof inside the lower saloon. This would normally be used to hold the lower saloon glazing in place. However, I found on my model that it protruded across the saloon quarter lights. I decided therefore to glue the glazing in place and to put aside the false roof.

The inside and outside of the model were painted including the dashes, platforms, floors and roof. The whole thing was given three coats of matt white. The lower parts of the inside of the upper and lower saloons and bulkheads doors were painted in dark brown (Humbrol HR142). The whole lot was then given a coat of varnish. Masking the car in the ways previously described, I gave it a coat of matt and then gloss red (Humbrol matt 19 and gloss 19) while the solebar was painted red oxide (Humrol HR110). It was at this point I realised that the model looked very wrong. I had glued the waist rail far too high. This meant that the red upper rocker panel was narrow compared to the white lower panel. It was so bad it had to be corrected and so I cut off the waist rails. These had just been glued in place, and I thought that they would come off easily. Not so, I had to cut and cut before I could release them. It did show just how well the glue works. I smoothed the sides and repositioned the waist rail. Then the whole area was re-painted. The result was worth the extra effort as it now looked like the real thing.

The lining was added using strips cut from the appropriate colour of self-

The six major sub-assemblies of the Type T car ready for the next stage of construction (D. Voice).

adhesive tape (gold on the red panels and black on the white panels). Numbers and the crests were chosen from the Mabex range. The style of livery I used was that introduced around 1920. This was carried by all cars until the late 1920s when an experimental livery was tried on a few of the trams. The experimental livery used large white triangles on the dashes and the lower rocker panel was painted red. However, this was not liked and a new form of livery very similar to the one I adopted was used for the last few years of LUT operation. The main change between this and the 1920s livery was that the crest was replaced with the title 'London United'. As it takes many years for new liveries to be adopted by the whole fleet, I am sure that there were cars running in the old livery right through to London Transport days. To my mind it had a long life and was eminently suitable for modelling purposes. The final job before giving the car its overall varnishing was to add the little white triangle to the dashes. This was a warning triangle which proudly stated 'Eight Wheel Brakes', one word on each side ('Eight' to the left, 'Wheel' to the right and 'Brakes' on the bottom bar).

The usual reason for giving the car another coat of gloss varnish was to fix the lining and transfers in place. However, in this model there was a second advantage. The proper livery of the vehicle was red and broken white. I have always found that matt white changes nicely into broken white by the application of a couple of coats of clear varnish. The varnish is in reality a very pale brown which nicely takes away the sharpness of the white. When the varnish was dried the upper and lower saloons were glazed using clear acetate sheet. Whilst making this model I was given the tip that glazing material could be fixed more easily in place using double sided adhesive tape. I thought I would give this technique a try and stuck some to a piece of scrap plastic (I used the type with the removable backing strip). This I cut into suitable widths with a craft knife and steel rule. The strips were attached to the top and bottom of the glazing material. The protective strip was removed and the glazing material stuck in the correct position inside the saloons. I found that it seemed to take a little longer than my usual method of using glue, because the tape had to be cut into strips before being used. However, the distinct advantage was that there was no risk of getting glue in the wrong place. Now, on average, I have to replace one glazing strip during the making of a model due to glue getting across a visible part. This time all was fitted with no worries at all. I was very pleased with the result and on reflection it probably took no longer than using glue. It was certainly far less frustrating. I then cut my usual plastic figures to form the passengers. They were glued to the floor of the lower saloon and painted appropriate colours. Then the floor was screwed in place, hopefully for the last time. Seats for the upper saloon were cut 10 mm long from BEC seating strip. After painting dark brown they were fitted in the upper saloon and suitable seated figures painted and added.

The distinctive 'Robinson' stairs were obtained from Meadowcroft (BEC do the castings for this type of stair). I was most grateful for this as the thought of making them had sent shivers up my back. But there was one addition to make. The Type T tramcars had what I can only describe as a kicking strip around the middle platforms. The casting respresents the open version (see the model described in Chapter 6). So I added this feature using 5 mm wide thin brass strip. I expect that I could have glued it in place but at the

Top *The body has been assembled and painted, this view clearly shows the Brill 22E bogies* (D. Voice).

Above left *The finished model of the LUT Type T car, with the white safety triangle on the dash* (model and photo, D. Voice).

Above right *Although the BEC Kits etched brass mesh could be used, I decided to construct the handrails around the balcony from wire* (D. Voice).

time I was demonstrating model tramcar building at an exhibition and so used it as an opportunity to show low melt soldering. I tinned the inside of the brass strip with ordinary solder and then gave it a second tinning with low melt solder before bending it to shape. Putting the strip in place was much harder than I had thought and it took about a dozen tries before I got it. By that time I was well into muttering under my breath. Something not recommended as a public spectacle. Anyway I did manage the first, and surpris-

The Palace car doing service duties at an exhibition and proving what an elegant car the prototype was (model and photo, D. Voice).

ingly, the other was fixed on the first try. I can only assume that there must have been one correct way of holding it in place and I went through eleven failures before finding it. The stairs were then painted with several coats of matt white followed by two of gloss varnish. The treads of the steps were picked out in mid grey (matt 64) as were the balcony and platform floors and steps. The pip under the step casting was filed off and the stairs were glued in place.

The rails around the balcony were next to be fitted. It would have been possible to use the etched brass mesh available from BEC Kits but, I decided to construct the complete handrail assembly. I used the fine straight brass wire available from specialist model shops. The uprights were cut over length and glued to the inside of the balcony dash. Then the curved horizontal rail was soldered to the uprights. The four shorter uprights were cut to length and the whole thing painted black. The lower part of the uprights were painted white to match the inside of the balcony dash. The wire mesh was added using netting material obtained from my local milliners. A strip, the right height, was cut and simply glued over the vertical handrails. The remaining staircase handrails were soldered together and bent to shape. (The photograph shows the detail). They were painted black and glued in place. The balcony seats were made, painted and glued in place. The destination boxes were painted dark brown and fitted to the mesh at the end of the balcony. To finish the upper part of the model the roof was taken and my usual small piece of fine brass tube fitted to take the trolley pole. A trolley plank was added from plastic card. The roof was given a few coats of mid grey (matt 64) and then two coats of gloss varnish and screwed in place after cutting the tall uprights to length.

Finally the detail parts were added. The controllers were BEC spares, while the handbrake and platform handrails were made from the same wire as the other handrails. The fenders were made from brass strip. This was curved to shape and glued under the front of the platform. The lifeguards, lifetrays and central dog guards were made from thin brass strip, painted red oxide, and fixed in place. Finally the motor unit was taken, the bogie sideframes painted red oxide, and the unit fitted to the body. To ensure protection of such an attractive tramcar I made my usual special box to store and transport the model. I quite looked forward to the opportunity of using this tramcar at the next exhibition. It certainly had all the Edwardian elegance of the real 'Palace' tramcars.

Chapter 5

Leyton, Walthamstow and West Ham councils' tramways

The Leyton, Walthamstow and West Ham systems form the major part of the municipally run tramways serving East London. The remainder are described in the next chapter. Although technically individual districts, the spread of housing and industry linked these communities with London by the early 1900s. This resulted in the need for public transport between, as well as within, the districts. The tramways soon responded to this demand and the tracks were connected across boundaries allowing through running and route sharing. They all wanted to have direct routes into the central London termini. But it was not until the 1920s that London County Council completed through running agreements with the last of the East London municipal systems. This meant that the lines carried a range of different design cars carrying different liveries, and makes an interesting possibility for the modeller. It would be quite legitimate to run different systems cars on the same layout. Thus giving the added interest of a variety of liveries.

Leyton Urban District Council (later Corporation) Tramways

Leyton Council had two horse tramways operating within its boundary. Part of the North Metropolitan Tramways Company and most of the Lea Bridge, Leyton and Walthamstow Company operated in the district. In the late 1800s the council had thoughts about running its own trams. However, nothing was done until 1905 when the Lea Bridge, Leyton and Walthamstow Company was taken over. The horse tramcars continued to run under council control, but preparations were soon made to electrify and extend the system. The horse trams had been numbered 1 to 10 and so the first electric cars were given the numbers 11 to 50. These 40 tramcars were delivered in 1906, the same year that the Council took over control of the North Metropolitan lines within the district.

The design chosen by the council was the standard four-wheel, three window balcony car, but with a long 8 ft 6 in wheelbase. The stairs were direct 180°. The electric trams were evidently very popular and in 1907 a further twenty were ordered. Numbered 51 to 70 they were exactly the same design and made by the same manufacturer as the first batch. In 1910 there were through running arrangements to Aldgate over LCC conduit track and to meet their commitment cars No 51 to 70 were fitted with plough carriers. These were found to be insufficient so a further twenty cars (Nos 31 to 50) were also equipped with plough carriers.

These trams can be modelled from BEC Kit No 4. The chassis will need to be changed to the correct 8 ft 6 in wheelbase. The trucks were Mountain and Gibson radial and will probably need to be fabricated by the modeller. This could be carried out using parts cut from the truck side casting provided in the kit. The upper balcony dash panels were very low and it will be necessary to remove about 2½ mm from those supplied with the kit. Apart from these modifications the kit can be assembled as supplied. As a model these tram-cars are a most attractive proposition and it would be quite legitimate to mix them with LCC models running on conduit track. The dark green and primrose livery of Leyton would make them very distinctive. Indeed the

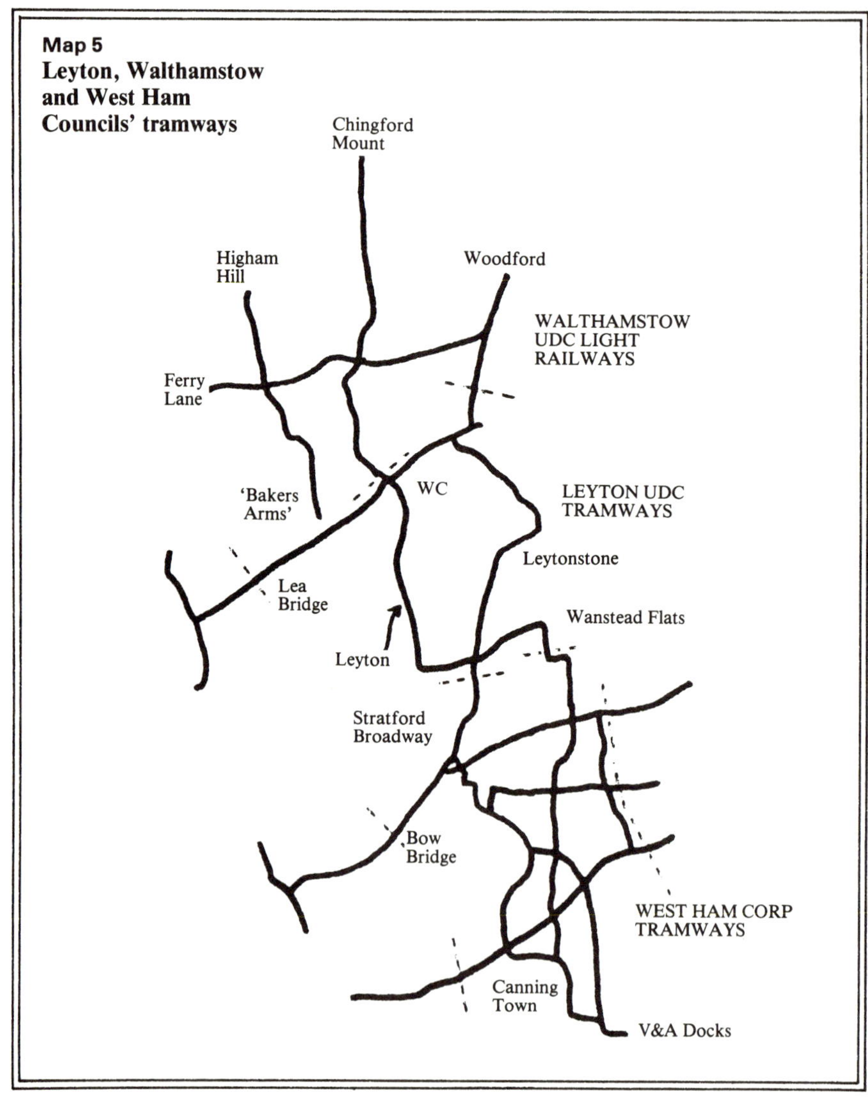

prototypes themselves must have added a splash of colour to the central London termini.

In 1915 two tramcars were loaned to Erith Council but the arrangement was short-lived and within a year they were taken back. This was the first sign of problems that grew greater. No doubt exacerbated by the long wheelbase radial trucks (which never lived up to their manufacturer's claims) the council found itself with around twenty unserviceable tramcars and many more needing major overhauls. Eventually in 1921 the LCC took responsibility for maintaining the rolling stock, overhead and track. Leyton Council were to re-lay track and renew overhead as part of the agreement. The first thing that the LCC did was to remove those tramcars unfit for service. A total of 19 trams were removed and stored at Hampstead (they could not be scrapped by the LCC as they were still the property of Leyton). The LCC introduced 20 of the E/1 Class as replacements and these operated from Leyton Depot. The remaining Leyton trams were overhauled. The LCC retained the Leyton livery and at the insistence of Leyton Council the elaborate monogram (LUDC) was kept on the upper rocker panel. However, the fleet name 'Leyton District Council Tramways' was removed and 'London County Council' added in small letters at the bottom left of the rocker panel.

After some track renewal in 1922, Leyton Council asked for improved services. This was achieved in 1925 by using West Ham Corporation tramcars on the joint route between the Victoria Docks and the *Bakers Arms*. The LCC replaced the West Ham tramcars with their own bogie cars. This complicated arrangement was necessary because the LCC was unable to spare any

Leyton tramcar No 27 of the 11-70 series. This photo shows the early livery with the council fleet name (courtesy I. Hodgson).

Above *In 1921 the LCC took over maintenance of the Leyton fleet. This photograph is of a balcony car from the 11-70 series. Note the absence of fleet name (although the monogram is retained). On the lower rocker panel, in small letters, is the name of the London County Council* (courtesy C. Withey).

Below right *Leyton Class E/3 No 191 in the LCC livery seen at Aldgate in 1931. Note the experimental cover plates over the bogie sideframes. These were added to give a more modern appearance. They were later removed to allow easier repair and maintenance* (G.N. Southernden).

of their own four-wheeled cars. Leyton Council became a borough in 1926 and the monogram was changed to 'LBC'. In 1927 six of the Leyton cars were re-trucked with Brill 21E 6 ft 6 in trucks from scrapped B Class cars. In 1930 Leyton Corporation decided to investigate the purchase of new tramcars. They examined some of the latest LCC cars and ordered 50 to the E/3 design. These were delivered, with metal vestibules from 1931 and had the then standard LCC livery of red and cream. They were numbered in the LCC fleet (161 to 210) but had the LBC monogram in place of the usual LCC coat of arms.

The variety of tramcars in the streets of Leyton was increased in 1930 with the transfer of six LCC M Class cars (Nos 1721 to 1726). They were joined in 1931 by a further 11, Nos 1427 to 1437, and another six (Nos 1438 to 1443) in 1932. This matched the withdrawal and scrapping of equal numbers of the original four-wheel cars. The remaining four-wheel Leyton cars were withdrawn and scrapped with the introduction of the newly acquired bogie cars. However, within two years of seeing the first of the new trams in service the Leyton Corporation found their system taken over by London Transport and their new trams transferred elsewhere! In modelling terms the Leyton E/3s and the LCC cars have all been covered in Chapter 2.

Table 6: Leyton Urban District Council (later Corporation) Tramways 1906-33

Number	Class/ type	Year built	Body type	Trucks/Bogies	LT Nos	Scrapped, sold or changed
1-10			Horse tramcar			1908
11-70		1906/07	Balcony top	4 W 8 ft 6 in M&G	—	1921-31
161-210	E/3	1931	Totally enclosed	MT Bogie EMB	161-210	by 1952

Notes
EMB Electro-Magnetic Brake Co; **M&G** Mountain and Gibson; **MT** Maximum traction; **4 W** Four-wheel.

Livery
1906-33 Dark green and primrose (dark cream). Gold lining on the green and black and green lining on the primrose. Letters and numbers gold shaded blue. Trucks green with yellow lining. Fenders and controllers black.
1931-33 The E/3 cars were painted in the same livery as the LCC cars (red and cream). They carried the Leyton arms in place of the London arms of the other LCC cars.

Walthamstow Urban District Council (later Corporation) Light Railways

Walthamstow is the most northerly of the council operated systems in East London with the boundary reaching out to Epping Forest. There was no history of horse tram working in the area and it was left to the council to acquire a Light Railway Order in 1903. Construction of the system proceeded quickly and all the routes were giving public service in 1905. To provide the initial service, 32 tramcars were ordered from Brush Electrical and Engineering Company. These were the standard design of four-wheel, three-window open-top car on a 6 ft 0 in wheelbase truck. Numbered 1 to 32 these tramcars remained in their original state until 1922. By this time the vehicles were in need of a major overhaul. Indeed such was the state of some of the cars that complete re-building was necessary. This was done over the next few years with those cars needing the most work being given extra

Above *Walthamstow open-top car No 3 which was later given a balcony top cover* (courtesy C. Withey).

Left *Walthamstow No 28. Although still in open top condition this car has been rebuilt with extra window pillars to strengthen the body* (courtesy C. Withey).

Above right *The final version of the 1-32 series with six-window upper and lower saloons. This car was photographed soon after acquisition by LPTB as it carries its new owner's name on the lower rocker panel, but is still in the old livery* (London Transport).

strengthening pillars, turning them into six-window open-top cars. Nine of the trams retained their 6 ft 0 in trucks while the other 23 had their trucks lengthened to 8 ft 0 in.

In 1928 No 2 was re-built with a matching balcony-top cover (six-window) with two trolley poles. This formed the basis for a second phase of re-building and by 1932 all the cars had become balcony top, covered, with six-window upper and lower saloons. Two of the re-built cars, Nos 22 and 23,

were given 8 ft 6 in Peckham P35 trucks. There were now three different sizes of truck in the class, but the bodies were all externally similar. Despite the numerous rebuilding exercises on this car the modeller is well served. In the original form, of an open-top car with a 17 ft 0 in three-window saloon, the Keil Kraft kit is ideal. The kit will be slightly over-width and must be modified to the open-top state by removing the upper saloon adding seats (from Tramalan), and mesh (BEC). The truck side will also have to be removed and replaced by a 6 ft 0 in wheelbase one from BEC Kits, who could also supply the appropriate powered chassis, or the 26 mm Tenshodo power bogie could be used. In its six-window open-top state the BEC Kit No 6 is recommended with the stairs changed to the direct 180° type. In the final balcony top version BEC Kits again produces the ideal kit in No 7. The construction of this kit is discussed in detail at the end of the chapter. This is an interesting car for the modeller, particularly as the whole class survived to be re-numbered in the London Transport fleet.

At the same time as the passenger tramcars were delivered a works car was supplied. The car was a combined water and sweeper type. The purpose of the tramcar was to damp down the dust and sweep the tracks during dry weather. We are so used to tarmac roads that we forget that in the early days the roads were covered in mud (and horse manure) and it was likely that the only part of the road actually surfaced was the tram track. In the summer, dirt would be thrown up by other road vehicles. The dirt lay over the tracks getting into the all important grooves. Use of the water car would assure that the trams ran smoothly. With its 6 ft 0 in wheelbase four-wheel truck it has a simplicity of design that would prove to be a good model to build as a first exercise in scratchbuilding. The modeller could make use of BEC chassis and truck sides, controllers and lifetrays from the same manufacturer's range of spares. The works car never carried a number during its early Walthamstow days but by 1933 it had received the number 63. However, it did not last long in the London Transport fleet, being scrapped soon after acquisition.

In 1909 through running started on a route that crossed Leyton to terminate in West Ham. The route was served by Walthamstow and Leyton tramcars. Originally a Saturday only service it was extended to a daily service in 1910. At this time Leyton insisted on Walthamstow using top covered cars and to accommodate this, six new tramcars were purchased. Numbered 33 to 38 these were three-window balcony-top four-wheel cars with 8 ft 0 in trucks. Like the previous class they were re-built between 1930 and 1932. Although at least one (No 34) had a three-window lower saloon with a six-window upper saloon. They all survived to be re-numbered in the London Transport fleet.

In modelling terms BEC Kits again provide the answer. For the original version Kit No 4 should be used (check that the stairs are of the 90° direct type and change the chassis and truck sides to the necessary 8 ft 0 in wheelbase). In the later version of car No 34 I would recommend using the No 7 Kit (changing the chassis and truck side as before) and cutting out the extra pillars in the lower saloon. Alternatively, the lower half of Kit No 4 could be combined with the top half of Kit No 7.

Walthamstow found itself short of serviceable tramcars after the 1914-18 war. Six tramcars were hired from London United Tramways. They were Nos 226 to 230 and 232 of the Type W still in open top condition. In 1920 the council purchased these cars. They were repainted in Walthamstow livery and numbered 47 to 52. They gave only about ten years' service before being scrapped between 1930 and 1932. For the modelling comments see the previous chapter.

The missing numbers 39 to 46 are accounted for by the purchase in 1920 (between the hiring and the purchase of the LUT cars) of eight single-deck bogie cars from Rotherham. These had six-window bodies with equal-wheel bogie trucks. Models of these cars would normally need to be scratchbuilt. However, if the modeller had an old K's MET E Kit and was willing to

A model of the Walthamstow balcony car in London Transport livery. This uses the same BEC Kit that is the basis of the description later in the chapter (model M. Pamphilon, photo D. Voice).

West Ham car No 39 in its balcony-top condition, having been rebuilt from the original open top (R. Elliot).

compromise a little on the exact dimensions, a conversion can be achieved. The Kit is about 5 mm short and would need to be modified with the removal of the quarter lights and truck sides. Equal wheel bogies can be obtained from BEC Kits and fitted in the same way as described for the LCC subway car. Suitable bogie sides can be obtained from the Tramalan range.

By 1926 through running arrangements had been extended so that West Ham, Leyton and LCC cars were all seen in Walthamstow. As part of the agreement with the LCC, Walthamstow agreed to provide tramcars that could run on conduit track. Rather than convert existing tramcars, twelve new cars (Nos 53 to 64) were purchased from Hurst, Nelson and Company. They were generally similar in design to the 1922 LCC E/1 Class. The most noticeable differences were a large stencil route box and larger than usual controllers. When delivered, and during their life with Walthamstow, they were unvestibuled. The modeller can use BEC Kits No 12 to make these trams. Apart from the modifications already mentioned the only other major change is to remove the vestibules.

The last tramcars to be purchased by Walthamstow were eight bogie cars similar to the LCC E/1. They were given the now redundant numbers 39 to 46. Broadly similar to Nos 53 to 64 they were delivered equipped with vestibules. This makes them even easier to model as only minor modifications are needed to the BEC Kit No 12. Remember that the plough carriers were only ever mounted on the body, so there is no need to file short one set of bogie sides.

Like Leyton, the citizens of Walthamstow had only just begun to see the benefits of this modernisation when the system was taken over by London Transport and their newest trams were transferred.

Table 7: Walthamstow Urban District Council (later Corporation) Light Railways 1905-33

Number	Class/ type	Year built	Body type	Trucks/Bogies	LT Nos	Scrapped, sold or changed
1-32		1905	OT later BT	4 W 6 ft Brush later 23 cars had 8 ft Brush	2004-2024 2031-2041	1936-37
33-38		1910	BT	4 W 8 ft HN (21E Type)	2025-2030	1937
39-46		1919	Single-deck (built 1902 ex-Rotherham)	EW Bogie Brill 27G	—	1932-34
47-52		1920	OT ex-LUT Type W built 1902	MT Bogie Brill 22E	—	1932
53-64	E/1	1926	Enclosed top	MT Bogie HN	2042-2053	1952
39-46(ii)	E/1	1932	Totally enclosed	MT Bogie Brush	2054-2061	1952
None later 63	Works	1905	Water car	4 W 6 ft Brush AA	63K	1935

Notes
BT Balcony top; **EW** Equal wheel; **HN** Hurst, Nelson; **OT** Open-top.

Livery
Crimson lake and chrome yellow. Gold lining on the crimson lake and brown lining on the chrome yellow. Letters and numbers gold shaded red. Trucks and undergear black (red oxide on the E/1s). Fenders, controllers and trolley standards black. Opening window frames and destination boxes, wood.

West Ham Corporation Tramways

The North Metropolitan Tramways Company (North Met) had been running horse tramways in West Ham from 1870. The corporation had decided to take over the company lines and, after obtaining the appropriate powers in 1898, began negotiations for the purchase of those lines inside their boundary. It was a protracted affair and it was not until 1903 that an agreement was reached. Whilst the lines were served by horse trams the North Met continued to operate. As and when the corporation electric cars were ready to take over, the North Met was paid for that route and ceased operating it. The first corporation electric route (Stratford Broadway to Canning Town) was opened to the public in 1904. The last North Met horse tram ran in West Ham in 1908.

Initially the corporation purchased fifty tramcars (Nos 1 to 50) in 1904 ready for the opening of the first electric routes. The manufacturer was George Milnes and the cars were the standard pattern three-window, four-wheel, open-top type with 180° direct stairs. The livery was very similar to that of the LCC except that the number was carried below the headlamp. The tramcars carried rotating hexagonal destination indicators. This was most unusual for London and was made more so by using black lettering on a white background. From 1907 the cars were re-built with balcony-top covers. There was one exception which was No 35. By this time the cars had the more usual roller type destination boxes. Following agreement on through running with the LCC, 25 of these cars were fitted with plough carriers. At the same time the trucks were extended from 6 ft 0 in to 7 ft 0 in wheelbase. The class was given another re-building programme in two batches (the first starting in 1914, the second in 1922, to become Type A) but apart from strengthening the body the main design remained the same. There were some minor changes made such as the destination indicators; the later batch had single line boxes with combined route number boxes. As always the modeller is recommended to follow a photograph of the prototype car being modelled.

With these standard design cars the modeller is well served by BEC Kits. The version as delivered can be modelled using Kit No 3 with 180° direct stairs and a 6 ft 0 in truck (removing the plough carrier as necessary). The truckside and chassis should be 7 ft 0 in wheelbase if the first conduit equipped cars are to be modelled. The rebuilt cars can all be modelled using Kit No 4. Again the wheelbase needs to be checked and some of the detail, such as destination boxes may need to be changed. BEC make a whole range of destination boxes which more than cover the requirements of this class. However, the original design would need to have a scratchbuilt hexagonal indicator. This is easy to make if you have access to a photocopier with reduction facilities. The six destinations can be typed out and reduced to scale size. Then the paper can be folded to form a hollow hexagonal tube. The black typing on white background is, of course, correct. The hollow tube of the destination indicator can be filled with milliput to give added strength. The completed model indicator can then be mounted on wire ready for fixing to the car. A similar type of indicator fitted to a Liverpool car is shown on the photograph. The cars were fitted with double line indicator boxes (BEC Part 27 with the lamps filed off) in 1907, at the same time as being given balcony tops. The first batch of re-builds (from 1914) were given single line indicators (BEC Part 29). The second batch of re-builds (from 1922) had single line indicators with route number box (BEC Part 28). There is also the plastic kit (by Keil Kraft) of the balcony version. Note that this kit is to 1:72 scale (slightly large for '00' gauge).

Very soon the corporation realised that more trams were required and another 35 were bought in 1905 (Nos 51 to 85). The bodies of these cars were to the same three-window standard open-top design as those first purchased. No 51 was fitted with an 8 ft 6 in radial truck while the remainder had 6 ft 0 in wheelbase trucks. In 1907 No 51 was given a balcony top and three years later the radial truck was changed to a rigid axle type (possibly 7 ft 0 in wheelbase). Nos 52 to 58 were fitted with balcony tops and 7 ft 0 in trucks with plough carriers in 1911. Five trams (Nos 70, 76, 77, 79 and 80) were withdrawn from service between 1914 and 1918. During this time spares were very scarce and these trams were cannibalised to keep the rest of the fleet going. Numbers 51 to 59 were re-built in 1922 as Type D but externally the design was unchanged with the exception of open-top car No 59 which was given a balcony top to match the other eight. Around this time there was some re-numbering of cars, taking the numbers from those cars in the batch that had been scrapped. No 51 was experimentally given enclosed ends on the top-deck. The bulkheads were left in place (presumably to save the cost of removing them). No other cars in this batch were given the same treatment. Nine more cars were scrapped in 1923 and the class now consisted of one totally enclosed top, eight balcony top, and twelve in open-top condition. By now all the cars had 7 ft 0 in wheelbase trucks. Gradually the open top cars were reduced in number and they had all been scrapped by 1931. The top covered cars lasted to be re-numbered in the London Transport fleet.

The modeller can treat this series in very much the same way as the 1 to 50 batch. For the open top condition BEC Kit No 3 should be used with 180° direct stairs and a 6 ft 0 in wheelbase truckside and chassis. A double line destination box (BEC Part 27 with the lights filed off) should be fitted. For the plough carrying cars a 7 ft 0 in) wheelbase truck side and chassis are needed. The balcony condition can be modelled directly using BEC Kit No 4 with a 7 ft 0 in wheelbase and single line destination box (later with combined route number).

The next batch of cars was bought in 1906. Numbered 86 to 93 these eight cars were similar in design to the previous tramcars except that the saloons were 1 ft 4 in longer. The trucks were 8 ft 6 in radial. These tramcars were re-built within a year to give them balcony top covers. Like the previous cars they were re-built at different times, but retained the three-window balcony-top style. During one such re-building in the 1920s to Type B the radial trucks were converted to fixed axle although the wheelbase was kept at 8 ft 6 in. Numbers 90 and 92 were fitted with plough carriers for through running with the LCC. These were the only two cars in this class to be so converted. The modeller is not so well served for an accurate model of this car. To be strictly to scale the model will need to be scratchbuilt. Of course, many of the items available as spares could be used to good effect. However, the difference between a true scale model and the standard BEC Kit would be just 5 mm on the saloon length (and, of course, on the overall length). If this difference is acceptable then the comment regarding the previous batches of West Ham cars will be equally valid. Alternatively the Keil Kraft kit would be very close in size with the exception of the trucksides (motorise with a BEC traction unit). It is worth noting that I have seen a photo of No 86 fitted with a one line destination box under the canopy (that is just above the driver's head) and a route number box fitted under the ends of the roof.

Also purchased in 1906 was a batch of seven cars delivered with balcony tops, (numbered 94 to 100). However, it is necessary to consider these cars in two parts. Numbers 94 to 97 had three-window lower and upper saloons. The upper saloons were very much shorter than the lower saloons, giving large balconies. Numbers 98 to 100 had the normal three-window upper and lower saloons. In both batches the lower saloon was of the longer type found on the 86 to 93 series and the trucks were again 8 ft 6 in radial (which proved troublesome). By the 1920s they had been either fixed or replaced by new, rigid types. Numbers 95 and 98 were fitted with plough carriers at around the same time. Originally fitted with two line destination boxes the cars were given route number boxes in 1917/18. They were re-built in the early 1920s to Type B specification.

Like the previous batch the modeller will need to scratchbuild to make a scale replica of this series. Numbers 94 to 97 with the short upper saloon would make most distinctive models. Again the many parts that are available from the kit manufacturers would be most useful. The extra length of the lower saloon is found in the Keil Kraft kit. Alternatively for numbers 98 to 100 BEC Kit No 4 should be used, taking into account the comments previously given. For numbers 94 to 97 I would suggest BEC Kit No 11. The stairs will need to be modified to 180° direct and the wheelbase checked. The upper saloon sides should be cut to remove one window. The new short three window upper-deck side should then be mounted centrally over the lower saloon and the bulkheads fitted. The balcony panels will need to be extended to fill in the gap now created (use metal strip or plastic card). Similarly the edging around the underside of the ends of the roof will need extending. A double line destination indicator should also be fitted.

West Ham Corporation continued their habit of buying small batches of tramcars with their next purchase in 1910. These six cars (numbered 101 to 106) were of an 'all weather' design. The special feature of these four-wheel, balcony-top cars, was the lower saloon. This had six windows per side each of which could be opened independently to give plenty of ventilation in warm weather. The cars were mounted on 7 ft 0 in wheelbase radial trucks and were equipped with plough carriers. Apparently the feature of independently opening large lower saloon windows was not the hoped for success. Passengers seemed divided about the weather and there were arguments over opening or closing the windows. So when the council re-built the cars in 1921 (to Type D) the lower saloons were given the more usual three window design with quarter lights, while the transverse seating was replaced by longitudinal seating to match the rest of the fleet. At the same time the radial trucks were made into fixed axle. All the cars were taken into the London Transport fleet and re-numbered. Four were scrapped in 1937 and the other two withdrawn in 1938. One of these was scrapped but happily the other was kept in New Cross Depot as a preserved vehicle. Thus West Ham No 102 (now London Transport No 290) joined the London Transport collection and can be seen in its London Transport livery in the LT Museum, Covent Garden. This is also the prototype that the Keil Kraft kit was modelled on.

The 101 to 106 batch had standard length saloons and so the BEC Kit range

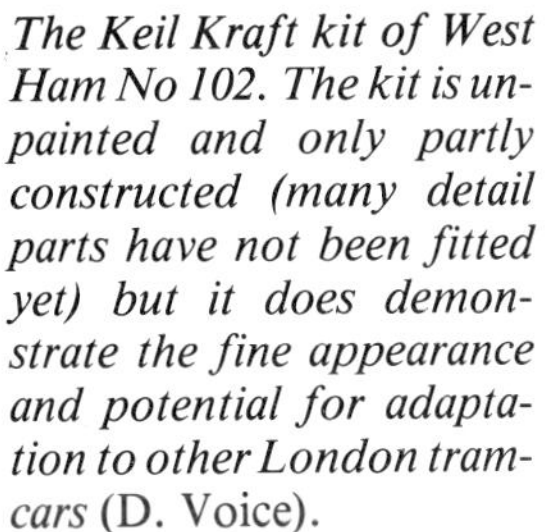

The Keil Kraft kit of West Ham No 102. The kit is unpainted and only partly constructed (many detail parts have not been fitted yet) but it does demonstrate the fine appearance and potential for adaptation to other London tramcars (D. Voice).

can be used. The original version could be made in two ways. The model could start with Kit No 4 with the lower saloon windows replaced in the manner described in Chapter 8. The other way would be to combine Kits Nos 4 and 7 using the three-window upper saloon with the six-window lower saloon. The small top lights in the lower saloon need to be cut away and filed smooth to give full height windows. With either method the chassis and truck side should be 7 ft 0 in, the stairs 180° direct and the indicator boxes double line. The later re-built version can be modelled directly from Kit No 4. By this time single line destination boxes with combined route number boxes had been fitted.

For their next purchase the council decided upon their first bogie cars. This was another small batch of twelve cars numbered 107 to 118. Broadly similar to the LCC E Class cars, the main differences were that the West Ham cars had balcony tops, 180° direct staircases and eight windows in the lower saloon. They were delivered in 1911 and had two line destination boxes. These were replaced by a single line destination indicators with route number boxes in 1913. The bogies were Hurst, Nelson maximum traction with one bogie fitted with a plough carrier. In 1922/23 the tramcars were re-built as Type C and the corporation changed the lower saloon to the more conventional (for London) four window style. They retained the balcony top and unvestibuled platforms. All twelve cars passed into the London Transport fleet and were scrapped in 1938. Both versions of this batch can be modelled using BEC Kit No 12. The Class E version should be used with the upper-deck modified to open balcony. The necessary bulkheads can be formed from BEC spares or scratchbuilt from plastic card. The eight window lower saloon can be made by adding extra verticals to the kit using strips of metal or plastic card. For complete accuracy a thin card backing should be cut to represent the frames of the drop light windows. The rebuilt version will not need these modifications to the lower saloon.

The next six tramcars were built by the corporation as Type E and were numbers 119 (built in 1923 and re-numbered 64 in 1925), 60 to 63 and 65 (built in 1925). This series was the last four-wheel design to enter West Ham service and had totally enclosed upper decks. They had 7 ft 0 in wheelbases

Left *Modelling the hexagonal type of destination indicator. This particular one is on a model of a Liverpool car, but the method of construction is as described in the text. (model and photo, D. Voice).*

Above right *The final car in the West Ham fleet, No 68 (London Transport).*

and the trucks were all fitted with plough carriers. In tramway terms these cars had a short life. They were taken over by London Transport and scrapped by 1938, a working life of some thirteen years. To model this series BEC Kit No 2 provides the basis from which to start. The chassis and truck sides should be the appropriate 7 ft 0 in wheelbase. The ends of the upper-decks will need to be modified as the window arrangement of the kit does not match up with this series (the technique described in Chapter 8 can be used). Alternatively the suitable window spacings can be fabricated using plastic strips (note that 119(64) had a wider upper end central window). The destination indicator and route number box will need to be scratchbuilt into the end upper dashes. Otherwise the kit can be built in accordance with the instructions.

In 1925 six more cars were purchased, the manufacturer was the United Electric Car Co (by then part of English Electric Co) and the cars were numbered 119 to 124 (and became Type F). These enclosed top bogie cars were delivered equipped with plough carriers for conduit operation. They all survived, to become numbers 325 to 330 in the London Transport fleet. All were withdrawn from passenger service in 1940, although numbers 326, 327 and 330 (by now fitted with vestibules) continued to run as staff cars at Charlton depot. They were withdrawn from duty and scrapped in 1950, still retaining the plough carriers on their bogies. These six cars can be modelled using BEC Kits No 12 as a basis. The majority of the kit can be used as supplied (the Class E version) with the necessary modifications to the upper-deck ends, including the addition of scratchbuilt destination and route number boxes.

The corporation embarked upon an increase in their fleet by building some cars and buying others. However, they were all to a common external design (Type G) and for our purposes can be considered as a single series. The total

Half the West Ham works fleet in action in 1907 as No 1A lays the dust (D. Voice collection).

number was 32 and they entered service in the following order. Numbers 125 to 138 entered public service between 1925 and 1929; No 76 to 85 were purchased in 1929; Nos 69 to 75 entered service in 1930 and West Ham's last car No 68 was seen for the first time in 1931. All the cars had bogies, totally enclosed upper-decks and unvestibuled platforms (except No 68 which entered service as a totally enclosed tramcar). They all had plough carriers and numbers 68-85 and 138 had two trolley poles. Numbers 69 to 85 were fitted with vestibules between 1931 and 1932. The whole series passed into London Transport hands and many of them continued to give service, moving onto South London routes until the final year of London's tramways.

This series of the West Ham fleet can be modelled using BEC Kit No 12. In the unvestibuled condition the Kit will need modification on the upper-deck ends. The small double window at the start of each end should be cut and filed to form a single window the same size as the others in the end. The destination and route number boxes will probably need to be scratchbuilt to suit the West Ham design. These modifications will be needed for the vestibuled type and in addition to the modeller will need to modify the E/1 vestibule to fit the E body. The blank panel by the stairs will need to be partially cut away to give an extra window.

There were two works cars in the West Ham fleet. The first was purchased in 1905, numbered 1A and was a combined water and sweeper car. It was little more than a 2,000 gallon water tank mounted on a four-wheel tram truck. The car did last to London Transport days, but was scrapped in 1934 without being renumbered. The second car was another water car with a slightly smaller tank (1,200 gallons). Numbered 2A, it lasted long enough to become number 055 in the London Transport fleet, finally being scrapped in 1938.

Table 8: West Ham Corporation Tramways 1904-33

Number	Class/ type	Year built	Body type	Trucks/Bogies	LT Nos	Scrapped, sold or changed
1-50		1904	OT later BT	4 W 6 ft Brush A later 6 ft 6 in Brush A	211-258	1929-37
51-85		1905	OT later 8 cars BT then 1 car ET	4 W 6 ft M&G later BT cars 7 ft M&G	259-267	1914-38
86-93		1906	OT later BT	4 W 8 ft 6 in M&G	274-281	1937-38
94-100		1906	BT	4 W 8 ft 6 in M&G	282-288	1937
101-106		1910	BT	4 W 7 ft Peckham	289-294	1937-38
107-118		1911	BT	MT Bogie HN	313-324	1938
119 (later 64(ii) & 60-63(ii) & 65(ii)		1923-25	ET	4 W 7 ft West Ham	268-273	1937-38
119-124		1925	ET	MT Bogie HN	325-330	1946-50
125-137		1925-29	ET	MT Bogie HN	331-343	1951-52
138 & 69-85(ii)		1928-29	ET 69-85 TE in 1931-32	MT Bogie HN	344 & 296-312	1940-52
68(ii)		1931	TE	MT Bogie HN	295	1952
1A	Works	1905	Water and sweeper car	4 W 5 ft 6 in M&G	1A	1934
2A	Works	1906	Water car	4 W M&G	055	1938

Notes
BT Balcony top; **ET** Enclosed top; **HN** Hurst, Nelson; **M&G** Mountain and Gibson; **MT** Maximum traction; **OT** Open-top; **TE** Totally enclosed; **4 W** Four-wheel.

Livery
1904-16 Munich lake and pale cream (ivory). Gold lining on the munich lake and brown lining on the ivory. Letters and numbers gold shaded blue. Red diamond surround to headlamps and the car number was below the headlamp, bracketed by the lining. Trolley standards, trucks and undergear red oxide. Opening windows and destination boxes wood. Fenders, controllers and handrails black.
1916-33 Main colours changed to maroon and deep cream. Trucks, undergear, fenders and handrails maroon. Fleet title omitted. Other colours as before.
1930-33 Numbers 68 and 92 had the lower rocker panels painted maroon. Their trucks and undergear were pale green. Other colours as before.

A Walthamstow six-window tramcar

I have always been attracted by the Walthamstow six-window tramcars. As previously explained these cars were delivered as standard three-window, four-wheel open-top vehicles. During the late 1920s they were re-built twice and emerged from these experiments with balcony-top covers and the body strengthened by the addition of extra window pillars becoming six-window cars, which gave the trams a far older, period look. In my view this added much charm and individuality to the trams, which were now in such good repair that they were absorbed into the London Transport fleet in 1933 and ran in the red livery until 1937. In modelling terms this is a very straight-forward project. BEC Kit No 7 is a scale replica of this particular prototype, so there are no changes to be made to the kit. I did decide to add extra detail and this will be made clear in my description. You will see that my method of construction is different from the instructions in the kit. This is a personal preference and I have seen excellent results obtained by modellers following the kit instructions.

The first thing, as always, is to check that all the parts are in the kit and that none are damaged. I must say that of the very many kits that I have had there has never been need to go back to the manufacturer and ask for missing parts. I did on one occasion have to write to ask what a couple of the parts were! It turned out that they were balcony seats. However, I always do such a check on the parts as it is the most effective way of identifying which bit of the kit is which. Construction of a BEC Kit is made more easy by the inclusion of a clear explanatory diagram showing exactly where each part fits.

My method for this type of four-wheel model is to assemble the upper and lower saloons and ends (parts Nos 1A, 3C, 4, 5, 6, 17, 20C, 21, 22). Access to the interior of the lower saloon is through the open floor and to the upper saloon through the gap where the roof will fit. The roof, of course, is fitted at a much later stage. On this particular model I assembled those parts using low melt solder. It so happened I was demonstrating modelling techniques at an exhibition at the time. Low melt soldering has the advantage that there is no waiting for glues to set and if things do go wrong you can have another try. If you are not familiar with this technique I would reassure you that the majority of my models have been constructed using contact adhesive throughout (I use the original type brown Evostick) and I have never had any problems. No matter which method you use there will inevitably be small gaps where white metal parts butt together. These should be dealt with before any painting is started. I filled the gaps with plastic filler (the type used by plastic modellers when altering their kits). I push it well in and make sure there is excess overlapping the edges of each part. It is left to dry overnight and then smoothed down. I remove large amounts of excess by filing or, in some cases, cutting away with a craft knife. The final smoothing is done using wet and dry paper. Then the whole assembly was given a coat of matt white inside and out. When this was dry I checked the body for any missed gaps, odd spots of filler or glue and these were cleaned off.

I then painted the exterior cream (Humbrol HR103) and the interior in dark brown (HR142). The cream required its usual three or four coats in order to get the true depth of colour, whilst the brown only needed two. I used the same brown to pick out the window frames of the upper-deck, the drop lights on the lower-deck and the bulkhead windows and doors. This was the usual awkward job needing a small brush. As always I ended up getting paint in the wrong places. However, with matt paint it was easy to keep

Above *The BEC Kits Walthamstow car takes shape and has its first coat of paint* (D. Voice).

Right Diagram 16: *Curved seat for the end of the top deck of the Walthamstow car (it can also be used for similar seats on other cars).*

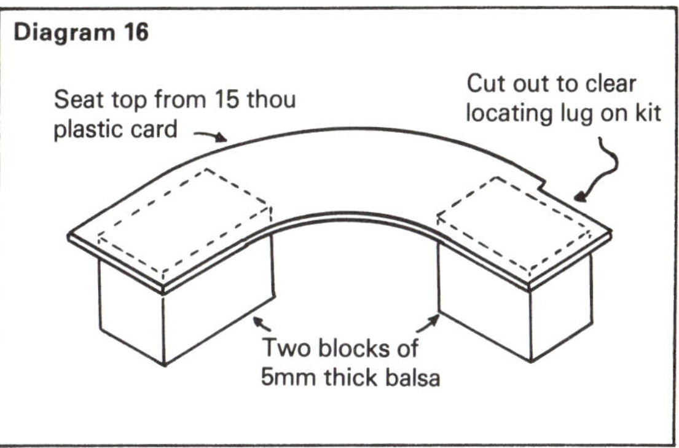

Below *The lining tape being applied. The strips of self adhesive gold tape are left for a few hours to allow the stretch to shrink out, then the ends are cut to length* (D. Voice).

touching up the frames until I was satisfied with the result. Whilst I was waiting between coats of paint I worked on the parts that were left, including the cutting of the seats to size (seven seats 9 mm long and seven 5 mm long). The undergear and resistance box (parts 12, 13 and 32) were painted red oxide (HR110). Controllers and side number boxes were painted black. The seats were given the same dark brown as the interior as was the route indicator box. The stairs were painted in crimson lake (HR116) on the sides and underside with cream risers and dark grey (matt 67) treads. In line with my preference I picked seven sitting figures for the upper-deck passengers and made the strips with the upper half of plastic people for the lower saloon. These and the driver and conductor were all painted in various colours finishing with flesh colour for the hands and faces.

My attention turned back to the body. I masked off the cream in my usual way and painted the crimson lake (HR116). This included the rocker panels, strips on the bulkheads, dashes and the narrow strip between the upper and lower-deck. The crimson lake was also used on the solebar of the car and so I painted a strip to represent it on the lower rocker panel. The truck sides and fenders were painted black. When I was satisfied with the body colours I lined the dash and upper rocker panel with gold tape. The lower rocker panel was lined out using the black Scotch 3M plastic tape. The crest came from Mabex and the number (I chose to model No 20 as I had a photograph of it) from Blick dry press transfer. I then gave the car a coat of gloss varnish inside and out, using a new tin. The saloons were glazed and the seats and passengers fitted. The balcony and platform floors were painted dark grey and the inside of the lower dash was given two coats of red oxide. I made curved seats from plastic card and balsa (see Diagram 16) to fit the curve inside the balcony. I painted them brown, gave them a varnish and fitted them into place. I glued one of the sitting male figures on the front balcony to represent a tram enthusiast having an enjoyable ride.

After putting two strips of gold lining on the outer side of the stairs and varnishing over the top I fitted the stairs in place. The controllers and handbrakes (brass wire) were also glued in place. I cut the etched brass mesh to fit exactly around the balcony (taking equal amounts from each end). I then soldered the two vertical handrails and the destination support rails to the appropriate places on the mesh. I left plenty of wire below the mesh to assist fixing it in place. I glued the destination box to the support and then fitted the whole assembly inside the balcony. The vertical handrails were left oversize in order to trim them when the roof was fitted. I painted the mesh black, having thinned the paint to prevent it clogging the fine holes in the

Right *The etched brass mesh has been added, as have the destination boxes and upright handrails. The latter are left oversize until the roof is fitted* (D. Voice).

Below left *Seating strip and passengers painted and ready to be put into the model. Note that they are fitted to represent the appropriate longitudinal type of seat* (D. Voice).

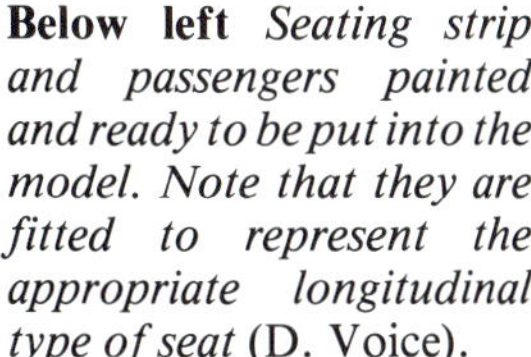

etching. I then turned my attention to fitting the handrails on the stairs. I started by cutting the lower vertical pole to size and gluing it in place. The upper end was secured inside the balcony dash while the lower end fitted between the stairs and the dash plates. I took a couple of pieces of brass wire and curved them roughly to the shape of the stairs. One was bent at the top to form a vertical support that could be glued to the side of the bulkhead door. The lower rail was then soldered half-way along this upright. The upright was glued in place and when it had set I made the final adjustments to the wire so that the two handrails curved down to meet the vertical rail already in place. I then touch soldered the three pieces of wire together. This may seem to have been tempting fate as the soldering iron could easily have melted the white metal kit. The technique I used was to just quickly touch solder the parts in place being very careful not to allow the soldering iron to touch any other part of the tram and not to let the iron rest too long on the wires. When not actually soldering I kept the kit and the soldering iron well apart. The curved wires were trimmed to length and a second vertical fitted and again touch soldered to the curved rails. The rail in the middle of the balcony protecting the stairwell was bent to shape from brass wire and glued in place. I went underneath the tram to glue the steps, lifeguards and lifetrays in place and painted them black. The grab rails by the step were cut to size and glued in place.

I had the usual problem with the destination. I checked the possible routes and found that the through route to Victoria and Albert Docks was worked by these cars. I knew that one of the Mabex destination transfers included 'DOCKS'. This was ideal and the appropriate route number 7 was taken from the Mabex range of white numbers on black background. The route number was also fitted to the side boxes. These seemed a bit frail so to add strength to the fixing I glued a strip of black card to the back extending upwards and glued inside the lower edge of the balcony.

The roof was painted cream on the underside and dark grey on the upper. I cut a notch in the understrip to allow the trolley hooks, fabricated from

Above *The completed model in service with all the period charm of these six-window cars* (model and photo, D. Voice).

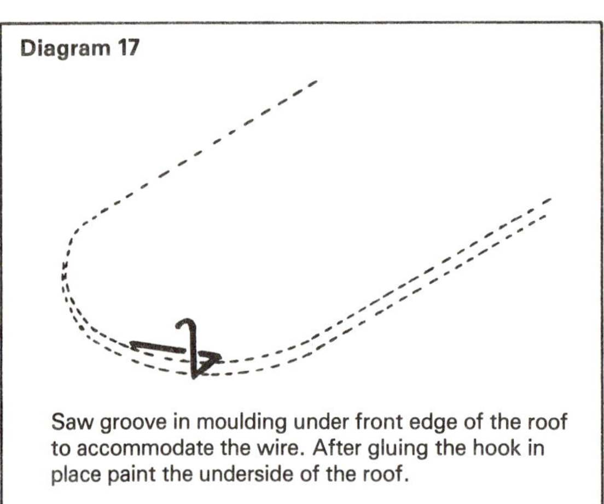

Diagram 17

Saw groove in moulding under front edge of the roof to accommodate the wire. After gluing the hook in place paint the underside of the roof.

Left Diagram 17: *Trolley retaining hook for the Walthamstow car. The hook is bent up from nickel silver wire and glued to the upper-deck canopy.*

nickel silver wire, to be fitted, (see Diagram 17). I decided to omit the upper cantrails (parts 24A) as the moulding on the underside of the roof looked just right as it was. I picked out this moulding in crimson lake. The catwalks, previously painted black, were glued in place and drilled out for the fine tubing which formed the trolley holder. The two trolley poles were made to my usual design. The roof was glued in place. The chassis was painted black (not painting the moving parts or the bearings) and fitted in place. Finally two suitable Mabex advertisement transfers were chosen and fixed in place.

Chapter 6

Barking, East Ham and Ilford councils' tramways

These three corporation-operated systems form what could be called the 'Far East' of the London network. The East Ham system with its neighbour West Ham formed the hub of the six tramways in the eastern part of the London area. Indeed, the close co-operation and working between East and West Ham could almost deserve a chapter in itself.

The through running agreement with the LCC makes the inner London terminus Aldgate a very attractive place to form the basis of a model layout. If the model is set in the period around 1912 it will be appropriate to run not only the munich lake of the LCC but also the greens of Barking and Leyton, the brown of East Ham and the munich lake of West Ham. All these systems ran their cars through to Aldgate. An added advantage is that it was a conduit operated terminus. Therefore, there is no need to worry about constructing overhead wiring. In this respect the Conrad ready-to-run tram track can be used with a strip of black self-adhesive tape to represent the conduit slot. This can be cut from wider tape in the way described for lining tramcars or a roll of ready cut thin strip can be obtained from specialist model shops.

Barking Urban District Council Light Railways

After a protracted construction period the Barking electric tramways opened in 1903 with two outstanding features. The most famous was the bascule bridge over the River Roding (Barking Creek). This bridge had three sections, the centre one of which lifted. It had large wheel-like structures at one end which rolled and raised the centre section rather like half of Tower Bridge. Behind these wheels was a large operating cabin mounted high over the bridge. The lifting section prevented the overhead wire from spanning the length of the bridge. In the early days a side conducting rail was fitted allowing a special skate on the tramcar to pick up the electric current. Later this arrangement was removed and the cars coasted across with the conductors holding the trolley poles down. Indeed I understand that it became a matter of honour to get the trolley pole back on the wire before the car came to a rest.

The other feature, the depot, is less well known. In the original plans the depot was to have been built at the end of the bridge. However, when the first batch of tramcars was delivered, there had been delays in the building of the

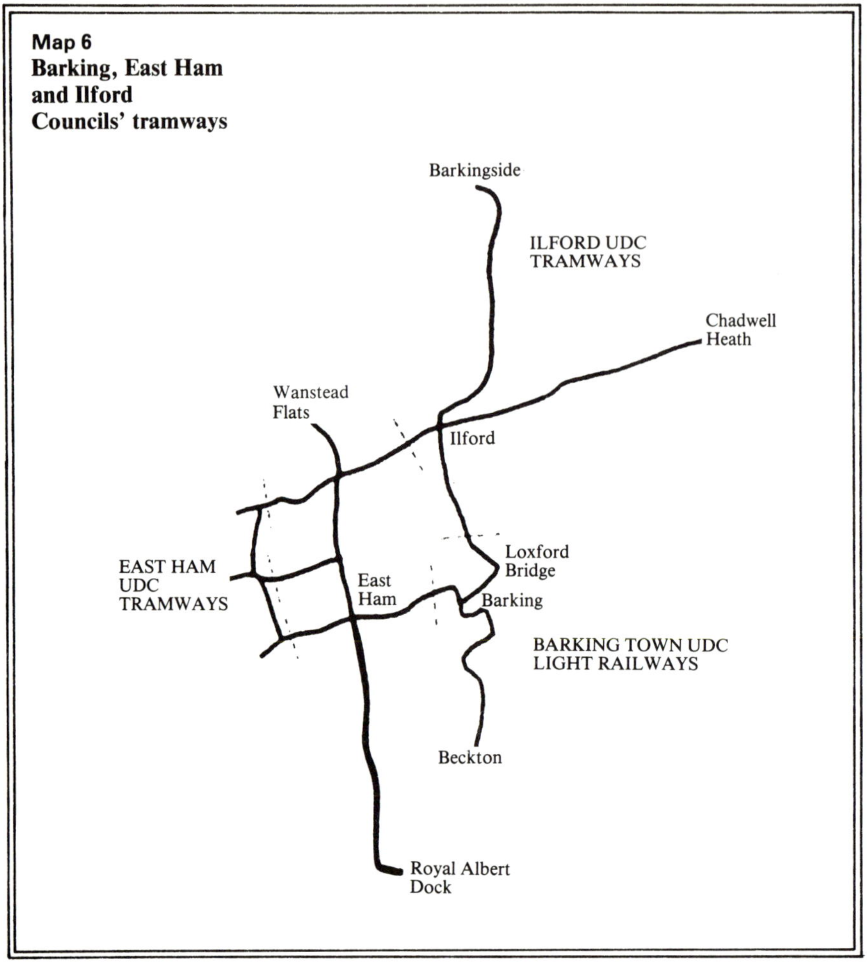
Map 6
Barking, East Ham
and Ilford
Councils' tramways
Barkingside
ILFORD UDC
TRAMWAYS
Chadwell
Heath
Wanstead
Flats
Ilford
Loxford
Bridge
EAST HAM
UDC
TRAMWAYS
East
Ham
Barking
BARKING TOWN UDC
LIGHT RAILWAYS
Beckton
Royal Albert
Dock

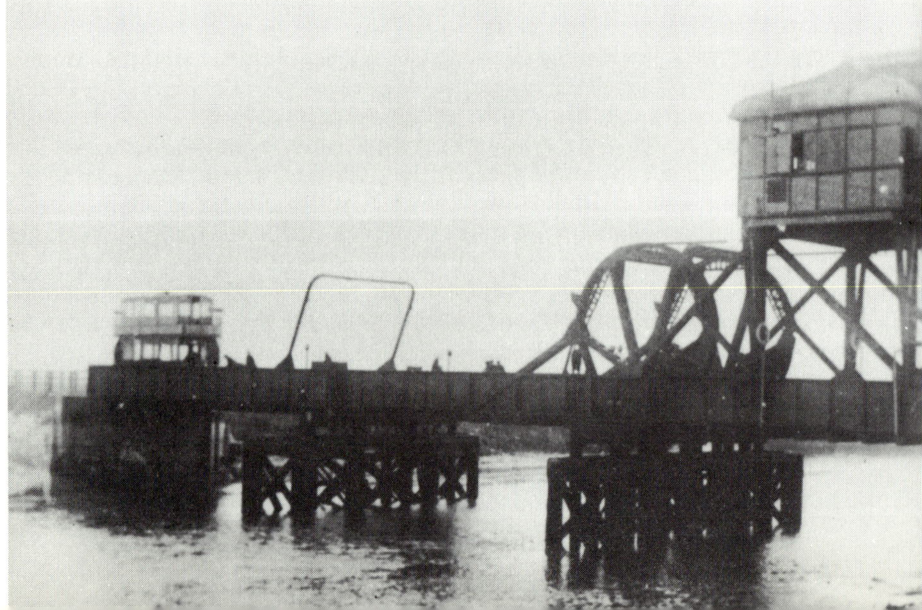

Above *Barking tramcars Nos 3 and 5 in the 'temporary' tram depot* (courtesy D. Sibley).
Below left *The bascule bridge over the River Roding (Barking Creek). Note the tramcar, which is one of the Bellamy-roof cars* (courtesy D. Sibley).

trackwork. Not only was the planned depot not built, but the track had not reached that section. So the tramcars were assembled in the open at the exposed Beckton end of the line. Hurriedly the Council arranged for a temporary corrugated iron tram shed to be built there. As is the nature of such things this tram shed was never replaced. This part of the system would make a good basis for a model layout. The four-track tram shed lay alongside the terminus stub. In the model the feature would be the shed with cars working in and out, while a service would be operated to the terminus. The other end of the layout could be either a street terminus or the track could disappear into a fiddle yard. If space permitted, the bascule bridge could also be modelled. Think of the added interest if the bridge could be made to operate.

For the opening of the tramway Barking purchased seven tramcars in 1903. Numbered 1 to 7 these were standard four-wheel, three-window, open-top design cars with reversed stairs. The wheelbase was 6 ft 0 in on a Peckham design truck. Very quickly four of the tramcars were modified. In 1904 numbers 2 and 3 were given Bellamy-type top-covers with the upper saloon and roof extending only over the lower saloon. The balcony ends were left exposed. At the same time numbers 1 and 7 were fitted with the more conventional type of balcony top. In 1911 these four tramcars went back for further modifications and all become standard design three-window, balcony-top cars with 90° direct stairs. The headlamps were taken from the dashes and placed on the balcony ends. The trucks were changed for longer 7 ft 0 in wheelbase Peckham 10A types at the same time. The other cars, numbers 4 to 6, were also fitted with the extended wheelbase truck during 1911/12. The covered top cars were fitted with plough carrying equipment in

1912 for the through working arrangements with the LCC. The next change came in 1922 when numbers 1 to 3 were converted back to their open-top condition, owing to the deterioration of the vehicles. In the same year numbers 4 to 6 were given 90° direct stairs. Numbers 4 and 5 were withdrawn and scrapped in 1926, while the remainder ran until the end of the Beckton line in 1929.

The modelling of these cars is complicated only by the choice of condition. In the open-top state BEC Kit No 3 can be used with the only alteration being to the wheelbase and type of stairs. These will depend upon the date and individual fleet number of the tramcar being modelled. The Bellamy roof condition of numbers 2 and 3 would make unusual models for London. I would recommend using BEC Kit No 3 as a basis and adding the Merseyside Tramway Preservation Society's Bellamy roof conversion kit. This kit is made to fit on BEC Kits. The other balcony top version is a straightforward model from BEC Kit No 4. The later version will need modification to the headlamps. The destination boxes were fitted under the canopies on these cars.

A short length of line was opened in 1905 from Barking Station to meet the Ilford system. Since this was isolated from the rest of the Barking system (waiting for the road bridge to be built over the railway line by the station) the tramway was leased to Ilford. The next move by Barking Corporation was to build a line to connect the centre of Barking, between the station and the Broadway, with the East Ham system. This opened in 1905 and was operated by both East Ham and West Ham tramcars and, at the beginning was separate from the rest of the Barking system. The three parts were eventually joined in 1907 and the Ilford operation ceased.

Barking Council purchased a further two cars in 1911. Numbered 8 and 9

A heavily retouched makers photograph, probably of No 8. It shows the Peckham radial truck very clearly (Brush official).

they were three-window, balcony-top cars with 7 ft 0 in wheelbase trucks and 180° direct stairs. Both of these cars were fitted with plough carrying equipment in 1912. Their life with Barking was short as in 1915 number 8 was sold to Ilford (it became number 28) and number 9 to East Ham, becoming number 46. These cars can be modelled directly from BEC Kit No 4.

Through running on LCC tracks to Aldgate began in 1912. Barking fitted all the covered cars with plough carriers and purchased the final car in their fleet, Number 10. It was the same design as cars numbered 8 and 9 except that it was fitted with a plough carrier when delivered. Its life at Barking was even shorter as it became number 27 in the Ilford fleet in 1914.

By 1914 Barking Council decided to restrict their own operation to the Beckton line, hence the sale of the last three tramcars. The other routes were leased to Ilford and East Ham. Operation of the Beckton route was un-eventful but it was never financially successful and was closed in 1929. The Barking fleet was scrapped and the corporation ceased to be a tramway operator. Of course, they still owned the lines through the centre of town and these continued to be operated by the adjoining corporations.

Table 9: Barking Town Urban District Council Light Railways 1903-29

Number	Class/ type	Year built	Body type	Trucks/Bogies	LT Nos	Scrapped, sold or changed
1-7		1903	OT later Nos 2 & 3 Bellamy top, 1 & 7 BT later OT	4 W 6 ft Peckham later 1-3 & 7, 7 ft Peckham	—	1926-29
8 & 9		1911	BT	4 W 7 ft Peckham	—	1915
10		1912	BT	4 W 7 ft Peckham	—	1914

Notes
BT Balcony top; **OT** Open-top; **4 W** Four-wheel.

Livery
1903-06 Crimson lake and cream. Gold lining on the crimson lake and black lining on the cream. Trucks and undergear red oxide. Letters and numbers gold shaded blue. Controllers and fenders black.
1906-07 As above but with brown replacing the crimson lake.
1907-29 Holly green and ivory. Dark green lining on the ivory. After 1918 the fleet title 'Barking Council Tramways' omitted. All other colours as before.

East Ham Urban District Corporation Tramways

East Ham was served by the North Metropolitan Tramways Company horse operated line to Manor Park. This line was opened in 1886 and continued to operate until 1908 when it was purchased by East Ham Corporation for integration into their electric tramway network. This system started in 1901 with the opening of lines from the Ilford boundary near the Broadway to Manor Park and the level crossing in East Ham Manor Way near the Docks;

East Ham depot at the opening of the system with the first series (1-35) of tramcars, all open top (London Transport).

and from the West Ham boundary to the Barking boundary near the Broadway. In doing so East Ham became the first electric tramway in London under municipal ownership and only became the second of London's electric street tramways by a matter of months.

In the first year of operation 20 tramcars had been purchased. These were given the numbers 1 to 20 and were three-window, four-wheel, open-top cars to the standard 'Preston' design with reversed stairs and a wheelbase of 6 ft 0 in. In 1902 a further ten tramcars (numbers 21 to 30) of exactly the same design were purchased and to these a further five (numbers 31 to 35) of the same design were added in 1903. For simplicity these can all be regarded as one batch of 35 tramcars. Written research conflicts in some details on these cars, I have used the most recently published. Number 31 was re-built with a balcony-top cover using a six-window upper saloon and at the same time was given 180° direct stairs. Unusually for London it was given a dome roof. Between 1905 and 1909 the rest of the batch were similarly re-built with the exception of numbers 1, 2, 4 and 7 which remained open-topped. In 1910 cars numbers 17, 19 and 21 to 33 were given extended 7 ft 6 in wheelbase trucks fitted with plough carriers in order to work over LCC conduit track to Aldgate. Numbers 10 to 14 were given similarly re-constructed trucks in 1912 and 3, 15, 16, 18, 34 and 35 in 1921. The need to use these cars on conduit service ceased when the new bogie cars were delivered and so the plough carriers had been removed by 1928. By this time seven of the class had been scrapped (numbers 5, 8, 17, 19, 20, 23 and 33). Some renumbering took place and in 1928 numbers 1 to 4, 6, 9 and 20 were also withdrawn. Number 26 had its truck removed in 1928 and the body was used as a hut in the depot. Number 14 was scrapped in 1931. The remainder of the batch lasted to London Transport days but ten were quickly withdrawn and had been

Some of the open-top cars of the first series were rebuilt with domed roof balcony-top covers. This view is of car No 19 (R. Elliott).

scrapped by 1934. The remaining ten were given the new livery and numbered 46, 48, 49, 53, 56, to 61. Of these numbers 53 and 58 were sent to Erith to work while the rest stayed at East Ham. However, they did not last much longer and all ten had been scrapped by 1935.

Modelling these tramcars in their open-top condition is quite simple. BEC Kit No 3 can be used with the appropriate stairs and chassis. The construction of the kit requires no further modifications. However, the balcony version is more of a problem. I suggest using BEC Kit No 7 as a basis. The wheelbase of the chassis and truckside should be checked and, if necessary, replaced by the correct 7 ft 6 in size. The staircase is the correct 180° direct type. Next, the modeller can either purchase the correct three-window type of lower saloon directly from the manufacturers or modify the six-window side by cutting the unwanted uprights away. The edges of the window frames should be filed smooth. It is on the upper saloon where most work is required. The number of windows is correct but because the East Ham cars had deeply domed roofs the cast windows are too high. I suggest cutting away the upper horizontal frame and replacing it in the correct lower position with either brass or plastic strip. The top of the upper-deck bulkheads will also need to be lowered. Then a new roof will have to be made using the same technique that is described in Chapter 9. The destination box should be the single line type without route number and one trolley pole should be fitted.

The first through running agreement came in 1904 when East and West Ham jointly operated the route from Canning Town to the Barking boundary. This was the first of many close working relationships between the two corporations. Traffic increased, and East Ham purchased five tramcars in 1905. These were numbered 36 to 40 and were delivered in balcony-top condition. They were to the same design as the covered top version of the previous Class of tramcar but on 7 ft 0 in wheelbase trucks. These cars were never re-built and they gave service until the 1920s. Two of the series were withdrawn in 1921 (numbers 39 and 40), two more in 1922 (numbers 36 and 37) and the final one in 1928 (number 38 which had been re-numbered to 8 in 1922). The modelling remarks for these cars are the same as the 1 to 35 Class.

East Ham tramcars began working to Ilford Broadway in 1905, following agreement with that council for through running. In the same year Barking arranged for the joint East and West Ham service to be extended to Barking Broadway. The East and West Ham co-operation was extended in 1907 by the connection at Plashet and further through running of West Ham cars. The North Metropolitan Tramways Company horse route from Manor Park to Green Street was purchased in 1908 and electrified. The new route was opened in 1909 and in the following year through running commenced to the inner London terminus at Aldgate.

To cope with the extra route mileage the corporation purchased five new cars in 1910. These were numbered 41 to 45 and were again four-wheel, balcony-top trams similar in design to the previous batch. That is they had three windows in the side of each lower saloon and six windows in the side of the upper saloon. These new cars were delivered with 7 ft 6 in wheelbase Brill 21E trucks already fitted with plough carriers. The stairs were the 90° direct type. In 1922 the plough carriers were removed from numbers 43 and 45 whilst number 42 lost its carrier in 1928. Number 43 was accidentally burnt and subsequently scrapped in 1929, its number being taken by 28. On being taken over by London Transport in 1933 numbers 41 to 43 were scrapped almost immediately, whilst the remaining two (numbers 44 and 45) were re-numbered and lasted a further two years before being scrapped.

The modeller can make use of BEC Kit No 7 to make this class of tram. The stairs, trucksides and chassis need to be checked and changed if required. The modifications to the height of the upper-deck and construction of the domed roof have already been described, as has the modification of the lower-deck to the three window style. The addition of plough carriers will depend upon the individual vehicle and period being modelled.

From 1910 Barking tramcars were seen in East Ham, working on the route to Poplar. This was extended to Aldgate in 1912 and the inhabitants of East Ham were now treated to the sight of LCC, West Ham and Barking tramcars joining in operation with their own fleet. However, as has been seen, Barking withdrew from the through running in 1914, but still allowed working by the other Councils to Barking Broadway. In 1915 Barking sold their car number 9 to East Ham. This was re-numbered 46 although it retained its old livery for some time. This tramcar had its plough carrier removed in 1923 when it was re-numbered yet again to number 35. It survived to be taken over by London Transport and acquired its fourth number (70) and its third livery. It was scrapped in 1935. This tramcar had a flat roof and has been previously described in the Barking section of this chapter. It can be modelled directly from BEC Kit No 4.

With the scrapping of unfit cars after the Great War, replacements were needed. Ten tramcars were bought in 1921/22 becoming numbers 47 to 52 and 37 to 40 (the latter numbers having been made vacant by scrapping or re-numbering). These were standard design, three-window (upper and lower saloons) with four-wheel, 7 ft 6 in wheelbase trucks (fitted with plough carriers) and open balcony on the upper-decks. They were fitted with 180° direct stairs. These cars had the more usual flat roof. In 1923 numbers 51 and 52 were re-numbered 36 and 46 respectively. They remained unchanged, and all were absorbed into the London Transport fleet. They were re-numbered and given new liveries but again their days were limited. They were all scrapped in 1935. Like the previous cars, this class can be constructed straightforwardly from BEC Kit No 4. Again attention should be paid to the trucksides, chassis and stairs.

The next tramcars to be purchased were East Ham's first bogie cars. They were delivered in 1927/28 and numbered 51 to 70. In general design these were the same as the 1922 series LCC E/1 Class. The major difference was in the route number indicator. The East Ham cars had roller blinds in place of the LCC large stencils. All twenty cars of this class were taken over by London Transport. They were re-numbered and given the LT livery. Later they all had vestibules fitted. They ceased running in the East Ham area in 1939. However, their life was not at an end and they ran south of the Thames right up to the last day of tramway operation in London. With the use of BEC Kit No 12 modelling these tramcars is made simple. The E/1 version of the kit should be used but for the East Ham days the vestibule will need to be removed. The plough carrier for this period should be fitted to the end of one of the bogies.

Table 10: East Ham Urban District Council (later Corporation) Tramways 1901-33

Number	Class/ type	Year built	Body type	Trucks/Bogies	LT Nos	Scrapped, sold or changed
1-35		1901-03	OT later 31 cars BT	4 W 6 ft Brill 21E later some 7 ft 6 in Brill 21E	46, 48, 49, 53, 56-61	1922-35

East Ham bogie car No 56 built to the design of the LCC E/1 Class (R. Elliott).

Number	Class/ type	Year built	Body type	Trucks/Bogies	LT Nos	Scrapped, sold or changed
36-40		1905	BT	4 W 7 ft Brill 21E	—	1921-28
41-45		1910	BT	4 W 7 ft 6 in Brill 21E	68 & 69	1933-35
46 later 35(ii)		1915	BT ex-Barking No 9	4 W 7 ft Peckham later 7 ft 6 in Brill 21E	70	1935
47-52 & 37-40(ii)		1921-22	BT	4 W 7 ft 6 in Brush	71-80	1935
51-70	E/1	1927-28	ET from 1938 TE	MT Bogie Brush	81-100	1952

Notes
BT Balcony top; **ET** Enclosed top; **MT** Maximum traction; **OT** Open-top; **TE** Totally enclosed; **4 W** Four-wheel.

Livery
Rich reddish brown and yellow cream. Gold lining on the brown and sepia and black lining on the cream. Letters and numbers gold shaded blue. Trucks, undergear and trolley standards red oxide. Handrails, fenders and controllers black.

Ilford Council (later Corporation) tramways

The first proposals for tramways in Ilford came in 1898 for a 3 ft 6 in gauge system. No moves were made to build it until the council were prompted by the opening of the East Ham line to their boundary. In anticipation of joining with their neighbour, Ilford had already amended their powers to permit a gauge of 4 ft 8½ in and so they began construction. The first routes opened in 1903 with 18 tramcars. These cars were of two types. The first

The first car in the London area to be fitted with a covered top was Ilford No 9. This was originally an open-top car, which had this short Magrini-type upper saloon fitted in 1903 (D. Voice collection).

twelve (numbered 1 to 12) were open-top, four-wheel vehicles. They had three tudor-arch windows in the lower saloons, reversed stairs and trucks of 6 ft 0 in wheelbase. Later in the same year a further four tramcars were delivered to the same design. These became numbers 19 to 22 and the two batches will be considered as a single class. In 1903 a Bellamy type top cover was purchased and fitted to car number 9. This became the first tramcar in the London area to have a top cover. The upper-deck had three tudor-arch windows matching the lower saloon. The trolley standard was not removed but stuck through the roof, a feature common in the early days of top covering. Obviously this was considered a beneficial move as cars numbered 1, 4, 10, 11, 12 and 19 to 22 were fitted in the same way in 1904. In 1906 the remaining cars Nos 2, 3 and 5 to 8 were fitted with balcony-top covers having domed roofs and three arched (curved arch not tudor) windows. From this point it is clearer to consider this class in two parts according to the type of top cover fitted.

The Bellamy roof tramcars were re-fitted in 1911/12 and had the trolley standards removed. The roofs were sealed and the usual trolley pole mounted. At the same time numbers 9 and 21 were given depot built 6 ft 6 in wheelbase trucks. Number 1 was taken out of passenger service in 1920 to become the permanent way vehicle. The upper and lower saloons were removed and a truck type body fitted. The trolley stood on a mast in the centre of the car. In the same year numbers 4, 9 and 21 were scrapped, while numbers 20 and 22 were re-numbered 29 and 30. In 1921 a further four cars were scrapped (numbers 10, 11, 12 and 19). The two cars remaining in passenger service, numbers 29 and 30, were scrapped in 1925, whilst the works car survived to 1932.

The domed roof cars had an even more complex life. In 1911 numbers 3 and 6 were given new 6 ft 6 in trucks made in the depot. The next year number 8 was given lengthened platforms and a front entrance with a 7 ft 0 in depot built truck. In view of the further complications of re-numbering, each of these six cars will be looked at separately. Number 2 was re-numbered to 20 in 1920, again in 1924 to number 40 and yet again in the following year to 29. In 1929 it received 180° direct stairs and square top windows in the lower saloon. In 1933 it became number 41 in the London Transport fleet and was scrapped in 1937. Number 3 became number 22 in 1920 and was given 180° direct stairs and square top lower saloon windows in 1929 and then in 1930 it was re-numbered to 39. In 1932 it became number 31 and in the following year number 43 in the London Transport fleet and was scrapped in 1937. Number 5 became number 21 in 1920, then number 41 in 1930 and was scrapped in 1931. Number 6 became number 9 in 1920 and number 19 in the following year. In 1924 it became number 39 only to became number 30 the following year. In 1929 it was given 180° direct stairs and square top windows to the lower saloon. In 1933 it became London Transport number 42 and was scrapped in 1937. Number 7 became number 17 in 1921 and number 37 in 1924. The following year it became number 31 and was scrapped in 1932. The last tramcar in this saga, number 8 (the 1912 front entrance experiment) became number 18 in 1921. In 1924 it became number 38 and in the following year number 32. This car was given 180° direct stairs in 1929 but kept its original tudor-arch windows in the lower saloon. It passed into London

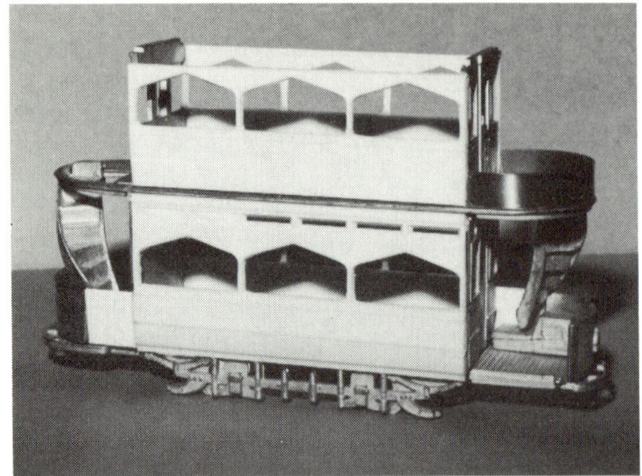

Using lower saloon sides from the Blackpool Standard plastic kit a model can be made of the first covered-top car in the London area. The truck-sides, platforms, upper-deck floor, dashes and bulkheads are all BEC Kits parts (D. Voice).

Transport hands in 1933 to become number 44 and was finally scrapped in 1937. It could well be said that never have so few tramcars carried so many numbers.

Modelling these tramcars has been made considerably easier by the introduction of the Blackpool Standard plastic kit. Although there appears, at first sight, to be little in common between the plastic kit and the Ilford cars, the main features are similar. The use of this kit to make the similar bogie cars is described at the end of the chapter. For these four-wheel cars the plastic sides need to be cut to three windows with the end pillar being slimmed to match the others. The easiest way of making the open-top version would be to use BEC Kit No 3 and replace the lower saloon sides with ones modified from the plastic kit. The modification will have to include making the tumblehome as described for the bogie car model. The Bellamy roof cars can be made by adding further sides from the lower saloon of a second plastic kit to the upper-deck. The photo of a model under construction illustrates the method. For the dome roof cars I would recommend BEC Kit No 4 with the lower saloon replaced as before and the white metal upper saloon windows being given plastic card arches. The upper-deck will need to be lowered in height and a domed roof made in the same way as described for the East Ham tramcars. The final version with the square top lower-deck windows is even easier as BEC Kit No 4 can be used with the lower saloon quarter light covered with a piece of plastic card. The upper-deck would need to be modified as before. In all cases the stairs, chassis and trucksides should be appropriate to the period modelled. The earliest 6 ft 0 in wheelbase trucks can be modelled using the appropriate BEC Kit chassis but the truck sides will need to be scratchbuilt owing to their design. The re-built permanent way car (ex-number 1) would be nice to model. I have not found any photographs of it in this condition but a drawing appears in Len Thomson's *Trams and Trolleybuses in Ilford*.

The next class of tramcar to be described is not as complicated. These were the open-top bogie cars numbers 13 to 18 delivered in 1903. They had four tudor-arch windows in each saloon and were un-canopied with double flight straight stairs. The maximum traction bogies were mounted in the reversed position. These gave considerable problems in running and in 1910 number 17 was fitted with a 9 ft 0 in wheelbase, four-wheel truck. Number 16 was given a longer wheelbase, depot built four-wheel truck in the same year. In 1911 numbers 16 and 17 were given 180° direct stairs although remained uncanopied. At the same time number 14 had its under frame strengthened and the bogies turned to the more normal position with the pony wheels innermost. This proved successful and the others were similarly modified including numbers 16 and 17. In 1915 numbers 14 and 16 were taken over by the War Office and converted into searchlight cars. They remained under War Office control (working in Ilford) until 1919 when they were converted back, and returned to passenger service. The cars were re-numbered in 1921 taking numbers 31 to 36. During 1923-25 they were all given an extensive re-building programme. The upper-decks were extended the full length of the platforms and direct 180° stairs fitted, although they remained as open-top cars. At the same time the bogies were removed and 9 ft 0 in four-wheel trucks fitted. In typical Ilford style numbers 31 and 32 were given new numbers during re-building and became 37 and 38. The cars all remained in this form until being withdrawn and scrapped in 1932. The modelling of this class of tramcar is described in detail at the end of this chapter.

The other tramcar to be delivered in 1903 was a bogie water sprinkler/sweeper car. It appears it looked very much like a stores van, the 1,800 gallon tank being hidden by a wooden body. It had Brill 22E maximum traction bogies mounted in the normal position. However, these were taken off in 1911 and the truck from car number 21 fitted (probably still 6 ft 6 in wheelbase). It was fitted with attachments for snow plough duty and in its

Four of the original tudor-arch windowed cars were rebuilt in 1929 and given square top windows. This shows one of the cars in London Transport livery. Note the Ilford built truck (courtesy I. Hodgson).

latter days carried the number 1 (previously it was un-numbered). In 1932 it was given yet another truck, this time the 9 ft 0 in wheelbase one previously under car number 34. In this state it entered London Transport service in the following year to become number 057. It was scrapped in 1937 still in its green livery. This works car is another good exercise as a start in scratchbuilding. It had simple clean lines and there is opportunity to use component parts from the manufacturers. I would particularly recommend either of the later four-wheel versions which would be easier to motorise than the early bogie version (this is simplified by the Meadowcroft Models Brill 22E mechanism).

As has been mentioned before, through running began in 1905 and East Ham cars were seen in Ilford. In the same year Ilford cars ran on the Barking rails to Barking Station, but this only lasted to 1907. In the following year the single track on the Ilford Lane route was doubled. This stretched the resources of the fleet and with the problems caused by the bogies of the 13 to 18 Class, Ilford decided to purchase four new cars. These were numbers 23 to 26 and were delivered in 1910. They were to the standard three-window (upper and lower saloons), four-wheel (7 ft 6 in wheelbase), balcony design with direct 180° stairs. Unlike the previous classes, these tramcars remained very much in their original form. In 1930 number 23 was re-numbered 40 and again re-numbered 28 in 1932. All four cars entered the London Transport fleet in 1933 and became numbers 28 to 30 and 32 and were re-painted in the new livery. They all gave further service until 1938 when they were withdrawn and scrapped. Unlike the earlier cars these can easily be modelled directly from BEC Kit No 4.

In 1914 Ilford cars began working once again in Barking, this time a little further to Barking Broadway. In the same year Ilford purchased Barking car number 10 and a year later car number 8. They were given the Ilford crest and numbered 27 and 28. However, they remained in the green of the Barking livery. It was noticed that this paint kept in better condition than the crimson lake. Thus it was decided to change the Ilford livery to sage green and ivory. By 1917 the whole fleet had been given the new livery except for the two searchlight cars that were not re-painted until 1919. The Barking cars have already described earlier in this Chapter. Ilford re-trucked them in the 1920s but otherwise they worked on unchanged. Number 28 was scrapped in 1930 but number 27 went on to become number 31 in the London Transport fleet, finally reaching the end of its life in 1938. The modelling comment on these two cars are as described in the Barking section of this chapter.

With the scrapping of most of the older cars, Ilford needed new trams and six were purchased in 1920. These new cars were given the numbers 1 to 6. A further ten were obtained in 1921 (numbers 7 to 16), four more in 1924 (numbers 17 to 20) and three more in 1930 (numbers 21 to 23). They were all built to the same basic design and will be considered as a single class despite the 10 year spread of purchase. These cars were to the three-window, four-wheel, balcony-top type of design but with longer saloons (18 ft 6 in in length, some 2 ft 6 in longer than the standard saloon size). They all had 8 ft 0 in wheelbase trucks except number 21 which was 9 ft 0 in. On some cars the upper-deck windows were unusual as the glass was split into three parts. There was a lower fixed section with two sliding panes above. The other cars

*The later Ilford cars were built with longer saloons (18ft 6in) and enclosed top covers.
This shows No 40, which was built in 1932 and sold to Sunderland in 1938* (R. Elliott).

had the more usual single pane drop light windows. Some cars were fitted
headlamps on the dashes, while others had no headlamps. The trucksides and
dog guards also differed from car to car, so the modeller is strongly
recommended to obtain the necessary information from a photograph of the
particular car being modelled. The details of these cars were not changed and
they all entered the London Transport fleet in 1933 becoming numbers 5 to
27. They were all scrapped in 1938.

With their long saloons these tramcars are difficult to model. There are no
kits available and the modeller will need to scratchbuild. Even the longer Keil
Kraft kit is 6 mm short. It might be practical to use any BEC Kit of a four-
wheel balcony car and replace the sides with scratchbuilt ones. But the upper-deck floor and roof would need lengthening and the chassis retaining parts
would also need modification. However, I am sure that the project would be
a satisfying one as the extra 10 mm of length would give the model a striking
appearance over the standard size tramcar.

The last tramcars to enter service for Ilford Council were purchased as late
as 1932. By this time it was well known that they would be losing their system
to London Transport. Eight tramcars were added to the fleet becoming
numbers 33 to 40. These were similar in design to the previous class except
that the new cars had totally enclosed top covers and the sliding type of
window. Their life as Ilford cars was very short, but they were the only non-
LCC passenger cars to retain their original numbers without suffix in the
London Transport fleet. With the development of trolleybuses in Ilford they
became surplus to needs by 1938. They were sold to Sunderland, where they
served until scrapped in 1954. The modelling remarks are as for the previous
class. The only difference is that if a BEC Kit is to be modified then number 2

should be chosen. However, the enclosed top-deck ends will need adjustment to suit the design of the Ilford cars.

Table 11: Ilford Council (later Corporation) Tramways 1903-20

Number	Class/type	Year built	Body type	Trucks/Bogies	LT Nos	Scrapped, sold or changed
1-12 & 19-22		1903	OT later Bellamy roof then BT heavily re-numbered	4 W 6 ft HN later various	41-44	1920-37
13-18		1903	OT later re-numbered 31-36	MT Bogie HN	—	1932
23-26		1909	BT	4 W 7 ft 6 in Brush	28-30 & 32	1937-38
27-28		1914-15	BT ex-Barking 8 & 10	4 W 7 ft Peckham	31	1930-38
1	Works	1903	Sweeping and water car later stores van and snowplough	MT Bogie Brill 22E later 4 W	057	1937
1920 (New series)—1933						
1-23(ii)		1920-30	BT	4 W 8 ft Peckham except 21 which was 9 ft	5-27	1938
24-26 & 28(ii)		1909	OT old Nos 23-26	4 W 7 ft 6 in Brush	28-30 & 32	1937-38
27-28		1914-15	BT see above	4 W 7 ft Peckham	31	1930-38
29-32		1903	BT survivors of the original 1-12 series	4 W 7 ft (?)	41-44	1937
33-38		1903	OT originally 13-18 series	MT Bogie HN later 4 W possibly 9 ft	—	1932
33-40(ii)		1932	ET	4 W 8 ft 6 in Peckham	33-40	1937-38
1	Works	1903	Sweeping and water car, later stores van and snowplough	MT Bogie Brill 22E later 4 W	057	1937

Notes

BT Balcony top; **ET** Enclosed top; **HN** Hurst, Nelson; **MT** Maximum traction; **OT** Open-top; **4 W** Four-wheel.

Livery

1903-18 Crimson lake and cream. Gold lining on the crimson lake and brown lining on the cream. Letters and numbers gold shaded blue. Trucks and undergear maroon. Fenders and controllers black. Destination boxes wood.

1916-33 Sage green and ivory. Gold lining on the green and maroon lining on the ivory. Trucks and undergear red oxide. Other colours as before.

Ilford Council Tramways open-top tramcar No 17

I chose this class of car in order to use the Blackpool Standard plastic kit produced by Hadfields Limited. This Class of Ilford tramcar basically went through three variations of design. The first is the condition as delivered. That had the top deck covering only the lower saloon (there were no canopies), the double flight straight stairs and maximum traction bogies. Depending upon the period selected the bogies could be pony wheels outermost or innermost. The second condition had the experimental four-wheel trucks under numbers 16 and 17. Whilst going through this experiment these cars had their stairs changed to 180° direct. The final condition was the extensive re-building in 1923 to 1925 where the upper-deck was extended over the platforms and all the cars fitted with 180° direct stairs and 9 ft 0 in wheelbase four-wheel trucks. At all times these cars remained in the open-top condition.

Choice of a model is always a very personal thing. I decided that the four-wheel version would make an attractive model. I really wanted to have the straight double-flight stairs and short upper-deck. In fact it was possible to get all this by modelling Number 17 in the year of 1910. This is the project that is described in detail. Any version can be modelled in the same way. With the same body and the type of chassis described in Chapter 2 or Chapter 7 the original state can be modelled. By building the extended upper-deck using the methods described in Chapter 7 then the later condition can also be modelled.

The Blackpool Standard tramcars had similar windows to the tudor-arch Ilford cars. This allows the Hadfields plastic kit to be used. The two upper sides in the photograph are from the platic kit. The one on the left has had its lower saloon windows modified as detailed in the text. The lower side in the photograph is a scale etched brass component from the R. Collins kit and can be used as a comparison (D. Voice).

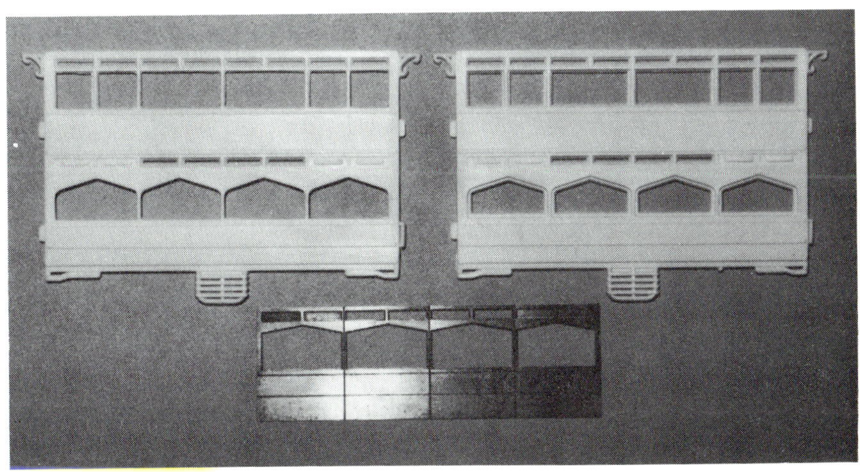

The first thing that I noticed on opening the kit was the lower saloon windows. These really looked far too small. However, I soon realised that by cutting away the inner frame the correct size of window can be made. The plastic is quite soft and easily removed. Using the main thickness of the window as a guide I soon cut the inner frame away and the whole side was transformed, as the photos show. I decided to use the BEC Kit bulkheads, (part No 4). For the few pence that they cost there is enormous saving in modelling time (and I probably could not equal the detail). At the same time I ordered an 8 ft 6 in traction unit, matching truck sides (and a set of four axle boxes), straight double-flight stairs, seating strip and destination boxes. You may also wish to take advantage of the cast lifeguards and lifetrays (I had decided to make my own).

Once the windows were adjusted, the sides of the kit were modified to suit my purposes. I cut the bottom edge flush, removing the dog gate and the odd mouldings at each end. Then the side was cut to 36 mm high. That is, cutting along the top of the horizontal moulding below the upper-deck windows. Using a sharp craft knife this was simple due to the softness of the plastic. The inside edges of the corner pillars were champered to match the BEC bulkheads. The Blackpool Standard has a very straight side, whilst the Ilford car has a tumblehome on the rocker panels. I had been a little worried about

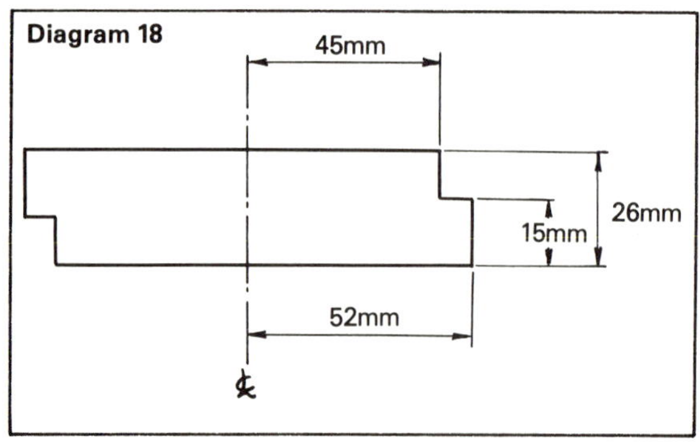

Above *The modified kit with BEC trucksides (8ft 6in). The strip of plastic card in front of the model is about to be used to cover the quarter lights (D. Voice).*

Left Diagram 18: *Upper-deck floor for Ilford tram-car. Cut out from 40 thou plastic card.*

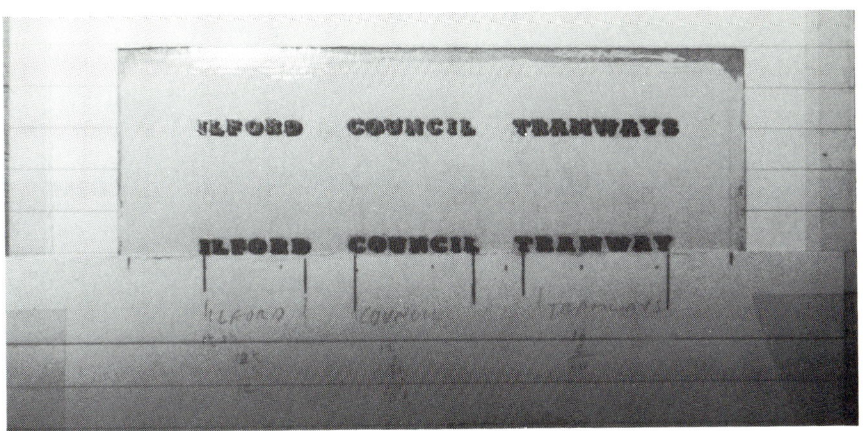

this aspect but it was easier than I had thought. With the craft knife I cut through half the thickness of the side immediately below the waist rail. Then the lower rocker panel was bent inwards and the sides glued to the bulkheads. For this I used my favourite adhesive, the original brown Evostick. I find this handles the metal to plastic combination very well. A word of warning; it does attack the plastic so care must be taken not to get any on surfaces which will be on view. It should also be used sparingly as it can distort plastic, particularly plastic card. I then cut the upper-deck floor from 40 thou plastic card to the shape shown in Diagram 18. This was glued over the bulkheads and the locating lugs on the inside of the plastic sides. Once this is in place it holds the sides and bulkheads securely in position. From the same sheet of 40 thou plastic card the two chassis retaining pieces were cut to the shape shown in Diagram 19 and glued inside the lower edges of each end of the saloon. The platforms were cut off the plastic kit moulding, leaving enough behind the platforms to allow a good gluing surface to the chassis retaining pieces. The holes for the handrail were filled in. The lower-deck dashes were then modified to suit the Ilford car. They were sawn to give a height of 12 mm. The windscreens were put aside to my bits boxes in case they could be used at a later date. I cut away the little bit of rear light that was left to leave a smooth dash, apart from the headlamp. Since I did not intend to use the

Above *Making the fleet name using single letters from a transfer sheet. There is always the problem of making a mistake, in fact I thought I had finished when I took this photo. Only later did I realise that there was a letter missing* (D. Voice).

Right Diagram 19: *Chassis retaining pieces, cut from 40 thou plastic card. Before fitting second part in place check the fit of the chassis and adjust as necessary.*

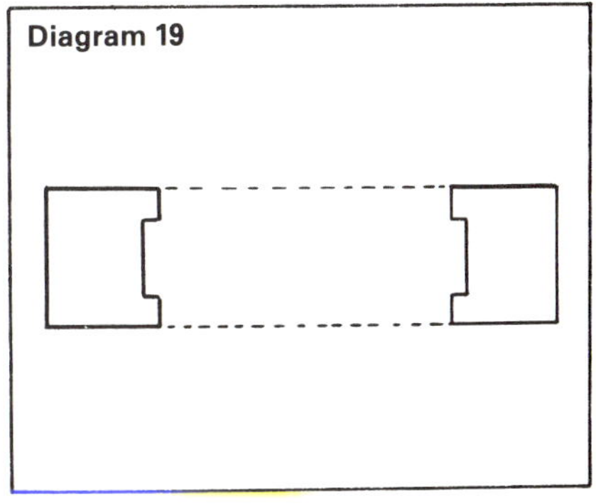

jewels for the headlamps I filled the deep part of the hole with filler to leave just a smooth indentation. The modified dashes were glued to the platforms and then these sub-assemblies were glued to the saloon.

The wheelbase of both this experimental car and the post 1923-25 versions was 9 ft 0 in. Unfortunately, there is no suitable commercially available chassis to this size. However, BEC Kits make an 8 ft 6 in traction unit and matching truckside. So I decided to use this. The model trucksides are cast with roller axleboxes and so I had also purchased a set of four plain bearing axleboxes. I treated these tiny parts with great care as I did not wish to lose them. The roller axleboxes on the truckside were carefully filed off and the

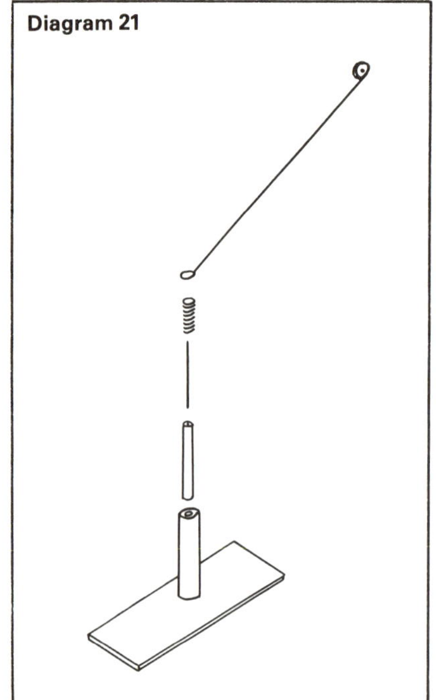

Diagram 21

Above *The BEC Kits 8ft 6in chassis in front of the car* (D. Voice).

Right *One of the attractive features of this particular car is the Robinson type stairs. The handrails require patience during construction, but are well worth it.* (D. Voice).

Left Diagram 21: *Trolley standard and trolley pole for open-top cars.*

Below Diagram 20: *Strip to cover the quarter lights of the kit sides. Cut from 15 thou plastic card.*

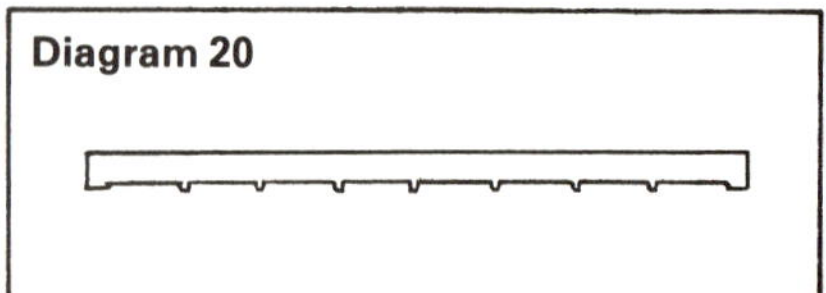

Diagram 20

new boxes glued in place (the two little knobs are on the upper part). Then the truckside extension plate (used to glue the truckside in place) was cut to allow it to be fitted in the gap left between the chassis retaining pieces. Both trucksides were glued in place. The upper-deck decency panels were completed using strips of 40 thou plastic card. These were cut to size and glued in place, taking care on the butt joint of the extension of the kit side. When the glue had set the butt joint was smoothed off. The little curved roof extension at the ends of the upper-deck floor were shaped from 40 thou plastic card and glued under the floor extension. A strip of 15 thou plastic card was cut to cover the quarter lights (see Diagram 20). Immediately above and below it a piece of straight brass wire was glued to represent moulding.

The trolley standard was made from a piece of flat brass and some tubing as described in my previous book. I have included the diagram of the construction of this and the trolley (Diagram 21). Again the now standard Meadowcroft trolley wheel has been used. A hole was drilled in the upper-deck floor and the trolley standard fitted from below. The body was given two coats of matt white paint followed by two of gloss ivory (Humbrol 41). The inside of the saloon was painted dark brown (Humbrol HR142) and the ceiling was painted white. The outside of the car was masked off in my usual way for the darker colour. For this I used three coats of crimson lake (Humbrol HR116). This was applied to the dashes, upper rocker panel and upper-deck decency panel inside and out. The masking was removed and the bulkhead doors and windows painted dark brown and the solebar and truck sides maroon (Humbrol HR144). The floors and platforms were painted mid

grey (Humbrol matt 64). The stairs were given the same matt white followed by gloss ivory treatment. The treads and half landing were picked out in mid grey. The controller (it is moulded on the inside of the dash) was picked out in black with a gold top. The lower rocker panel had to carry the title 'Ilford Council Tramways'. I decided to use the technique I had developed for awkward panels like this. I took a large self-adhesive address label and gave it three coats of ivory paint. Then I surrounded it with card on which I had marked the size of the panel. Then another strip of card was marked with the letters and the positions of the words. I used the small size of gold letters with blue shading from a sheet of Tangley water slide transfers. The words were built up letter by letter. I kept checking that all was well as it is very easy to miss-spell or drop letters. In fact I very nearly put one panel on without the final 'S'. The second set of words were place on the label then both panels were cut carefully to size, that is, to fit over the whole of the lower rocker panel.

The lining was applied in my usual way. Gold tape was used for the crimson lake panels and black for the ivory panels. The white disc carrying the crest was taken from a piece of self-adhesive address label painted white and punched out with a paper punch. This was stuck in place. The numbers were added from the Tangley sheet. On the Ilford cars they were unusually large and mounted to the right and slightly higher than the headlamps. The crest was added from the Mabex range of waterslide transfers. The headlamps were picked out in white and the car was given a coat of gloss varnish to hold the lining and transfers in place. I was now able to glue the stairs into place. This was followed by the window glazing and the lower-deck passengers. On this car I used the new low height BEC Kit 8 ft 6 in mechanism which allowed me to cover the whole of the lower saloon. This I did with two pieces of 15 thou plastic card painted dark brown with the top parts of plastic figures glued in the appropriate places. The latter were painted to represent clothing. Pieces of matchsticks were glued to the inside of the saloon below the windows. When the glue had set the floors were put in position and glued to the matchstick pieces. The joint in the centre was hidden by a third piece of plastic card, painted dark brown and glued underneath and across the joint. The sides of the traction unit were painted

The handrail detail, which was soldered in situ (D. Voice).

The model seen at an exhibition. A most attractive car which draws much favourable comment (model and photo, D. Voice).

black and the unit fixed in place using a small self-tapping screw. This fitted into a hole drilled in the plastic chassis retaining pieces.

The upper-deck and railing was tackled next. As with other open-top cars the BEC Kit etched brass mesh could be used. However, I decided to build my own handrail from thin straight brass wire. The uprights were glued in place and the upper rail soldered in position. Then the uprights were cut to length. The upper-deck lights were made from small roundhead screws. These were soldered to a length of wire for the upright and then the shank of the screw was sawn off. The wire was placed in position and soldered to the horizontal rail. The handrails were painted black with the flat part of the lights painted white. The mesh was added from netting material purchased from my local milliners. The handrails around the stairs were added by fabricating them flat on a scrap of paper then bending them to shape and cutting the length to fit the stairs. They were painted black and glued in place.

The trolley standard was painted maroon. Then the seats were cut from the BEC Kit seating strip. 19 were cut 10 mm long and one 5 mm long. They were painted dark brown, varnished and glued in place. Suitable plastic figures were painted and fitted in place as passengers, including the conductor. The handbrake and platform handrails were fabricated from brass wire and glued in place. I used the platform steps from the plastic kit but made up my own lifeguards and lifetrays using thick brass strip. The step was painted mid grey and other undergear maroon. Finally the driver and trolley pole were added and the car given its inaugural run on the layout. I must admit to a distinct preference for tudor-arched windows, so I fully expect that this car will be doing more than its fair share of exhibition duty.

Chapter 7

Croydon Corporation and South Metropolitan Tramways

In the history of London's tramways each local authority either operated its own system or agreed to one of the company owned systems running the tramways. The exception to this rule was Croydon Corporation who, through an unusual course of events, had company operated routes as well as its own system. The relationship between the company and the corporation had its ups and downs. However, there was surprising co-operation, even during times when relationships must have been strained. This combination of company and corporation did not readily improve connections outside the respective systems. It was not until 1926 that through running agreements with the LCC enabled the citizens of Croydon to travel to central London without changing tramcars.

South Metropolitan Electric Tramways and Lighting Company Limited

It has been said that the size of any tramway system is in inverse proportion to the length of its name. This rule certainly works with the South Metropolitan Electric Tramways and Lighting Company Limited (henceforth to be called Southmet). The official title was the longest in London and the system was the smallest. The history of the Southmet begins with the run-down of Croydon Tramways Company horse tram system. When British Electric Traction Company Limited (BET) made approaches to purchase the system, Croydon Corporation stepped in quickly and bought the system themselves. They decided to electrify it and then to lease the lines to the BET. The new electric tramways opened under BET control in 1901. The BET then set up the Southmet (in 1904) with the intention of using this company to develop electric tramways throughout the south of London.

Under the leasing agreement between the corporation and the BET, ten tramcars were to be supplied initially by BET and 35 by Croydon Corporation. A further 15 tramcars were purchased in the first year of operation and five of them were provided by the BET. The company-owned cars are described first while the corporation-owned cars are described later in the chapter. This total of 60 tramcars provided the service until Croydon Corporation decided to terminate the lease in 1906. This option had been written into the lease from the beginning. During this period the BET had been planning and building extensions beyond the Croydon boundary. To the west two lines were laid, one through Carshalton to Sutton and the other through Mitcham to Tooting Junction station. To the north-east a line went through South Norwood to split, one branch going to Crystal Palace and the other to Penge. Unsuccessful negotiations prevented extensions into Beckenham. The Crystal Palace and Penge line was connected to the main Croydon route at West Croydon. However, the Tooting and Sutton routes were not completed until after the Corporation had withdrawn the lease. These routes joined in Croydon Old Town and then ran to West Croydon. The lines here were not connected to the corporation lines in London Road. In 1906 the BET, who were by now operating through the Southmet, had their system split into two by the landlord, Croydon Corporation. Because the corporation was unable to purchase the lines outside its boundary the

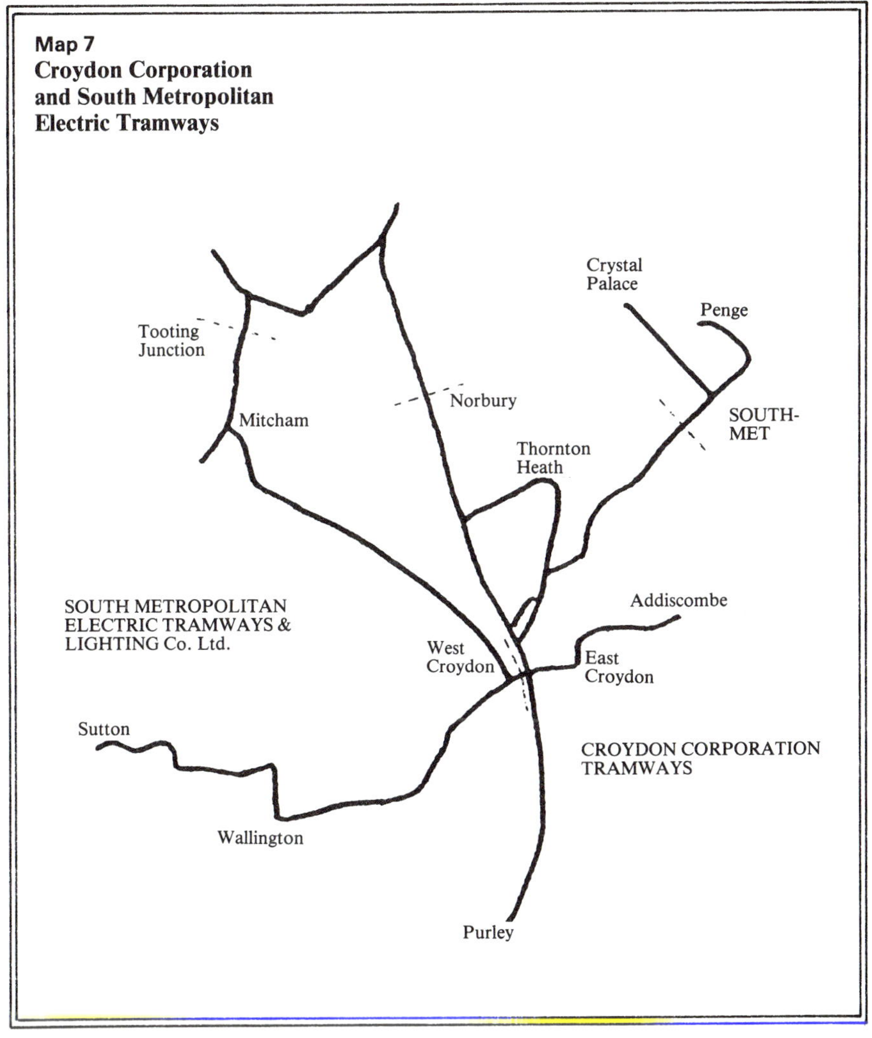

Tooting and Sutton lines were operated by Southmet over the short section of municipal track to West Croydon, whilst the Crystal Palace and Penge lines were only operated to the Croydon boundary. It was soon realised that it would be beneficial to all concerned to enter into through running agreements, but the corporation still refused to allow the Tooting and Sutton routes to join with their lines. So Southmet tramcars at their respective termini, faced each other across a road but could not run onto the other's lines.

The first ten cars were delivered in 1902 for running on the leased lines. They were painted in the Croydon livery of munich lake and ivory but with the BET wheel and magnet device on the bulkhead. The cars were numbered 36 to 45 in the fleet and were of the standard three window, four-wheel, open-top design with 180° direct stairs. The wheelbase of the Milnes girder truck was 6 ft 0 in. The headlamps of the cars were fitted to the upper deck decency panelling. In 1906 the cars left the Corporation lines to work the Sutton route and were based at the Sutton depot. In the Southmet fleet they were given the numbers 17 to 26. Later in the classification scheme that was applied from 1916 they were designated Type K. Under Southmet control the headlamps were moved from the upper-deck to the more usual dash position. Later the destination boxes were positioned under the canopy (directly above the driver's head). The cars ran for several years in the Croydon colours but were eventually repainted in the Southmet brunswick green and cream. The cars were not liked by the drivers and after 1914-18 got into a poor state. They were refurbished in 1926 to 1927 except No 17 which was scrapped. Later No 20 was transferred out of the Southmet leaving eight cars to be taken over by London Transport in 1933. These were broken up before they could be re-numbered, except for No 19 which became a works vehicle. Although not rebuilt or modified, it was used as a breakdown towing vehicle at Sutton depot. It was given the suffix 'S' (becoming No 19S) but it was scrapped soon after in 1934.

The standard three-window, four-wheel car makes a straightforward model. BEC Kits No 3 can be used with a 6 ft 0 in wheelbase chassis and truckside. The latter will need to be modified to represent the distinctive Milnes girder type. To represent the original condition the headlamps will need to be filed off the dashes and new ones put on the upper-deck. After 1918 the cars were fitted with large hoops (called 'Spencer' hoops) over the upper-deck canopies. These devices were fitted to some open-top tramcars of the period in order to protect passengers in the event of the trolley spring failing. If the trolley pole did drop it would be held above the passengers' heads by the hoop.

Demand on the newly opened electric tramway was such that more tramcars were needed and the BET bought five open-top bogie cars which were numbered 56 to 60 and again painted in the munich lake and ivory livery. The bogies were fitted with the pony wheels outermost and were the Brush BB Type. In 1906 they were taken into the Southmet fleet where they were numbered 27, 28, 29, 31 and 35. The cars had straight stairs with 180° turn and half landing. These cars gave problems in running as the bogies were prone to de-railing. In an attempt to remedy this No 27 had the bogies turned so that the driving wheels led. This was far more of an engineering job than

Southmet Type J No 1 seen at Croydon depot in the mid-1920s. (London Transport).

might be first imagined as the whole main frame had to be altered. It was not a success and the others were not altered although No 27 was not changed back. All five cars were withdrawn from service in 1931 and stored at Fulwell. When London Transport took over, the cars were left in storage until being broken up in 1934.

If a model of this type of tramcar is desired there is very little help available. It would be possible to splice two extra windows on a four-window BEC Kit side to construct the six-window saloon, or the body of the tramcar could be scratchbuilt using the techniques described elsewhere in this book. The chassis would best incorporate BEC bogies, obtained direct from the manufacturers. The bogie side frames are a problem as no manufacturer presently makes a casting of the Brush BB Type. Either scratchbuild or modify BEC bogies side frames (parts Nos 107A and B). The track brake will need to be removed and the whole thing filed to give it a much less substantial look.

With the beginning of the Southmet Penge routes in 1906, 16 tramcars were bought. these were considered the first cars in the company owned fleet and were numbered 1 to 16. These four-window, four-wheel, open-top cars were a little longer than the usual standard car. The saloon length was 19 ft 9 in compared to the more usual 16 ft 0 in. Later they were designated Type J. The single line destination boxes were fitted directly under the canopy ends. The trucks were a long 9 ft 6 in wheelbase and were to the radial design. After 1918 they were fitted with the 'Spencer' safety hoops at each end of the

upper-deck. All these cars were strengthened in the early 1920s and at this time No 16 was rebuilt with a five-window saloon (Type J/1). Then the whole class was rebuilt in 1928/29. They were given flush sides with metal sheeting replacing the mesh on the upper-deck. The destination boxes were repositioned to just above the upper-deck dash panels. Number 16 became Type J/2, but the others remained classified as Type J. The height of the dash panels themselves was also increased. Surprisingly, after these major construction works the 16 cars were still in open-top condition and so remained until taken over by London Transport. They were scrapped in 1935.

The modelling of the Type J tramcars is made difficult by the unusually

long bodies. For a true scale model the car will need to be scratchbuilt. The usual range of commercially produced items can help in the construction. If precise scale is not a major factor and the modeller is willing to overlook the 15 mm length difference BEC Kits No 8 can be used as a basis for the model. However, this would lose much of the character and presence of these cars.

In 1906, when the Southmet was purchasing cars, another tramway in the BET group was offering some second-hand bogie cars at a reasonable price. Thus the Southmet became the owner of four ex-Gravesend open-top tramcars with maximum traction bogies. The cars had been built in 1902 and when received by Southmet had reversed stairs, a five-window saloon and bogies in the reversed (pony wheels leading) position. They were renumbered 30, 32 to 34 but remained in the Gravesend livery of reddish brown for some time before getting the Southmet green. In the mid 1920s one of the tramcars (No 32) was rebuilt. The platforms were lengthened by 9 in each, the stairs replaced by 90° direct type and the dash height raised. The remaining cars were similarly converted in 1930. All four cars in this class (by now designated Type O) were fitted with metal panelling in place of the upper-deck wire mesh at this time. However, the remainder of their working life was very limited as they were all withdrawn from service in 1931 and scrapped in 1934. The modelling of the Type O is described in detail in the latter part of this chapter where I make a model of No 32.

The next batch of cars were purchased for the newly opened Sutton and Tooting routes. They were delivered to the Sutton depot in 1906 and numbered 36 to 51. They became the mainstay of the Crystal Palace service. These 16 cars (later classified Type M) were to the very standard three window, four-wheel design with 180° direct stairs and 7 ft 6 in wheelbase 21E trucks. These cars were fitted with 'Spencer' hoops in 1918. In the late 1920s car No 47 was withdrawn from passenger service and re-numbered 010 as a rail grinder in the MET fleet. In 1929 and 1930 Nos 37, 38, 41, 43, 46 and 48 were rebuilt at Hendon and given higher dashes and metal sheeting instead of the wire mesh. These cars were taken into the London Transport fleet and some were re-painted in the LT livery. However, they were not re-numbered but given the suffix 'S' to their existing number. They were scrapped in 1936 when trolleybuses took over the Crystal Palace route.

The saloons of these Type M cars were 16 ft 10 in long which allows the Keil Kraft kit of the West Ham Type A car to be used to model this 7 ft 6 in wheelbase tramcar. The upper-deck saloon and roof will need to be removed. This is easily done by cutting the upper windows off along the top of the lower panel and removing the upper-deck bulkhead. The correct type of trolley standard and pole will need to be added as will the wire mesh around the upper-deck and the seats. For those cars that received the higher upper-deck panelling this will need to be made of plastic card and added. The side route board will either have to be carefully cut away or extended to the centre of the end windows. The deep plank on the truck side should be removed. The neat scrollwork in the kit needs to be replaced with plain plastic card. Motorise using a BEC traction unit.

In 1912 Southmet joined the MET and LUT in the 'Underground' group. This had more significance in later years. As was mentioned in Chapter 2, the MET was trying to dispose of surplus Type E single-deck cars. In 1921 two of them, Nos 145 and 150, were loaned to the Southmet for trials on the Crystal Palace route. But neither this nor the Sutton route proved suitable for the cars which were returned in 1925. The Type E car was produced by K's as a kit some years ago and it is possible to find either kit or made-up models on the second-hand market. If one can be found it is a simple matter to make either of these cars. The headlamps were positioned on the roof and the title 'County Council of Middlesex' and the crest were very roughly painted out in a red that did not quite match the existing livery of the cars. No 145 carried

The final condition of the ex-Gravesend cars. This view was taken at Fulwell depot after they had been withdrawn from service (W. Gratwicke).

Car No 38 in North End. The headlight on the upper dash panel shows this to be the first series No 38 which was owned by the BET. In 1906 the car was transferred to the Southmet following the break-up of the leasing arrangement. The tower wagon on the left is the original horse-drawn works vehicle belonging to the tramway (commercial postcard).

an advertisement for 'Nugget Boot Polish' on one side with no advertisement on the other and a headlamp at one end only.

In 1927 Croydon Corporation offered 12 surplus tramcars at a very cheap price. These were cars Nos 13, 24, 34, 35, 43, 44, 62, 63, 64, 66, 67 and 69. Of these No 13 went to LUT as rail-grinder 006 while Nos 43 and 69 were re-numbered 07 and 09 in the MET works fleet having also been adapted to rail-grinders. Numbers 24, 34, 35, 62 and 63 were not used and were dumped at Fulwell. The other four, Nos 44, 64, 66 and 67 were the best of the dozen and after being refurbished at Hendon joined the Southmet fleet as Nos 17, 47, 52 and 53 and designated Type P. A little while later the bogie car No 21 was withdrawn from service and No 53 was re-numbered 21. These cars were now in the condition of being three window, four-wheel, open-top with 180° direct stairs and 7 ft 6 in wheelbase. They were fitted with 'Spencer' hoops. three of these Southmet cars were taken out of service in the early 1930s and scrapped, while the fourth became 47S in the London Transport fleet.

The modeller can use BEC Kit No 3 for this class of car. The chassis and truck side will need to be 7 ft 6 in and the staircase should be the 180° direct type. The destination box was the single line type fitted below the ends of the canopies. Do not forget to fit the distinctive 'Spencer' hoops. In all other respects the kit can be assembled to the instructions.

By 1931 Southmet were once again looking for more tramcars, preferably open-topped to match the rest of the fleet. Another 'Underground' company, the LUT, had recently converted some tram routes to trolleybus operation and had some surplus tramcars. The Southmet arranged for ten of the surplus Type U bogie tramcars to be transferred on a temporary basis. By this stage in their LUT life these cars were in a top-covered condition. It is difficult to be precise about the actual cars so transferred. This is because when vehicles required overhaul or repair they were returned to Fulwell and another car substituted in exchanged. However, it is known that the following cars did run on the Southmet, Nos 267, 268, 269, 271, 272, 276, 278, 286, 290, 293 and 299. During the period that they were loaned to the Southmet the cars retained their LUT red and white livery, numbers and also the fleet name. They were still on loan in 1933 when London Transport took over. All were eventually repainted and numbered in the LT fleet. However, some ran with their London Transport number although still in LUT style livery. They were withdrawn from the Sutton route in 1935 and transferred to Stonebridge Park. They finished their lives working in North West London finally being scrapped in 1936. The modelling comments on these cars have been covered in Chapter 3.

The Southmet had one powered works car, a street watering car that was BET owned and transferred from Croydon Corporation in 1906. It was the standard four-wheel Brush model and was painted a medium green livery. Little is known about this vehicle and no photograph suitable for modelling purposes exists. It is thought that this car was only kept for a short while on the Southmet system but its disposal is a mystery. It was probably sold to another BET system. If you do desire to add this particular car to your fleet then the lack of information does cause difficulty. My recommendation would be to use a photograph of any standard Brush 2,000 gallon watering car as a basis for the model. You can be sure that no-one will be able to argue about it with you.

Table 12: South Metropolitan Electric Tramways and Lighting Co Ltd 1906-33

Number	Class/ type	Year built	Body type	Trucks/Bogies	LT Nos	Scrapped, sold or changed
1-16	J	1906	Open-top	4 W 9 ft 6 in Brush	Suffix S	1933-35
17-26	K	1906	Open-top ex-Croydon built 1902	4 W 6 ft Milnes	Suffix S	1927-34
27-29 31 & 35	L	1906	Open-top ex-Croydon built 1902	MT Bogie Brush BB	In store	1934
30 & 32-34	O	1906	Open-top ex-Gravesend built 1902	MT Bogie Brill 22E	In store	1934
36-51	M	1906	Open-top	4 W 7 ft 6 in Brush 21E	Suffix S	1927-36
17, 21, 47 & 52	P	1927	Open-top ex-Croydon built 1907	4 W 7 ft 6 in Brill 21E	—	1931

Number	Class/ type	Year built	Body type	Trucks/Bogies	LT Nos	Scrapped, sold or changed
—	Works	1906	Street watering car ex-Croydon built 1902	4 W 5 ft 6 in Brush A	—	1907
19	Works	1927	Breakdown car ex-Type K Open-top	4 W 6 ft Milnes	19s	1936

Notes
MT Maximum traction; **4 W** Four-wheel.

Livery
1906-21 Dark holly green and pale ivory. Gold lining on the green and black and orange lining on the ivory. Letters and numbers gold shaded blue. Trucks, undergear and trolley standards red oxide. Fenders, controllers and wire mesh black. Drop window frames and destination boxes wood.
1921-29 Pillar box red and broken white. Gold lining on the red and black lining on the white. Numbers gold shaded black (no lettering). Other colours as before.
1929-33 Black lining on the red and red lining on the white. Wire mesh white. Lettering gold. Other colours as before.

Croydon Corporation Tramways

The early days of electric tramway operation in Croydon has already been covered in the Southmet part of this chapter. Under the original leasing

Models of the first series (1-35) of Croydon cars. Number 9 is a straightforward construction of a BEC Kit and is described in detail in Tram and Tramway Modelling. *Car No 34 shows the tram as it was when owned by the War Department and operating in the Great War as a mobile searchlight to combat the zeppelin menace (models and photo, D. Voice).*

Left *Number 34 showing detail of the upper-deck. The searchlight is a working example produced for the model boat trade. The remainder is a standard BEC Kit with plastic card additions. The box on the upper-deck was an armoured shelter in case of attack* (model and photo, D. Voice).

Below right *When the 36-45 series cars (owned by the BET) went to the Southmet in 1906 the Corporation replaced them. This shows the second No 40 in a specially posed view; a pity they forgot to turn the trolley!* (D. Voice collection).

arrangements the corporation had the option to take over the system in 1906. As we have seen this is exactly what it did. It may then be wondered by the corporation allowed the Southmet to keep the Sutton and Mitcham lines. It must be remembered that at the time of the ending of the lease the Sutton and Mitcham lines were still under construction. Croydon Corporation only had authority to operate tramways inside its own boundary. Even then the newly opened lines would have to have been bought at the full cost of laying the tracks and associated road works. In addition the corporation would have had to grant the company full through running rights. The Penge Council were in the same position regarding the lines recently opened within their boundary. Under such conditions it is not surprising that the lines were left to the company and that Croydon Corporation concentrated on running the originally leased routes.

Under the leasing arrangements in 1901 the corporation had supplied 35 tramcars for the opening of the line. Numbered 1 to 35 they were three window, four-wheel, open-top cars to the standard design of the day. Most noticeably they had reversed stairs and were delivered with two designs of 6 ft 0 in wheelbase truck. Numbers 1 to 8, 11, 12, 15, 23 to 26 and 35 had the Peckham 9A design. This was a much heavier looking piece of undergear than the Brill 21E fitted to Nos 9, 10, 13, 14, 16 to 22 and 27 to 34. (It is quite possible that during maintenance and repair trucks became swapped around and the numbers given were for 1921). When originally placed in service the cars were fitted with a 'Providence' wire-mesh lifetray extending in front of the dashes rather like American style cow-catchers. These were replaced within a year by wire mesh lifeguards and lifetrays in the more usual position. In turn these were replaced in much later years by the standard slatted wood type on some of the cars.

In about 1913 No 35 was rebuilt with 180° direct stairs. A year later two of this class were taken over by the War Office for military duties. Number 25 and 34 were converted for use as mobile searchlights. The searchlight equipment was fitted to the open upper-deck. A senior citizen who used to work on the trams at that time recalls that these two cars were painted an overall brown colour. One was based at Purley depot and only left for patrol duties. The lower saloon doors were padlocked and only soldiers, complete with rifles drove and manned the car. No corporation employee was allowed near them. At the end of the war they returned to the corporation. After a few years lying at the back of the depot they were rebuilt with 180° direct stairs and mounted on Brill 21E trucks. The whole class was withdrawn in 1927. Numbers 13, 24, 34 and 35 were, as we have already seen, sold to the Southmet and the remainder were scrapped. The saloon of No 8 was sold as a garden shed and a few years ago was acquired by enthusiasts with a view to restoration. Unfortunately, the remains were in too bad a condition to save and after stripping the useful parts the remainder was regretfully scrapped.

In modelling terms these cars are very straightforward if the type with the Brill 21E trucks is chosen. BEC Kits No 3 with 6 ft 0 in wheelbase chassis and trucksides and reverse stairs is all that is needed. I have described in full detail the assembly and painting of such a tramcar in my earlier book *How to Go Tram and Tramway Modelling*. If it is desired to construct the cars with the Peckham truck you will need to remove the casting supplied in the kit and scratchbuilt your own truck sides. The variations described in the rebuilding of three of the cars in this class are all easily achieved by using the appropriate BEC parts in combination with Kit No 3. The searchlight cars provide an unusual prototype and a replica could well come under the category of military modelling, as the photographs show.

As I have already mentioned it was soon realised that further tramcars

would be required to meet the demand from the public. As part of the agreement the corporation provided ten tramcars in 1902, these were numbered 46 to 55. This class of car comprised six-window, open-top bogie cars with Brill 22E maximum traction trucks, mounted normally, and straight stairs with a half landing and 180° turn. They ran in this condition until 1927 when there was a wholesale revision of the Croydon fleet and they became designated Class B2 and re-numbered 21 to 30. In 1928 the class began to be rebuilt and this included fitting top covers and two trolley poles. By 1930 the whole class had been converted. In this particular conversion the upper saloon and roof extended only the length of the lower saloon. There was a small canopied balcony platform leading to the uncovered staircase, which was unchanged. These cars were absorbed into the London Transport fleet taking Nos 365 to 374. They continued running on the Thornton Heath branch until they were withdrawn and scrapped in 1936/37.

These cars were so like the Southmet type L (originally Nos 56 to 60) that the modelling comments can be taken as applying to the Class B2 tramcars. The only extra comment concerns the power unit. The Corporation tramcars had Brill 22E bogies, so advantage can be taken of the motorised unit available from Meadowcroft Models. There are two types available. The first is the simplest for the modeller as it consists of a ready-to-run chassis using a centrally mounted motor driving the bogies through flexible shaft. The other type consists of a separate power bogie and unpowered bogie. In this case the modeller must make the mounting on his own chassis. In both instances the

Number 46 is one of the original cars purchased for the first years of operation. Evidently this view was taken at the same time as the previous one as the same error with the trolley pole has been made. Note the curtains in the lower saloon. These were later removed (D. Voice collection).

bogies are available already fitted with the correct 22E bogie castings.

The other cars delivered for the opening of the electric tramways system, that is Nos 36 to 45 and 56 to 60 and the street watering works car have all been considered in detail in the previous part of this chapter. This leads us to the problems of the numbering in the Croydon Corporation fleet. There were three distinct numbering schemes for the fleet. The first ran from 1901 to 1906, when the BET leased the system. When the corporation began operations they extended the original scheme and filled in the gaps. In 1927 the corporation undertook a complete fleet review. As a result many of the old cars were scrapped and the whole fleet was re-numbered, each class being given a classification letter. This scheme continued until 1933 when London Transport took over. For ease, the fleet is summarised under these three separate periods at the end of this chapter. The complexity is well illustrated by the tramcars which were introduced with numbers previously held by BET cars and and which were themselves re-numbered later. So if things get little confusing in the following text I hope you will be able to unravel the situation using the tables.

In 1906 15 cars were purchased to replace the trams that were the property of the BET. These were given the old BET numbers of 36 to 45 and 56 to 60. This class was comprised of four-wheel, three-window open-top cars with 180° direct stairs and 7 ft 6 in wheelbase trucks. The cars remained in their original state with only minor changes to the odd individual car. Under the re-numbering system in 1927 the class became designated W1 and re-numbered 10 to 20 (cars Nos 41 and 57 were scrapped and Nos 43 and 44 were sold to the Southmet at the same time). All the re-numbered cars lasted to be

The new bogie cars as delivered. These were the same as the LCC Class E/1 except for minor detail differences (D. Voice collection).

taken over by London Transport. However, with the possible exception of number 11 which may have received 355, they were not given LT fleet numbers. Instead they received the suffix 'E' to the Croydon number. They were taken out of service in 1933 and scrapped at Brixton Hill in 1934 except for 19E. Converted to a snowbroom it continued working in Croydon until 1937 when it too was scrapped.

The Class W1 is another model that is well catered for by BEC Kits. Kit No 3 can be used with the appropriate chassis, truck side and stairs. In all other respects except the addition of a ventilator window to each bulkhead the kit can be constructed in accordance with the instructions.

In 1907 the corporation found that they were still short of tramcars and purchased a further ten, numbered 61 to 70. In all respects these cars were exactly the same as the 36 to 45 Class, even to being given the same classification (W1) in 1927. At this time Nos 62, 63, 64 and 69 were sold to the Southmet and Nos 66 and 67 were scrapped. The remainder were given the numbers 6 to 9. These were kept in original condition and when absorbed into the London Transport fleet were given the suffix 'E'. They were taken out of service in 1933 and scrapped (at Brixton Hill) the following year without re-numbering or re-painting. The previous modelling comments for the other Class W1 tramcars apply to this batch.

A water car was purchased in 1907 to replace the one that had been taken by the BET when the lease ended. It was ordered from Brill and had a 1,500 gallon water tank mounted on 5 ft 6 in truck. In 1914 it was decorated to assist in the recruitment of volunteers for the Great War. By 1916 the need for a water car had declined and the vehicle was converted into a mobile welding unit. This consisted of removing the water tank and completely rebuilding the body. In this condition the car was painted an overall flat dark grey. It was taken over by London Transport in 1933, re-numbered 056 and sent to West Ham depot. At this time it was repainted a light grey livery with a white roof. But it did not last much longer being broken up in 1937.

Once again the early condition of this works car presents a problem to the modeller as no photograph of it is known. Since it only lasted nine years in the original condition and was probably very little used in the last few years, I would not recommend attempting to model it in this form. The rebuilt condition as a welding car is a quite different proposition. Since it lasted until 1937 photographs are available and indeed the design is evidently suited to modelling. It had planked straight sides and bulkheads, simple dashes and an open top style trolley standard mounted on the roof. A BEC chassis and truck side castings can be used (7 ft 6 in Brill 21E). Commercial sources can also provide the controllers and trolley pole (static from BEC or working from Tramalan or Meadowcroft). If it should be required BEC could also supply a roof to special order, the type used in kits 2, 4, 7, 9 or 11 is suitable. For the sides I would recommend scribing thin wood to get the correct effect although planked plastic card could be used with good effect.

The popularity and use of the tramway obviously continued to grow. By 1911 the corporation found that demand at Bank Holidays outstripped resources. So a further five tramcars were purchased. Once again these were to the standard three-window, four-wheel, open-top design as used in the 36 to 45 Class. The new cars were numbered 71 to 75. Like the previous cars they remained in original condition throughout their lives. Under the re-numbering scheme in 1927 they became Nos 1 to 5 and were again classified Type W1. When absorbed into the London Transport fleet No 4 in its Croydon livery and number, went to Brixton Hill for scrapping. The remaining four cars received a variation of the London Transport livery and were numbered 345 to 347 and 349. Number 349 was transferred to Erith in 1933 and ran there until being scrapped in 1935. Numbers 345 to 347 continued running in Croydon on the Crystal Palace route until they were replaced by trolley buses in 1936. The cars were then broken up in Anerley depot.

1922 saw the joining of the Southmet tracks (on the Sutton and Tooting route) with the Croydon Corporation rails at West Croydon. The roads were very narrow at this junction. Even today with wider roads it is an awkward spot, and the corporation did not allow regular running. The connection was only to be used for transferring tramcars from one part of the Southmet system to the other.

In 1909 the LCC had opened a route to Norbury. This terminated a short distance from the Croydon Corporation terminus. Right from the start there were transfer ticket arrangements. However, nothing further was done until 1922 when through running negotiations were successfully concluded. Work started on joining the tracks and the first through cars ran in February 1926. This does seem an inordinately long period for what was a short piece of track. But in fact the whole route from Norbury to Purley had to be upgraded and the road lowered under Norbury Railway bridge in order to take the taller top covered tramcars. As part of the arrangement Croydon Corporation agreed to provide 25 new trams to a design approved by the LCC. This, of course, meant that they were built to the LCC Class E/1 design. There were some small detail differences, like the large route stencils on the upper-deck. They were delivered in 1927/28, classified E/1 and numbered 31 to 55. When originally delivered the plough carrier was fitted to the inside end of one bogie. Around 1930 this was re-positioned to the centre of the under-frame. At the same time similar modifications were being made to the LCC E/1s. However, the Croydon plough carriers had large oval holes. This made for the easy identification of a Croydon tramcar, even showing its origins in London Transport days (except for those that later received LCC type plough carriers). These through running arrangements naturally meant that the Croydon tramcars ran on LCC lines to the Embankment. Whilst in return LCC cars ran through to Purley. When London Transport was formed the Croydon E/1s were only around six years old. They were all absorbed in the LT fleet and given the new livery with numbers 375 to 399. Numbers 376, 379, 380 and 398 were 'rehabilitated' and the remainder were given vestibules between 1938 and 1939. Number 396 was withdrawn in 1940 following bomb damage; No 376 was scrapped in 1945. The remainder continued to give service until 1951/52.

These cars were so similar to that LCC E/1 that the BEC Kit No 12 can be used. The kit includes all the necessary detail parts to make the Croydon tramcars. For the original version you will need remove the vestibule from the E/1 version of the kit and reduce the height of the dash. These are the only changes that are necessary to the kit to make the E/1 in the version used by Croydon Corporation.

Table 13: Croydon Corporation Tramways 1901-33

Number	Class/ type	Year built	Body type	Trucks/Bogies	LT Nos	Scrapped, sold or changed
1901-06 Leased to BET						
1-35		1901	Open-top	4 W 6 ft Peckham 9A & Brill 21E	—	1927
36-45		1902	Open-top went to SMET	4 W 6 ft Milnes	—	1906
46-55		1902	Open-top	MT Bogie Brill 22E	365-374	1936
56-60		1902	Open-top went to SMET	MT Bogie Brush BB	—	1906
—	Works	1902	Street watering car went to SMET	4 W 5 ft 6 in Brush A	—	1906
1906-27						
1-35		1902	Open-top	4 W 6 ft Peckham 9A & Brill 21E	—	1927
36-45		1906	Open-top	4 W 7 ft 6 in M&G 21E	SB	1927-33
46-55		1902	Open-top	MT Bogie Brill 22E	365-374	1936
56-60		1906	Open-top	4 W 7 ft 6 in M&G 21E	SB	1927-33
61-70		1907	Open-top	4 W 7 ft 6 in Brill 21E	SB	1927-33
71-75		1911	Open-top	4 W 7 ft 6 in Brush 21E	345-349	1933-35
—	Works	1907	Water car, converted 1916 to welding car	4 W 5 ft 6 in Brill 21E	056	1936
1927-33						
1-5	W1	1911	Open-top ex-Nos 71-75	4 W 7 ft 6 in Brush 21E	345-349	1933-35
6-20	W1	1906/07	Open-top from Nos 36-45, 56-70	4 W 7 ft 6 in Brill 21E	Suffix E	1927-33
21-30	B2	1902	Open-top, from 1928 enclosed top, ex-Nos 46-55	MT Bogie Brill 22E	365-374	1936
31-55	E/1	1927/28	Enclosed top	MT Bogie HN	375-399	1940-52
—	Works	1907	Water car, converted 1916 to welding car	4 W 5 ft 6 in Brill 21E	056	1936

Notes
HN Hurst, Nelson; **M&G** Mountain and Gibson; **MT** Maximum traction; **SB** See below; **4 W** Four-wheel.

Livery
1901-27 Munich lake (dark chocolate brown) and ivory. Gold lining on the brown and

black and orange lining on the ivory. Letters and numbers gold shadcd blue (shading changed to red from 1913). Trucks, undergear, trolley standards and destination boxes deep crimson. Controllers, fenders, handrails and wire mesh black.
1927-28 The first of the new E/1 had the main colours red (rich carmine) and ivory. Trucks and undergear red oxide. Other colours as before.
1928-33 Red (rich carmine) and medium pearl grey. Trucks and undergear red oxide. Other colours as before.

Southmet Type 'O' (ex-Gravesend)

This tramcar gives the modeller an opportunity to make use of the first moulded plastic kit ever produced of a British tram. This is the Blackpool Dreadnought manufacturerd by Hadfield Plactics. Although the Dreadnought is a unique design, only ever seen in Blackpool, the sides of the kit give a five-window saloon that looks right for the Type O. To be strictly accurate the kit is 10 mm too long for the Southmet tramcar. This only represents 2 ft 6 in in a total length of 36 ft 0 in. For modelling purposes it does give many advantages as the plastic kit is inexpensive and the conversion will be easier for those modellers who are used to working with plastic. It has also given me another opportunity to work in plastic, a medium that I have never really got to terms with (you have probably realised by now that I much prefer metal). However, I was well pleased with the result of this modification.

Once the kit has been purchased the first thing is to resist the temptation to build it as a Dreadnought tramcar. In fact by the time the Southmet model is built there will be plenty of parts left over. These should not be thrown away, but kept in a special box for such spare parts. I call this my 'bits' box, although by now I have half a dozen, each containing different sorts of parts. When modelling future tramcars you will find it very useful to be able to dip into your bits boxes in order to solve a construction problem.

To get back to the Southmet car, the Dreadnought needed to be modified. The slatted dog gates under the side were carefully cut off and put in a safe place. The small extension at the end of the saloon was cut away to leave a straight edge each end of the side. On the kit the rocker panels are quite straight and deeply inset with heavy moulding. I cut away the solebar (the

Starting the ex-Gravesend car with a side from a plastic kit of the Blackpool Dreadnought and the white metal bulkhead from BEC Kits. (D. Voice).

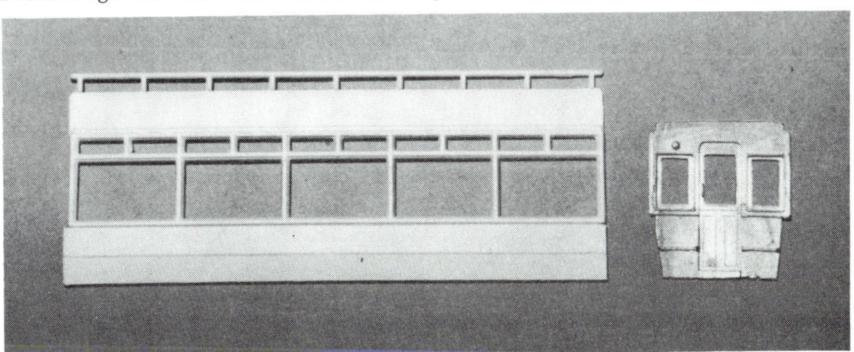

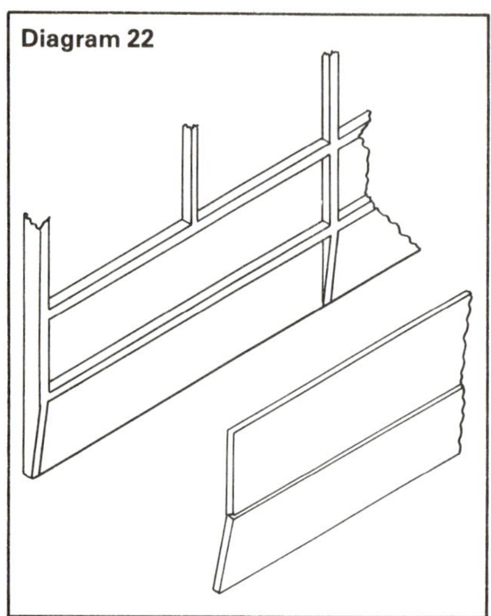

Diagram 22

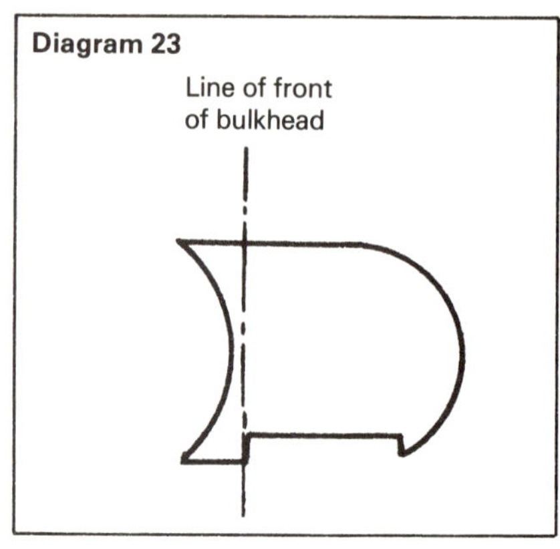

Diagram 23

Left Diagram 22: *Rocker Panel overlay. Made from 15 thou plastic card, scored and bent to give the required shape.*

Below Diagram 24: *Upper-deck floor for the Southmet Car, cut from 40 thou plastic card. Care should be take cutting the stairwells in order not to break the narrow strip.*

Above Diagram 23: *Pattern for the platform floors. Two are required, made from 40 thou plastic card. The width should be adjusted to give a good fit between the saloon sides.*

Diagram 24

lowest horizontal moulding). The bottom edge was filed and smoothed so that no part of the horizontal moulding remained. The vertical ribs on the lower rocker panel were filed to a taper. They matched the thickness of the middle moulded ridge where they met it and then get thinner, finally disappearing at the bottom of the side. A piece of 15 thou plastic card was cut to fit over the whole of the rocker panel. I marked the halfway line and scored (that it, cut half through the thickness) along the full length. The plastic card was bent along the score mark to give a slight bend to the two halves of the rocker panel. This was glued to the side making sure that the top of the plastic card fitted snugly under the window frame moulding and reached down to the bottom of the side. This now gave the appearance of the necessary curves to the rocker panel (see Diagram 22). The score line was used as a guide to glue on the beading of the waist rail. I used some brass wire

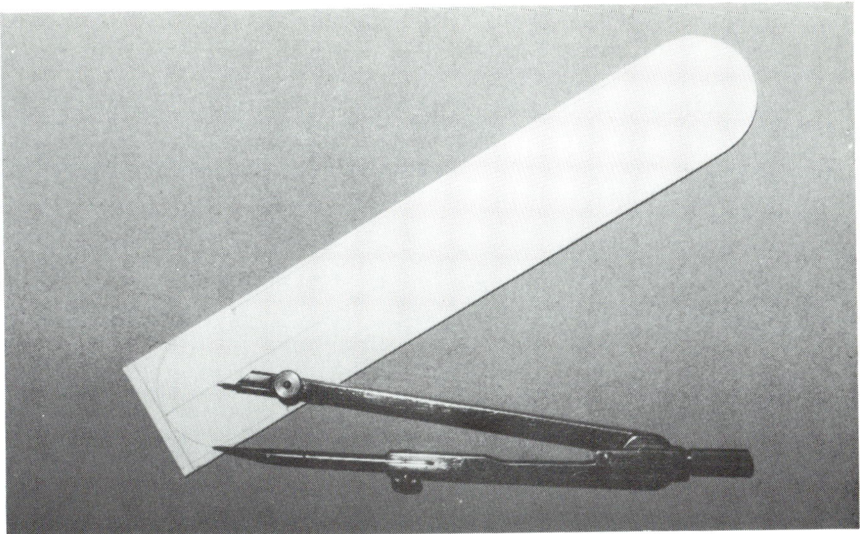

Making the upper-deck floor. The curve ends are scribed using the dividers, snapped to shape and then sanded smooth (D. Voice).

that happened to be handy, but thin plastic rod would do just as well. To complete the modifications of the side, the upper-deck decency panel was cut to leave a strip 3 mm high. The other side was modified in the same way and construction of the saloon could begin.

I had intended to make the bulkhead from plastic card. However, I realised that it was much easier, and more effective, to use a BEC bulkhead. These are available as separate items and I used part No 4A. I took the saloon side and filed the inside of the corner pillars in order to make a snug fit with the cast bulkheads. The upper-deck floor was taken from the kit and cut to the exact length of the inside of the saloon. The saloon sides, bulkhead and upper-deck floor were then all glued together. Platform floors were cut from 40 thou plastic card to the shape shown in Diagram 23. The curved ends were cut by scoring heavily with a pair of dividers and then breaking the plastic along the score line by carefully bending it backwards and forwards. The rough edges that were left were smoothed over with a file. The position of the front bulkhead was marked on the platform and it was glued in place. The upper-deck floor was cut to Diagram 24 from 40 thou plastic card. It was glued in place on the top of the kit floor. I had to file down the top of the bulkhead in order to get a good fit. 40 thou, plastic card was also used for the upper-deck decency panel and the dash.

I had decided to model the car in its final condition, that is after the two rebuilds. The first extended the platforms and changed the stairs from reverse to 90° direct and the second gave it higher decency panels and dash. I cut four strips from 40 thou plastic card, two 12 mm wide and the other two 15 mm wide, all four were at least 200 mm long. My next problem was to curve the strips in a way that would suit the model. It was possible to curve the strips to the correct shape but they had a strong tendency to return to the flat. I realised that this would pull away from any glue and what was necessary to fix the curve in some way. I had heard of modellers 'cooking' plastic card in order to achieve necessary shapes, so I thought I would give it a try. I cut a piece of wood the exact width of the inside of the decency panels of the model. I shaped the end into a semi-circle using a Surform and sanding block. The idea was to curve a strip around the block leaving an equal amount each side and to hold it in place by clamping two more strips of wood either side. This all worked out as I had expected and the next job was to cook it.

I pre-heated an oven to gas mark 3 (sorry, I do not know the electric equivalent) and had a go. Half a dozen strips later I found that it needed about two minutes at that heat. It was quite critical to get the time correct as too little meant that the strip sprang back whilst too much literally melted the plastic. Luckily plastic card is not too expensive and I did not have anything else planned for that evening anyway! I did manage to get the bits that I needed and I learned quite a lot about this technique. The centre of the upper-deck floor was marked out and I measured one of the decency panel strips around the floor and marked it at the centre. Then I cut it to length and glued it in place using the remaining 3 mm of the Dreadnought side and the edge of the rounded end of the floor to fix it in place. The other strip of the decency panel was cut to length and glued in place. The final result was a complete decency panel made in two parts with the joints in the centre of each side where there was least stretch. I clamped the pieces in place and left it overnight for the glue to set. The joints were filled with a small amount of Milliput and, when set, smoothed to hide any gaps. The dash panels were similarly cut to size measuring them against the appropriate platform. They were glued in place using both the edge of the platform and the butt joint with the bulkhead. Then two short strips were cut and fitted at the head of the stairs to represent the panels protecting the stairwell. Headlamps were made from 30 amp fuse wire bent around a suitably sized rod, cut to form a circle and then glued on to the dash.

When the glue had set the exterior and the saloon ceiling were given two coats of matt white, while the saloon interior was painted dark brown (Humbrol HR142). At the same time I painted the stairs (BEC part 55) matt

The model takes shape with the trolley standard and stairs about to be fitted (D. Voice).

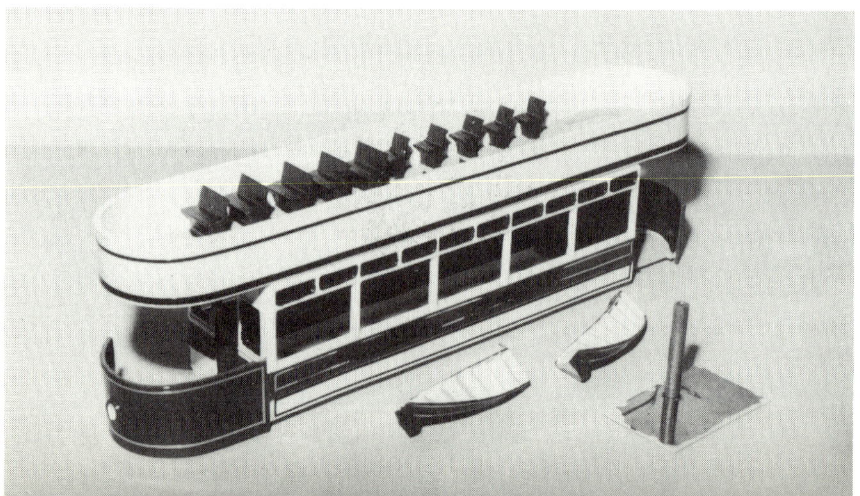

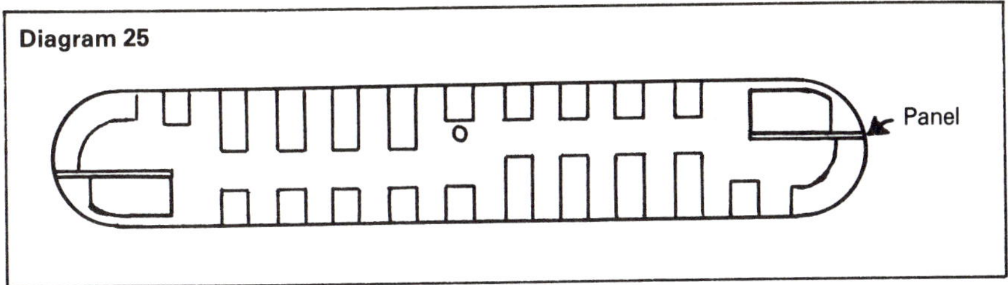

Diagram 25: *Seating plan of the upper-deck, also showing the offset trolley standard and the position of the protection panels by the stairwells.*

white. The outside of the car, saloon ceiling and stairs were then given two coats of ivory (gloss 41). The inside edges of the top quarter lights of the saloon sides and the bulkhead windows and doors were painted dark brown. The opportunity was taken to touch up any white or ivory paint that had strayed into the inside of the saloon. Using the masking techniques previously described the upper rocker panel and dash were painted matt red (matt 60) and then gloss red (gloss 19). The underside and sides of the stairs were similarly painted.

As usual I did some other work while the various coats of paint were drying. First the trolley standard and trolley pole were made. The method has been described in my previous book, but just in case I have included the appropriate diagram (21) in Chapter 6. The only difference is that now I have standardised on the Meadowcroft trolley wheels. In order to fit the trolley standard I drilled a suitable sized hole through the upper-deck floor. From photographs I had it was possible to calculate that the standard was offset to one side by 5 mm. This was quite usual on open-top cars where the trolley standard would often occupy the position of a seat in order not to block the gangway. It was fitted from inside the saloon by gluing the plate to the saloon ceiling.

Thinking of the upper-deck brought me to a knotty problem. I have been unable to determine the seating pattern as no suitable photographs were available. All the photographs of the cars in the earlier condition had so many seated and standing passengers that the seats were entirely hidden. The photographs of the cars in their later condition showed no seats at all as they were behind the high decency panel. I even searched for photographs of the cars before they left Gravesend and for others in the same class that were sold to Swansea and Jarrow, later South Shields, but without success. I was able to find that the upper-deck seating capacity had been quoted as 32, 33 and 34 depending upon which reference one took. In *The Tramways of Croydon* it states that the seating pattern was 2-2. However, it is clear from photographs that Gravesend four-wheel cars of the same period and exactly the same width had 2-1 seating. This factor combined with my own previous researches into the seating patterns of open-top cars leads me to believe that the pattern for these Southmet cars must have been similar to that shown in Diagram 25. This uses the space normally allocated for such seating in the 1900s. Had the company been able to squeeze in 2-2 seating then the capacity on the top deck should have been around 42. So I feel quite justified in the seating pattern I have used. I do not wish to labour this point but it does show the occasional problems the modeller faces when no photographs can be found. In such cases decisions that are made should be on as sound a basis as possible (especially if it is contrary to other opinion).

After this deliberation eight seats were cut 13 mm long and eleven seats 6 mm long. They were painted dark brown in readiness for the upper-deck. The upper-deck floor and platforms were painted mid-grey (matt 64). This was a departure from my usual practice of using dark grey and came about as a result of riding on LCC No 106 at the National Tramway Museum, Crich. I noticed that restoration team had painted all the flooring in mid-grey. Knowing the detail of research that had been undertaken when restoring this car, I felt that I should follow suit. My reason for choosing dark grey previously has been to convey the feeling of much use. I must say that I am still in two minds which is the better for models. I would leave it entirely to your personal preference. Whichever is chosen remember to use the same colour on the stair treads.

Back with the main body of the tramcar I lined the red panels with gold tape and the white rocker panel with black tape. I did this lining when it was in my mind, to represent car No 32 in its first rebuilt condition in the 1920s. However, later on and after more careful reading of the relevant parts in *The Tramways of Croydon* I realised that the extended upper-deck decency panels had not been fitted until 1930. This meant that the correct colour for the lining on the red panels was black. But by now it was too late for me to rectify it and it will remain as a deliberate error. I would be interested to see if anyone comments on it at exhibitions. The two thicker lines around the upper decency panelling were applied in the same way using the same Scotch 3M black plastic tape. I left all the lining oversize for 24 hours in order to allow any stretch to be taken out and then cut off the excess. The number and

Soldering the handrail in place. The ends will be curved to shape and cut to length before the final soldering is done (D. Voice).

Southmet name was applied using Blick dry letter transfers. The larger 'S' and 'T' were made by combining letters as described in Chapter 3. The inside of the dash was painted in red oxide (HR110). Then the whole of the car, except the floors, was given a coat of gloss varnish using a new tin. I fitted the seats to the pattern already described. This was another mistake as they should have been left until after the railing was fitted. The end seats were made from plastic card and balsa, painted and fitted.

I had decided that I would use BEC maximum traction bogies for this model. I already had a set of Brill 22E sideframe castings from Meadowcroft Models. These were the correct 4 ft 0 in wheelbase while the BEC bogies were 4 ft 6 in. So there was a 2 mm difference between the parts. However, when the sideframes were fitted the difference was not noticeable. In order to fit the sideframe castings I attached a brass strip around the bogies, soldering it on at the ends of the bogies casting. The sideframes were then soldered to this strip. In order to do this I tinned the brass strip with ordinary solder first and then used low melt solder for the rest of the job. I fitted the press studs at the same time. When the sideframes were painted red oxide and the rest of the bogie, including the brass fixing strip, painted black, the whole lot looked very neat indeed. The chassis was made in exactly the same was as described in Chapter 2, including my usual practice of fitting passengers. The saloon of the model was glazed and small pieces of wood glued just below the window line. I actually cut up a matchstick to make the pieces of wood. The chassis was now manoeuvred past the pieces of wood and dropped back on to them. I then checked that it fitted nicely and was the correct height for the bogies. I moved the chassis up and placed blobs of glue on the top of the blocks using a cocktail stick. The chassis was pulled back into place and the glue was allowed to set overnight.

Now I could delay it no longer, I had to tackle the upper-deck railing. I

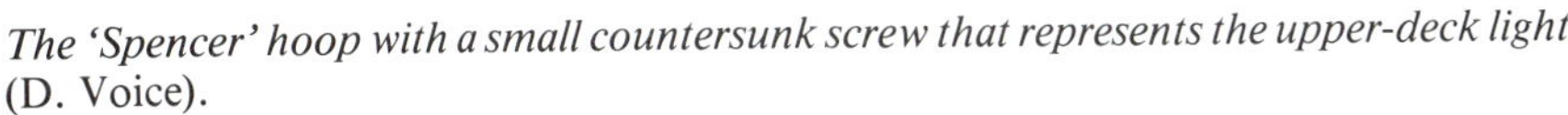

The 'Spencer' hoop with a small countersunk screw that represents the upper-deck light (D. Voice).

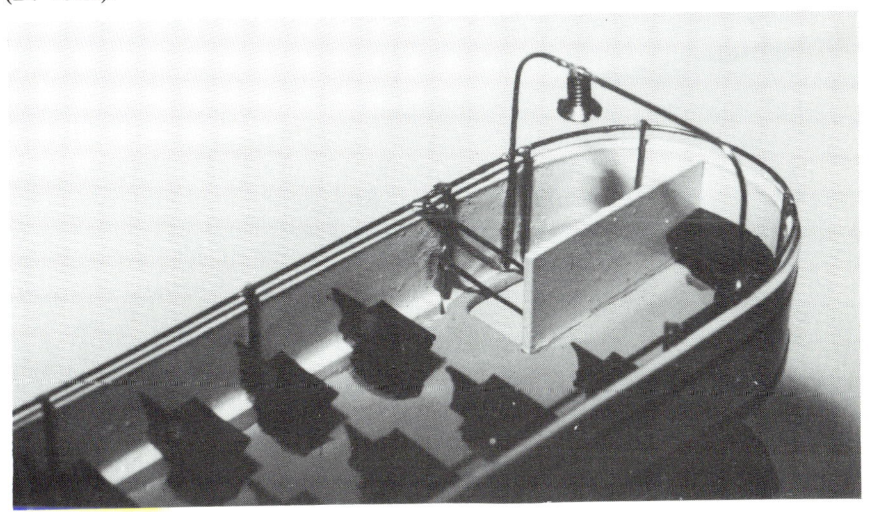

have already described how I have found it possible to solder wire whilst in situ on a white metal model. On the Southmet car the only way I could devise to fit the railing in a neat way was to push this technique even further. I decided to do all the soldering actually on the car. I cut uprights from brass wire leaving them all well over-length. These were then glued in place using a photograph as a guide. This is where I found that the seats got in the way. I actually had to remove some of them in order to fix the uprights and then had to glue the seats back in place. This is not recommended as the least you will have to do is to re-paint the upper-deck floor, so do fix the railing in place before putting the seats in. I laid a long piece of wire along one side and soldered it to the uprights. I put a dab of flux on each joint and kept the use of the soldering iron to an absolute minimum. Naturally I was extremely careful to keep the hot soldering iron separate from the plastic. When not actually soldering I put the iron well away from the model. In fact I was able to make strong joints on the wire without making any defect on the plastic. When I completed the one side I curved the wire around each end. I had already decided that the joint in the wire would be at the centre of one end so that it would be hidden by the destination box. The remaining soldering was completed, the wire cut to length and the joint made. Then the 'Spencer' hoops were fitted and two small countersunk screws were soldered under them to represent the lights. I deliberately made these larger than true scale in order to emphasise them. The uprights were soldered to the destination boxes, using low melt soldering. I made sure that they did not foul any of the other uprights or the panels above the stairwell. The over-height uprights were all now snipped to length.

The stairs were glued in place and the stair rails curved to match them. The lower ends of the stair rails were glued to the inside of the dash panelling and the upper end soldered to the upright at the top of the stairs. Then all the rails except the stair rails were painted black while the destination boxes were painted dark brown. I know that the BEC Kits transfer for the E and E/1 kit had the destination 'Croydon, Purley' and I decided to use the Croydon part and cut it out from the transfer. This was much too small for the whole of the space on the destination box. So I painted the front of the destination box gloss black and then applied the Croydon transfer. The trolley standard was painted red oxide and the trolley pole black with a red oxide spring. To complete the upper deck the destination boxes were glued in place and suitable passengers were added.

The handrails on the platform were added as were the controllers (BEC Part 7) and handbrakes fabricated from brass wire and fitted. BEC advertisements were fitted to either side. The small advertisements were taken from Tiny Signs photographs of enamel signs. I used double-sided adhesive tape to fix them in place. Next I turned to the undergear. The lifetrays and lifeguards under the platforms were fabricated from 1 mm wide brass strip. The steps were similarly soldered together using 3 mm wide strip for the actual step. These were all painted red oxide, bent and glued under the platforms. A strip of plastic card was fitted to the step to represent the vertical kickboard. The dog gates under the centre of the car were made from the original mouldings from the Dreadnought kit. One section was cut off and the remainder was painted red oxide. Then a piece of black card was glued behind the slats and

Model Southmet and Croydon cars pass while in service. This is a bit of modellers licence as they ran on different lines in reality (models and photo, D. Voice).

extended upwards to be glued inside the rocker panel. I found that to prevent the bogies fouling the dog gates it was necessary to bevel the inside of the ends of the slats.

The last job was to fit the fenders. These were made from 1½ mm brass strip bent around and glued in place. I am sure that plastic strip would have done just as well, but may not have stood up to the rigours of exhibition running. The fenders were painted black. This then completed the model of this Southmet tramcar in its final form. The same techniques and mostly the same parts could be used to construct earlier versions of this car. Indeed, it would be a very similar job to make the original version, as used in Gravesend. The main differences would be the lower decency panels, the need to fit mesh around the upper-deck, the shorter platforms, and the reversed stairs. I hope that this description has demonstrated just part of the versatility of the Dreadnought plastic kit. I have seen the kit used to produce a whole range of tramcars, all very different from the original Dreadnought prototype.

Chapter 8

Bexley, Dartford, Erith and Gravesend tramway systems

Beyond the south-east boundary of London the tramway needs were met by two municipally owned systems, one municipally owned and leased to a company, and one that was company owned. As it transpired the council-owned tramways joined each other and the London County Council lines and eventually formed part of the total London Transport tramway network. The company-owned system in Gravesend remained isolated and closed before the formation of the London Passenger Transport Board.

In this chapter of our look at London's tramways will be found the most devastating event ever to occur to any tramway system. In a single night a catastrophic fire destroyed every tramcar in the Dartford fleet. As will be seen, by the enormous co-operation of neighbouring councils the citizens of Dartford were without a tramway service for only one day. This demonstrated in a dramatic way the advantages of linking with neighbouring systems to form large, co-operative networks.

Bexley Urban District Council Tramways

Bexley never saw horse tramways. The nearest such system was the Woolwich and South East London Horse Tramway which terminated in Plumstead. So when the Bexley Council decided to construct their own electric tramway it was sensible to include in the Act of Parliament an extension beyond their boundary to meet with the existing horse tramway terminus. Thus this three-quarters of a mile of tramway route was included in the proposals. Since this section of line was on London County Council land, a proviso was added whereby should the LCC construct the line within a given period it would be under LCC control. As it happened they did not and so Bexley Council owned and ran a short section of tramway within the London boundary.

All the five miles of route were opened in 1903 and operation commenced with 12 tramcars purchased that year. These five-window, four-wheel, open-top tramcars were designated Class A and numbered 1 to 12. They were fitted with 6 ft 0 in wheelbase trucks, reversed stairs and, unusually for 1903, had large oil headlamps which fitted on clips on the dash. The lifeguard and lifetrays were the wire mesh type. The cars carried the coat of arms of Kent but did not have the Bexley name except on the 'legal' lettering on the solebar. There were no destination boxes, instead a large board with the main places on the route was fixed on the wire mesh at each end of the upper-deck.

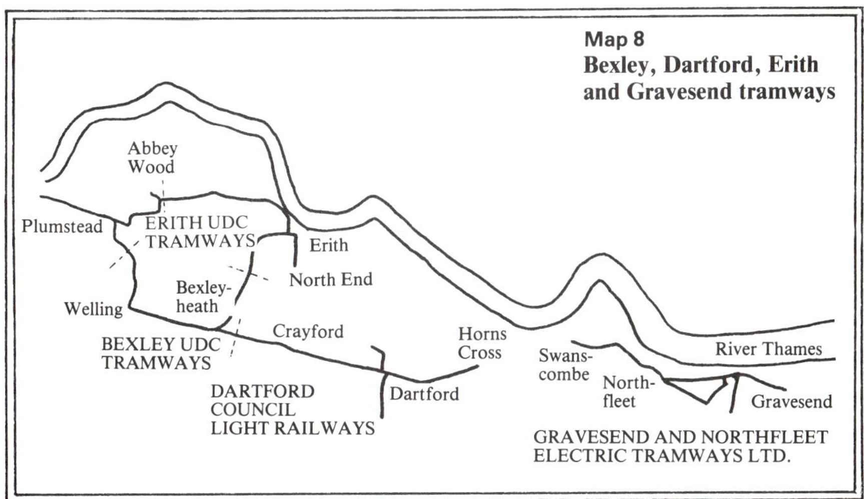

This used black lettering on a white background. There were also side indicator boards. By 1911 the oil headlamps had been replaced by the more conventional electric type fitted high on the dash with the car number below it. Also one line destination boxes had been fitted immediately above the upper-deck dash panel, in front of the wire mesh. The cars were given new 8 ft 0 in wheelbase Peckham P22 trucks in 1913 except No 9 which was given a 6 ft 0 in Brill 21E truck.

It was soon evident that the demand for the new tramway was greater than

Five-window Bexley car No 14. This photograph shows the high headlamp setting and the fleet number below it (H.A. Whitcombe).

While I was making my five-window Bexley model I came across this converted BEC Kit in a shop window in West Wickham. In this case the construction used plastic strip for the window frames. The car on the right is an LCC Class B as hired to Bexley, with direct stairs and a trolley pole. Modeller not known (D. Voice).

expected and a further four cars were purchased in 1904. These were to the same design as the previous tramcars and the numbers followed in sequence, 13 to 16. They were also designated Class A and had the same modifications as the 1 to 12 series. Thus by 1913 they had been fitted with 8 ft 0 in trucks. All the Class A tramcars remained in this condition until taken over by London Transport. Except for cars 3, 8, 13 and 15 they were all taken out of service within two weeks of new ownership. The twelve withdrawn cars were stored temporarily at Abbey Wood before going to Brixton Hill for eventual breaking up when financial terms had been agreed with the former owners. The four cars that did enter London Transport service were given the suffix C. But they lasted only lasted six months and by 1934 were also sent to Brixton Hill for scrapping. Modelling of this class is discussed in detail at the end of this chapter.

While Bexley had been developing their system the London County Council had been re-laying standard gauge electric track on the narrow gauge horse tramway. In 1908 they reached the end of the horse tramway and connected with the Bexley track in Plumstead. The LCC were planning to continued their route to Abbey Wood. This meant that the short section of Bexley track in the High Street was needed. Since it was in London the LCC acquired the track from Bexley. The latter lost no time to press home the opportunity to gain a through running agreement. Thus Bexley tramcars were operated over LCC metals to Woolwich. The Bexley route now ended in Beresford Square, outside the Woolwich Arsenal. At this time Erith had just been rebuffed by the LCC and so approached Bexley to reach through running arrangements. Bexley were more agreeable in this respect than the LCC and so, perhaps with an unconscious irony, Erith cars ran on Bexley tracks on the same day as the Bexley tramcars ran to Woolwich. But probably the need to release Bexley trams from the short Northumberland Heath route to work the longer Woolwich route was the reason for this arrangement. Relations with Erith were not smooth in the initial stages. The agreement ceased after one year and was restarted in 1910. The through running then continued to 1914 when the agreement came to an end again. The through running arrangements with the LCC were extended in 1914 by the lengthening of LCC route No 38 to Bexleyheath on Sundays. This route from London's centre was served by the top-covered bogie E/1 tramcars. The service finished in 1915 probably due to the necessities created by war. The war also emphasised the importance of the Bexley system as it was in the centre of the munitions industry. The Government put pressure on the councils and once again through running arrangements were made with Erith.

The demands on the Bexley system in 1915 began to outstrip the resources. The LCC was approached with a view to hiring some cars. As an interim measure five Class E/1 cars were hired until six Class B tramcars were fitted with trolley poles and made available to Bexley. These Class B tramcars had enclosed top covers and probably all had direct stairs fitted by this time. They retained their LCC livery and numbers for some time, but were eventually re-painted in Bexley colours and given the numbers 17 to 22. A further five Class B tramcars were purchased from the LCC in 1917 and were given the numbers 23 to 27. Further Class B tramcars were acquired later, and the story of the 17 to 27 series will be continued then.

The wartime period led to another through running arrangement, this time with Dartford. Bexley cars ran through to Crayford and Dartford tramcars ran on Bexley rails. Thus the residents of Bexleyheath were hosts to LCC, Erith and Dartford tramcars. However, they were not to see the Dartford tramcars for very long. The whole Dartford fleet was destroyed by a depot fire in 1917. Bexley stepped in immediately and, despite problems of their own, managed to provide an emergency service. Dartford was without trams for only the one day necessary to make the arrangements. In the following weeks it became evident that due to the war Dartford was not likely to be able to rebuild its depot and re-form its fleet. An agreement was reached where Bexley provided the necessary tramcars and carried out the maintenance. By this time Bexley was desperate for more tramcars and once again turned to the LCC, no doubt with the support of the War Department.

Twelve more Class B tramcars were hired at short notice. A year later Bexley purchased these cars and they became numbers 28 to 39 in the fleet. However, the repainting was evidently spread over a period as some tramcars were still carrying the LCC numbers in 1920! It is thought that some of the Class B tramcars carried the title 'Dartford Council Tramways' on the rocker panel. The situation in 1918 was that there were 23 Class B tramcars in Bexley hands, of which 17 were purchased and 6 hired. By 1920 the need for the six hired cars had passed (the Woolwich Arsenal had reverted to more normal production). So the tramcars were sent back to the LCC. This would normally have left a gap in the numbering of the fleet. But in fact the remaining cars were re-numbered either from their new Bexley number or directly

from their original LCC number. Thus the Class B tramcars became numbers
17 to 33. Under Bexley ownership the bottom half of the two line destination
box was painted out in black to effectively give a single line box. Apart from
this the tramcars were unchanged during their stay at Bexley. They were all
taken over by London Transport in 1933 and were given the suffix C to their
numbers. However, by the end of 1933 they had all been taken out of service
and sent to Brixton Hill for breaking-up.

All the Class B tramcars can be modelled using BEC Kits No 2. By the time
these cars ran on Bexley rails they had fully enclosed top covers and direct
stairs. They were fitted with a trolley pole and the plough carriers had been

Above *Bexley No 33, one
of the B Class cars pur-
chased from the LCC (R.
Elliott).*

Left *BEC Kits LCC B Class
car possibly in the con-
dition loaned to Bexley. At
the time of the Dartford
fire the LCC loaned some
B Class cars very quickly.
It is not recorded in what
condition these cars were
transferred. It is possible
that some reversed stairs,
enclosed-top cars were
fitted with trolley poles
(model and photo D.
Voice).*

removed before they passed into Bexley hands. The kit will need these small modifications. In addition the bottom half of the destination boxes should be blacked out. Apart from the tramcars that may have been carried the Dartford title for a short while, the remainder were in a plain livery. The lining on the brown panels was straw coloured paint rather than the more usual gold. The cars had no coat-of-arms or large title. The name of 'Bexley Council Tramways' appeared in small lettering on the bottom of the lower rocker panel (generally known as the 'legal' lettering).

Table 14: Bexley Urban District Council Tramways 1903-21 and Bexley UDC Tramways and Dartford Light Railways Joint Committee 1917-33

Number	Class/ type	Year built	Body type	Trucks/Bogies	LT Nos	Scrapped, sold or changed
1-12	A	1903	Open-top	4 W 6 ft Brush A later 8 ft Peckham P22 except No 9 with 6 ft Brill 22E	—	1933
13-16	A	1904	Open-top	4 W 6 ft Brush A later 8 ft Peckham P22	—	1933
17-39	B	1915/16	Enclosed top	4 W 6 ft 6 in Brill 21E	Suffix C	1933

Notes
4 W Four-wheel.

Livery
1903-10 Maroon (browner than LCC) and cream. Gold lining on the maroon and burnt sienna lining on the ivory. Numbers gold shaded red. Trucks, undergear, trolley standards and wire mesh red oxide. Fenders and controllers black.
1910-12 Rocker panels also maroon. Other colours as before.
1912-17 As 1903-10.
1917-33 Chocolate brown and ivory. Straw coloured lining on the brown. Other colours as before.

Dartford Urban District Council Light Railways

The first tramways in Dartford were horse-drawn, although probably never seen by most of the local population. A 4 ft 0 in gauge tramway was built in 1897 as part of the development of Joyce Green Smallpox Hospital and was entirely within the extensive hospital grounds. It linked the complex of Joyce Green, Long Reach and Orchard Hospitals. The tramways had ambulance trams to convey patients. Horses were used as the motive power until 1924 when a motor ambulance was used as a towing vehicle. This was a sign of things to come. The continued development of the motor ambulance meant that the need for the tramway declined and it closed in 1936. It is reported that sections of tram rail can still be seen in the hospital grounds.

Of more direct interest to us and certainly far better known was the

The ill fated Dartford depot and cars Nos 3, 7 and 12. This view was taken before the opening of the system, car 12 is not yet completely fitted out (D. Voice collection).

Dartford electric street tramway which opened in 1906 with 6½ miles of route. One end of the tramway reached the Bexley tracks although at this time the rails were not joined. The corporation decided that they did not wish to operate the tramway and instead leased the system to a private company. However, this arrangement has little effect on the modeller as everything appeared as if the corporation was running it all.

To open the system 12 tramcars were purchased in 1906. These were conventional four-wheel, three-window, open-top tramcars with Brill 21E 6 ft 0 in wheelbase trucks and 180° direct stairs. These tramcars were unaltered during their relatively short lives. Once again the modeller is well served by BEC Kit No 3. The correct direct stairs, chassis and truckside should be fitted. Otherwise the kit is assembled in accordance with the manufacturer's instructions. Purists will want to cut away the flat part of the dash panelling by the stairs and replace it with a wrought-iron screen.

As described earlier, it was soon realised that it was in everybody's interest to connect the tracks between Dartford and Bexley. Thus Dartford tramcars ran the extra short distance on Bexley rails in order to terminate in the Market Place, Bexley. When the war started in 1914 the munitions industry in and around the area led to an increase in traffic. One result was the sight of Bexley tramcars running on Dartford rails to Crayford. The history of the system in the other direction was not so fortunate. Although extensions to meet the Gravesend Tramways had been voiced on a number of occasions there was no real enthusiasm for a line through open countryside. The matter was dropped, much to the satisfaction of the South Eastern and Chatham Railway and so Gravesend remained an isolated tramway outpost.

In order to increase the fleet Dartford approached Erith with a view to acquiring two one-man operated demi-cars that had become surplus to requirements. Subsequently, in 1915, one of them was hired to Dartford for a year and then purchased outright. This became car No 13 in the fleet. The tramcar was totally enclosed with a four-wheel 5 ft 6 in wheelbase truck. In common with all one-man operated demi-cars the vehicle was front entrance. Modelling this car creates problems as there is no kit that can be modified. So it will be necessary to scratchbuild the car, including the chassis, unless you

Car No 10 in Dartford High Street (commercial postcard).

are willing to compromise with a BEC 6 ft 0 in chassis. To add to all these problems there are no known photographs of this design of car either under Erith or Dartford ownership. The modelling of this car is discussed in further detail when the Erith system is described.

The end of the Dartford fleet came very suddenly in August 1917. The night after a very busy Bank Holiday was the last for the tramcars and the depot. At three o'clock in the morning the alarm was raised when a fire was seen in the depot. Despite the prompt appearance of the fire brigade there was little that could be done. The depot and all thirteen tramcars were totally destroyed. The subsequent history of the Bexley operation of the Dartford system has already been covered.

Table 15: Dartford Council Light Railways 1906-17

Number	Class/ type	Year built	Body type	Trucks/Bogies	LT Nos	Scrapped, sold or changed
1-12		1906	Open-top	4 W 6 ft Brill 21E	—	1917
13		1915	Single-deck demi-car ex-Erith built 1906	4 W 5 ft 6 in Mountain & Gibson	—	1917

Notes
4 W Four-wheel.

Livery
Similar to Bexley, but officially described as maroon and yellow. Gold lining on the maroon and black or burnt sienna on the yellow (cream). Letters and numbers gold, colour of shading not known but probably red or blue. Trucks, undergear and trolley standards red oxide. Wire mesh, cream. Fenders and controllers, black.

Erith Urban District Council Tramways

Erith had no history of horse-drawn tramways within the council boundary. Interest in electric trams started in 1901 when the council began its first investigations. Even at this early stage the council was very keen to connect with the LCC tramway system (even though the LCC line in Plumstead was still in the planning stage). The matter was often pursued by Erith but the LCC were not keen and Erith tramcars only ran on ex-LCC rails. Under London Transport ownership a connection was made at Abbey Wood. Even then this was just a single track and only used by tramcars running into Abbey Wood depot.

To return to the early days. The tramway opened in 1905 and the initial fleet consisted of equal numbers of two designs of tramcars. The first was an open-top, four-wheel car of the standard design with a four-window saloon. For reasons that have been lost in the mists of time these cars were numbered 1 to 6 and 9. They had 6 ft 0 in trucks and 180° direct stairs. A single line destination box was mounted on the mesh (rather an ornate scroll work) on the front of the upper-deck. Sometime after 1918 the trucks were extended to 8 ft 0 in. Otherwise, in modelling terms, the cars were unchanged during their life. They all lasted into London Transport days. Although the name was painted out and they received the suffix 'D' to their Erith numbers. They were withdrawn after three months. They were never repainted or re-numbered in the London Transport fleet. Like so many municipal cars those from Erith joined the queues for the breakers at Brixton Hill.

Modelling these cars is made simple by BEC Kits. Kit No 8, with the chassis and truckside appropriate for the period, can be used without modifications. In the early apple green and primrose livery it makes a very attractive model. The colour is most unusual for London and, of course, they only ran in Erith, Bexley and Abbey Wood.

The second design was again very standard. The same style of four-window tramcar was used. The difference in the two batches was that the second batch was top-covered with balcony ends. In all other respects the cars were the same as the first batch, except for the numbers which were 7, 8 and 10 to 14. With the higher centre of gravity these cars were prone to even more pitching and rolling than the open-top cars. In 1918 one of the cars was modified with an 8 ft 0 in wheelbase truck. This improved the riding and soon the whole batch was converted. The open-top cars followed suit. Otherwise these cars remained unchanged until taken over by London Transport in 1933. The condition of the bodies must have been good as London Transport decided to keep this batch. However, it was recognised that some action was required concerning the trucks. At this time a Croydon Corporation tramcar was allocated to Erith while others were being broken up at Brixton Hill. These had sound Brill 7 ft 6 in wheelbase trucks. Seven were taken and fitted to the Erith cars which were re-painted in the London Transport livery. However, they were not numbered in the LT fleet but were given the suffix 'D' to their old Erith numbers. They ran in this condition until trolleybuses replaced the services in 1935. Again these cars are ideal for modelling. BEC Kit No 9 should be used. The chassis and trucksides will need to be changed according to the period being modelled. Otherwise the kit can be constructed as supplied. The apple green livery of the early days does make this an eye catching model.

The final car in the original delivery was a combined sweeping and water works vehicle. It had a square shaped water tank which was not roofed and the car was fitted with a four-wheel 5 ft 6 in wheelbase truck. It was not given

Top *Erith depot at the opening of the system (the far car carries on advertisement saying 'Brush, Loughborough', the manufacturers). Note that both open-top and balcony-top cars are in view* (D. Voice collection).

Above *Car No 10 seen in Erith carrying the later mahogany red livery* (Lens of Sutton).

a number for many years. Eventually it was numbered 19, after the arrival of the LUT tramcars but before the Hull car. When the latter arrived the works car was re-numbered 20. However, use of the car declined and by the time London Transport took over in 1933 the car was out of use. Under London Transport it was re-numbered 20D, although this may have been just a book exercise. It was scrapped in 1933. There is a photograph of this car, but it is not generally available. This does cause problems for the modeller who would in any case need to scratchbuild the model.

Erith balcony car modelled using a standard BEC Kit (Model D. Watkins, photo D. Voice).

In 1906 two further tramcars were acquired in order to work the lightly used route to Northend. Numbers 15 and 16 were one-man operated demi-cars. The tramcars were small single deck vehicles with a 5 ft 6 in wheelbase truck. The overall length was 22 ft 6 in and the totally enclosed bodies had front entrances. The Northend route was not a success and lost money. In order to increase their earnings the demi-cars were tried on the main line offering a flat fare of one penny; tickets being issued by automatic machines. But this also failed and the Northend service was reduced to Fridays and Saturdays only in 1908 with service ceasing in 1909. After a brief attempt to revive the route, it was abandoned in 1910 making the demi-cars surplus to needs. In 1915 one was hired to Dartford who purchased it in 1916. The other was sold to Doncaster Corporation Tramways in 1917.

As I mentioned in the Dartford section, these cars prove a problem to the modeller. The only guide is that they were probably very similar to the Maidstone demi-car No 18 which is described in *The Tramways of Kent-Volume 1* by Invicta, with a drawing of the car. However, from that point the modeller is on his own. The whole car, including the chassis, will need to be scratchbuilt, although a compromise could be reached using the BEC 6 ft 0 in chassis and truckside.

Through running with Bexley began in 1908 and the trials and tribulations have already been described. In common with Bexley and Dartford the Erith system found itself in great demand during the war years. This put a strain on resources and two tramcars were hired from Leyton Council. but they had to be returned after a year due to the shortages in Leyton. In the same year (1915) two cars were hired from London United. These were Type W1 and they were joined by a further two in the same year. These tramcars retained their LUT numbers (187, 192, 221 and 252), and the dark blue and broken white livery although the fleet name was removed. Erith purchased these cars in 1919 and re-built them in 1922. They were then given full length canopies and 90° direct stairs. There is a photograph of one of these cars waiting to be re-built and it was still in its LUT livery, so these tramcars probably did not get the Erith livery until after the re-building. At this time they were given new numbers and became 15 to 18 in the Erith fleet (the demi-cars 15 and 16 having been sold by this time). These tramcars lasted to be taken over by London Transport and were given the suffix 'D' to their numbers. However, they did not last long and had been withdrawn for scrapping within three months. The modelling comments on the LUT Type W1 are contained in Chapter 4. The re-built Erith version can be constructed in a similar way and certainly is much the more attractive design for these cars.

A year after hiring the LUT tramcars, Erith purchased a second-hand bogie car from Hull Corporation. It had been number 101 in the Hull fleet and had been given a top cover which only extended the length of the lower saloon. The roof was not extended beyond the upper saloon and so the small balconies and stairs were left exposed to the elements. The bogies were Brill 22E maximum traction type and the stairs 90° direct. Allocated number 19 in the Erith fleet the cars was put into service still in its maroon and cream Hull livery. The car never carried destination boxes, but did have side route boards. Although it received its new number, the Erith coat-of-arms and fleet name, it remained in the maroon livery all its life. Its use in Erith was limited to short workings, for technical reasons it was never allowed to run to Bexleyheath. This tramcar lasted until London Transport days and again it did not receive a new number, just the suffix 'D'. It only lasted a few months before being withdrawn from service and like so many other cars it went to Brixton Hill for scrapping.

Ex-LUT Type W car purchased by Erith and seen running in LPTB service with the D suffix to the number (M.N.A. Walker).

This unusual car is not one to be found in the kit manufacturers catalogues so the modeller will need to scratchbuild. The lower saloon was very similar to the six arched window LUT bogie cars. As has been mentioned in Chapter 4 it is hoped that a kit for the LUT cars will become available. If so, it will be far easier for the modeller as a simple conversion could be carried out to make this ex-Hull car.

The Erith system contains a number of attractive features for the modeller. In fact if the period around 1918 is chosen this small system can provide enormous interest. The full representation of the fleet can be realistically achieved by one modeller and the variety of liveries would be very colourful. For example, in the 1918 period the citizens of Erith would have seen the old apple green and primrose yellow, the new dark mahogany red and ivory, which would have been in contrast to the blue and white of the LUT tramcars and the maroon of the ex-Hull car. In my opinion a most interesting system to model and one that has not received the attention that it really deserves.

Table 16: Erith Urban District Council Tramways 1905-33

Number	Class/ type	Year built	Body type	Trucks/Bogies	LT Nos	Scrapped, sold or changed
1-6 & 9		1905	Open-top	4 W 6 ft M&G 21EM later 8 ft M&G	Suffix D	1934
7-8 & 10-14		1905	Balcony top	4 W 6 ft M&G 21EM later 8 ft M&G	Suffix D	1935
15-16		1906	Single-deck demi-car	4 W 5 ft 6 in M&G	—	1915-17
15-16(ii)		1922	Open-top ex-LUT Type W built 1902	MT Bogie Brill 22E	Suffix D	1934
19		1916	Uncanopied enclosed top ex-Hull built 1903	MT Bogie Brill 22E	Suffix D	1934
20	Works	1905	Street sweeping and watering car	4 W 5 ft 6 in M&G	Suffix D	1934

Notes
M&G Mountain and Gibson; **MT** Maximum traction; **4 W** Four-wheel.

Livery
1905-17 Apple green and primrose yellow. Gold lining on the green and black lining on the primrose. Letters and numbers gold shaded green. Trucks, undergear and trolley standards red oxide. Upper-deck scrollwork, primrose. Fenders and controllers, black. The ex-LUT cars and ex-Hull car remained in their respective liveries in this period.
1917-33 Dark mahogany red (weathering to deep sepia) and ivory cream. Upper-deck scrollwork, black. Other colours as before.

Gravesend and Northfleet Electric Tramways Limited

The Gravesend system is very much the odd one out amongst the London tramways. It was never connected to the rest of the network and indeed the enterprise closed four years before the formation of the London Passenger Transport Board. Nevertheless it is still of great interest both historically and from a modelling point of view. Tramways began in Gravesend with the opening of a 3 ft 6 in gauge horse tramway in 1883. This tramway saw the first experiments in the London area with electric tramway operation. In 1888 an extension was built to Northfleet which operated on a conduit system, designed by Short-Nesmith and called the 'Series Electrical Traction System'. This experiment lasted for about eighteen months until 1890 when it was replaced by conventional horse trams. Two electric tramcars had been provided for this experiment and they were of four-wheel, single-deck design. The conduit slot was in the groove of one of the running rails. It would be a simple matter to model this system using the commercially available Conrad tram track. There would be no need to modify the track as the groove would also represent the conduit slot. The advantage of such a model is that there is not need for overhead wires and the whole fleet of two cars could easily be scratchbuilt.

The horse tramway was purchased by the BET in 1901, who immediately named the system Gravesend and Northfleet Electric Tramways Limited. At the same time as electrification the street track was relaid to standard gauge. New extensions were also constructed and the system began its public service in 1902. Among various proposals that were being discussed at the time was a link with the Dartford tramways. However, as had already been described, the Gravesend system was destined to remain isolated.

For the opening of the electric tramways twenty tramcars were purchased from Dick, Kerr and Company Limited. These cars, numbered 1 to 20 were open-top, bogie vehicles with reversed stairs. The bogies were the Brill 22E maximum traction type mounted in the reversed position, that is with pony wheel outermost. But it was soon found that these vehicles were too large for the needs of the system and it was decided to sell them. In 1904 Nos 9 and 10 were sold to Jarrow. Four others went to Swansea and the final four to the Southmet. The last vehicle in this class was sold in 1906, having spent just four years in Gravesend.

The modelling of these cars in their later form has been covered in detail in Chapter 7. The same basic construction can be used for the original condition, in particular the parts from the Hadfields Blackpool Dreadnought kit. The ends of the model will each need to be 3 mm shorter and they should be fitted with reversed stairs (BEC parts 14 and 15). The dash and upper-deck decency panels will also need to be lower. Otherwise the construction can be as described.

At the same time as the bogie cars were purchased ten four-wheel, open-top tramcars were obtained from the same manufacturer. Numbered 11 to 20, these were the standard design four-window, reversed stair tramcar with a 6 ft 0 in wheelbase. They were originally fitted with two line destination boxes at each end of the upper-deck. The lifetrays were unusual as the slats ran lengthwise rather than across the car. Before 1915 these cars were heavily adorned with advertising and even the dash panels were covered in script

making the fleet numbers difficult to spot. This practise stopped after 1918 although some cars did carry advertisements on the lower rocker panel. Around this time the destination boxes were removed and a single line box fitted inside the lower saloon window. At the end of the upper-deck of the cars a large semi-circular advertisement was carried for the local newspaper the *Kent Messenger*. In 1920 numbers 15 to 20 were fitted with a three window upper saloon with open balcony ends. All the cars lasted until the end of the Gravesend system and the bodies of some were sold off to be used as sheds.

A model of this type of tramcar in its open-top condition can be made

Above *Gravesend No 11, showing the advertisements carried on the dash panels* (commercial post-card).

Left *Bogie car No 5 in service in Gravesend. The 1-10 series only lasted at most four years. Note that the lower rocker panel has been used for advertising purposes* (courtesy R.J. Appleton).

Right *Gravesend Demi-car No 9* (courtesy R.J. Appleton).

using BEC Kit No 8. The correct 6 ft 0 in wheelbase chassis and truckside should be fitted. A reversed staircase (parts 14 and 15) should be obtained. The distinctive lifetrays will need to be scratchbuilt using either plastic card or, for better strength, brass strip. The later balcony top version of this class of car is best modelled using BEC Kit No 9. Again reversed stairs will be needed and the lifetrays will have to be scratchbuilt. The upper saloon sides will also need to be changed. Three-window upper saloon sides should be purchased from the range of parts obtainable direct from the manufacturer. The tramcars had the top quarter lights fitted to the upper-deck windows and these will need to be added to the cast sides. This can be done either by using the brass strip technique described later in this chapter or by fabricating from plastic strip. The large windows in the upper-deck were unusual in that they were composed of two panes of glass which could slide sideways for ventilation. On the model this should be represented by using two strips of glazing material for each window with a small overlap down the centre. The lower saloon windows were the more traditional type.

With the realisation that the 1 to 10 Class bogie cars were too large, they were offered for sale. However, passengers still needed transport and so when the first two bogie cars were sold in 1904 they were replaced by two demi-cars. These were given the now redundant numbers 9 and 10. They were purchased in order to run on the low revenue routes and had front entrances for one-man operation. Being small single-deck vehicles they were much lighter and cheaper than the standard open-top, four-wheel tramcar. Operating costs were much reduced both in electrical consumption and the wages of the crew. These two cars were in regular use and came to the end of their operational life in 1921 when they were withdrawn and scrapped. They never received the later cherry red livery.

As with all these small demi-cars the modeller has to resort to scratchbuilding. In my view these two cars were a most attractive design with arched

entrances and a narrow arched window to one side and three main arched windows on the other. In modelling this car you would need to develop your own drawings from the photographs that are available. It may well be possible to use a three-window saloon side from BEC Kits or even three windows cut from a Hadfields Dreadnought, as a basis for the model. In both cases the top quarter lights will need to be removed and replaced with arched tops to the windows. Again BEC parts can be used for the chassis and trucksides if your are willing to overlook the 2 mm difference between the 6 ft 0 in chassis, which is the shortest in the BEC range, and the 5 ft 6 in of the prototype.

When more bogie cars were sold, Gravesend purchased four more open-top, four-wheel tramcars. These were given the numbers 1 to 4. Again these cars were to the standard design, except that the saloon had three windows and the stairs were 180° direct. The cars had the same type of lifetray as before, with the longitudinal slats. Originally these were fitted with destination boxes. Later, in line with the 11 to 20 Class, they received one line indicator boxes fitted inside the centre window of the saloon. Like the other cars they had semi-circular *Kent Messenger* advertisements mounted at each end of the upper-deck. The 1 to 4 Class remained unchanged throughout their life and were scrapped with the rest of the fleet when the system closed in 1929.

This is another very straightforward prototype to model. BEC Kit No 3 can be used with the correct 180° direct stairs and 6 ft 0 in wheelbase chassis and trucksides. Other than the position of the destination box and the style of lifetray the kit can be assembled according to the instructions. Fitting the destination box inside the saloon windows could be a problem. I would recommend making a new destination box from very thick card, painting it brown and fitting an appropriate destination. Then after covering the front with double-sided adhesive tape, the box can be fitted to the inside of the glazing material. I have used this technique on some Birmingham tramcars that are now three years old and the destination boxes are still as good as when they were first fitted.

The system was still in need of further vehicles and in 1908 two four-wheel, open-top tramcars were purchased second-hand from Jarrow Tramways. These cars were numbered 5 and 6 and at first glance looked exactly like the 1 to 4 Class. However, numbers 5 and 6 were actually slightly smaller. The saloon length was 14 ft 6 in against the more normal 16 ft 0 in. This reduced the overall length by 1 ft 6 in. The trucks were 6 ft 0 in wheelbase. The tramcars were originally delivered with a single line destination box fitted under the canopy. This was removed during the war and an indication box fitted inside the centre window of the saloon. Again the longitudinal type lifetrays were fitted. These cars too carried the semi-circular *Kent Messenger* advertisements. Other than these modifications the cars remained unchanged during their life at Gravesend. They were scrapped at the end of the operation of the system.

In strict modelling terms this prototype will need to be scratchbuilt owing to the smaller saloon. However, the difference scales to 6 mm and if this is acceptable to you then BEC Kit No 3 can be used with exactly the same modifications as the 1 to 4 Class. There is one additional modification for Nos 5

The modeller is able to rewrite history. Seen on the Tramway and Light Railway Society ¾ in to 1ft scale layout Gravesend Demi-car No 9 passes Bexley B Class car, No 33. Had the tracks actually been built to connect the Gravesend and Dartford systems this could have been reality (models R.J. Appleton and E. Budden, photo R.J. Appleton).

and 6. The truck was of a different design and the kit truckside will need a little alteration, mainly to replace the quarter elliptic springs at the ends with the full elliptic type. If the difference in size is not acceptable then I would suggest that the easiest way would be to use BEC Kit No 3 and shorten the saloon, upper-deck decency panel and upper-deck floor. The saloon sides would be best modified by cutting 6 mm out from the centre and rejoining the two parts. The windows would then need to be removed and a new set fitted using brass strip and the technique described later in this Chapter. The upper-deck floor should also have 6 mm removed from the centre and the two remaining parts rejoined, while the decency panel can just be cut to the correct length.

The last tramcars to join the Gravesend fleet were numbers 7 and 8. These cars were also second-hand, having been used by Taunton Tramways. They were bought in 1921 to replace the demi-cars that had reached the end of their life. The Taunton cars were small four-wheel, single-deck cars. The Taunton system was built to 3 ft 6 in gauge which meant that considerable conversion was required before the tramcars could be used by Gravesend. At this time the opportunity was taken to convert No 7 to one-man operation by making it a front entrance vehicle. For reasons that are not known, No 8 was left as a rear entrance vehicle, although it is known to have been used on one-man operated service. Number 7 had the headlamp mounted on the roof while on No 8 it was on the normal dash position. The roof has very square ends with a clerestory running the length of the saloon. These cars remained in these conditions until the end of the system.

In modelling these two cars it is again necessary to look at it in two ways. The length of the saloon was 17 ft 0 in and the overall length 25 ft 6 in. This brings them into what some modellers would consider to be acceptably close enough to be modelled using BEC Kit No 8 as a basis. The model saloon would be 4 mm short, but if this is accepted then the construction is made far simpler. The kit can be constructed in the usual way for the lower saloon. The platforms will need to be shortened slightly (5 mm each) and the straight portion of the dash panelling reduced accordingly. The windows in the saloon will need to have the quarter lights removed to leave four large windows. A 6 ft 0 in wheelbase chassis and trackside should be used. The roof and clerestory will need to be scratchbuilt from plastic card or balsa. The lifetrays will have to be the Gravesend type with longitudinal slats. Number 7 will need greater modification to the platforms in order to model the front entrances. The headlamps will also need to be taken from the dash and new ones made to fit on the roof. Once again if this is not acceptable then the modeller will need to scratchbuild these cars, although commercial chassis, truck sides and other parts can usefully be employed.

From 1920 the Gravesend system continued a fairly uneventful operation gradually sliding into greater decline. In the mid 1920s a car was decorated each year for the Gravesend Carnival. However, the increasing bus competition was proving irresistable. The end finally came in 1929. The fleet was broken up with many of the tramcar bodies being sold as sheds. One such body was acquired many years later with a view to preservation. Unfortunately, it proved to have deteriorated beyond saving and after stripping the useful parts it was scrapped.

Table 17: Gravesend and Northfleet Electric Tramways Limited 1902-29

Number	Class/ type	Year built	Body type	Trucks/Bogies	LT Nos	Scrapped, sold or changed
1-10		1902	Open-top	MT Bogie Brill 22E	—	1904-06
11-20		1902	Open-top later some CT	4 W 6 ft Brill 21E	—	1929
1-4(ii)		1905	Open-top	4 W 6 ft Brush Aa	—	1929
5-6(ii)		1908	Open-top ex-Jarrow built 1906	4 W 6 ft Brush Aa	—	1929
7-8(ii)		1920	Single-deck ex-Taunton built 1905	4 W 6 ft Brush Aa	—	1929
9-10(ii)		1904	Single-deck demi-car	4 W 5 ft 6 in Brush	—	1920

Notes
CT Closed top; **MT** Maximum traction; **4 W** Four-wheel.

Livery
1902-21 Maroon and yellowish cream. Gold lining on the maroon and black or sepia on the cream. BET 'Magnet and Wheel' badge blue and silver. Numbers gold shaded

(probably) blue. Trucks, undergear and trolley standards red oxide. Fenders and controllers, black.

1921-29 Cherry red and ivory. Yellow lining on the red and no lining on the ivory. Other colours as before.

Bexley 1 to 12 Class, five-window tramcar

I have chosen this prototype to demonstrate a simple modification of a commercial kit. The 1 to 12 Class tramcars of Bexley had five-window saloons. However, there are no five-window, standard open-top, four-wheel kits currently manufactured. The Glasgow Standard and Manchester Pilcher kits are of five-window prototypes. However, they represent a later specialised design and are not suited to this type of car. So for this model I started with BEC Kit No 3. The sides of the three-window saloon were the first parts to be taken. The window bars were sawn and filed out to leave one large hole. As can be seen in the photograph I kept the corner pillars in place. A sketch was drawn of the positions of the window bars on the five-window saloon (Diagram 26). Strips 1½ mm wide brass were cut 5 mm over-length for the uprights and 3 mm over-length for the horizontal. The uprights and horizontal were soldered together on the sketch. With a file I cut grooves in the white metal inside the saloon window frame where the brass strip would rest. The sub-assembly of window bars was low-melt soldered in place. I had a good look at the side and was not happy with it. The window bars were set back too far and looked clumsy. I was rather disappointed and happened to have the soldering iron in my hand, so I tried a little more drastic action. When the iron was really hot I pressed on the window bars from the back. The hot iron actually melted the white metal allowing the window bar to sink into the side. The technique I used was to remove the iron as soon as I saw the white metal start to melt. The danger was, of course, that the white metal casting would be damaged by melting too much. In fact, it worked out very well, despite the fact that I was rather impatient at the time. Actually all this

Modifying the BEC Kits side to convert it into the five-window saloon needed to model the Bexley car (D. Voice).

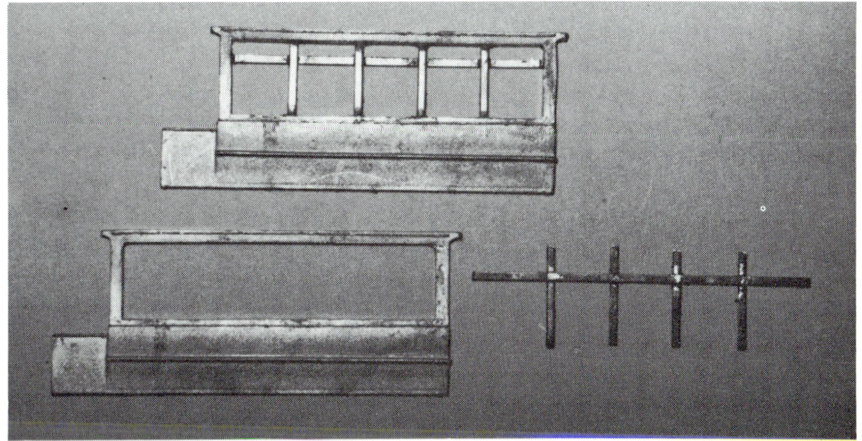

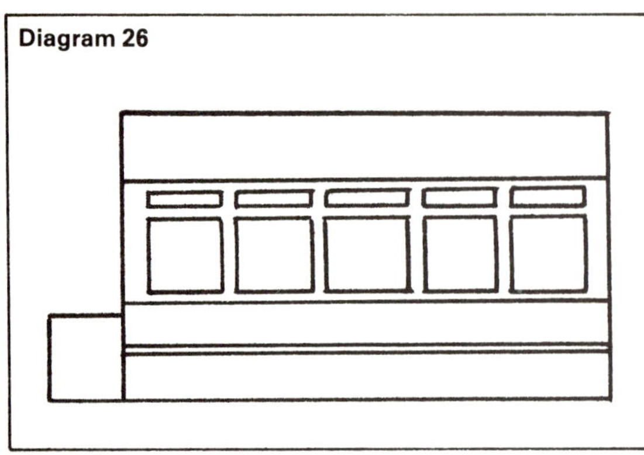

Diagram 26

Left Diagram 26: *Sketch of the modified BEC Kits side for the Bexley five-window tramcar.*
Below *The body gets its first coat of paint (D. Voice).*
Right *The model completed showing the later style of livery I used, with the brown extending over the whole of the upper-deck decency panels.* (model and photo, D. Voice).

was carried out during a demonstration of tram construction at an exhibition. While I had the soldering iron out I assembled the saloon, upper-deck floor, decency panels, platforms, dashes and trucksides using low melt solder.

The trucksides were 7 ft 6 in as was the chassis. I should really have obtained the correct 8 ft 0 in version (I was modelling the car in its final form). However, I happened to have the 7 ft 6 in chassis and truck sides handy and I felt that the odd 2 mm was an acceptable compromise. I filed away the headlamps on the dashes. New headlamps were made from 30 amp fuse wire formed into a circle around a suitably sized rod. These were glued on to the dashes in the higher position favoured by Bexley. As I had chosen the later years, the livery was the chocolate and primrose. I used Humbrol HR142 for the chocolate and HR103 for the primrose. The upper-deck and platform floors were painted grey (matt 67, I was back to dark grey for this car). I also put aside the very nice etched mesh supplied with the kit. I decided

to construct the distinctive handrails using the same method as described for the Southmet tramcar in Chapter 7. The uprights were glued in place first and the horizontal rail soldered and bent into position in situ. The extra rail at each end was bent to shape and soldered in place, as were the rails protecting the stairwell. All the handrails were painted black. The mesh was net material purchased from my local haberdasher. I was surprised at the range of useful netting material available. For this model I chose a brown material with holes that were almost octagonal in shape. It had a very fine appearance and, on the model, achieved just the effect I was after. I cut a strip carefully, using a metal rule and craft knife. The strip was glued to the upright leaving the joint at the centre of one end. It would be hidden later when the destination boxes were fitted.

The lining of the later livery has been described as being straw coloured for the chocolate panels instead of the more usual gold. For this I used the yellow plastic tape made by Scotch 3M. When cut into thin strips and applied using the technique described in previous chapters, the effect was very pleasing. The model has a rather plain appearance when compared to other models with gold lining, but this is very much in line with period descriptions of the prototype. The number I chose was 4 since I used a photograph of this car to check livery and other details. The remainder of the construction was exactly as described in the chapter on the Walthamstow model. The final remark concerns the destination blind. As can be seen in the photograph I chose the destination 'Horns Cross'. This was made up from two bus destinations from the Mabex range. I used 'Kings Cross' and 'Holborn'. The last letter of 'Kings' and the whole of 'Cross' was combined with the 'Ho' and 'rn' from 'Holborn'. Thus giving the required destination. This may seem a fiddley process but is well worthwhile as a poor destination can detract greatly from a model. If this is not possible then I would recommend using 'Tram Depot', or 'Special' or 'Reserved' which are all featured on the special tramcar destination transfer available from Mabex. Another possibility is 'Plumstead' from the South East London destination sheet from Tramalan (see Appendix 1).

Chapter 9

London Transport

Ever since the mid 1800s there had been proposals to co-ordinate all forms of public transport in London. However, it was not until the late 1920s that the first decisive moves were made towards unification. These proposals were to set up a single body to own and operate the bus, tramway, trolleybus and underground railway systems as a single entity. Thus it was that on July 1 1933 the London Passenger Transport Board (LPTB) was set up to be responsible for providing all the public transport within 25 miles of Charing Cross with the exception of the (then) four railway companies.

The tramway part of the new network combined no less than eleven independent systems with a total of 2,630 tramcars. It was somewhat of a mixed bag. There were the streamlined Felthams only a couple of years old, the even younger LCC Number 1 and some new tramcars from systems like Ilford, Walthamstow and West Ham. On the other hand some of the systems handed over some very old and run-down tramcars.

The tramway system was just part of the new overall public transport scene. It has been said that the newly created LPTB was bus dominated and, whatever the reason, the immediate plan for the tramways was consolidation, rationalization and contraction. The trolleybus conversion programme started by the LUT was to continue and be expanded to other parts of London. The first task of the new tramway managers was to absorb the many different tramcars into one fleet. Immediately following July 1 1933 the various individual fleets were given a suffix letter on the following basis:

C	Bexley	E	Croydon	G East Ham		K	Walthamstow
D	Erith	F	Ilford	H West Ham		S	Southmet

The LCC, LUT, and MET, tramcars retained their original numbers until the new fleet numbering system was developed. All the tramcars in service were given paper stickers showing the new owners and the old fleet names were painted out in more or less the appropriate colour. Before the end of 1933 the whole of the Bexley fleet and the older cars of Erith, Croydon, Southmet and MET, were withdrawn from service. Then the re-numbering scheme was implemented and, as can be seen from the details given in each chapter, it was based upon the existing LCC scheme.

In the first few years of operation by LPTB there was much swapping around particularly in the south and south east of the network. A total of 70 tramcars were withdrawn from service in the first twelve months of LPTB

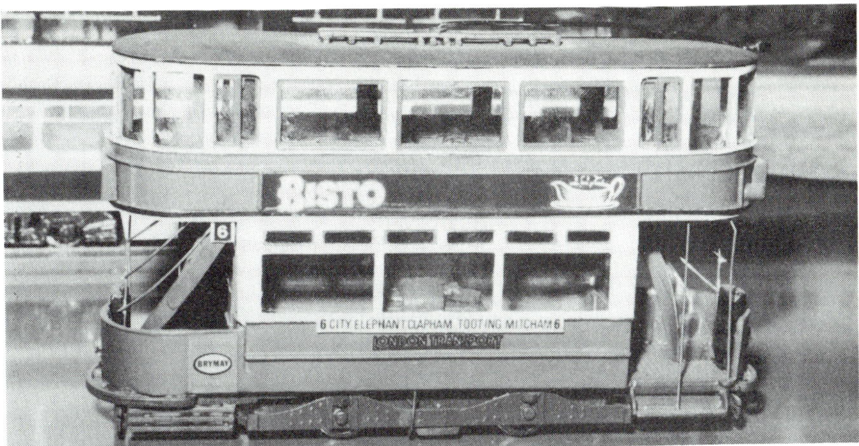

A model of an ex-LCC Class M car in London Transport livery. This has been made by converting a B Class BEC Kit. The truck sideframe is scratchbuilt (model D. Orchard, photo D. Voice).

control. The local population saw tramcars unfamiliar to them, like ex-LCC Class M, replacing their worn out vehicles. The unserviceable cars were stored in various depots awaiting disposal. As has been described in the

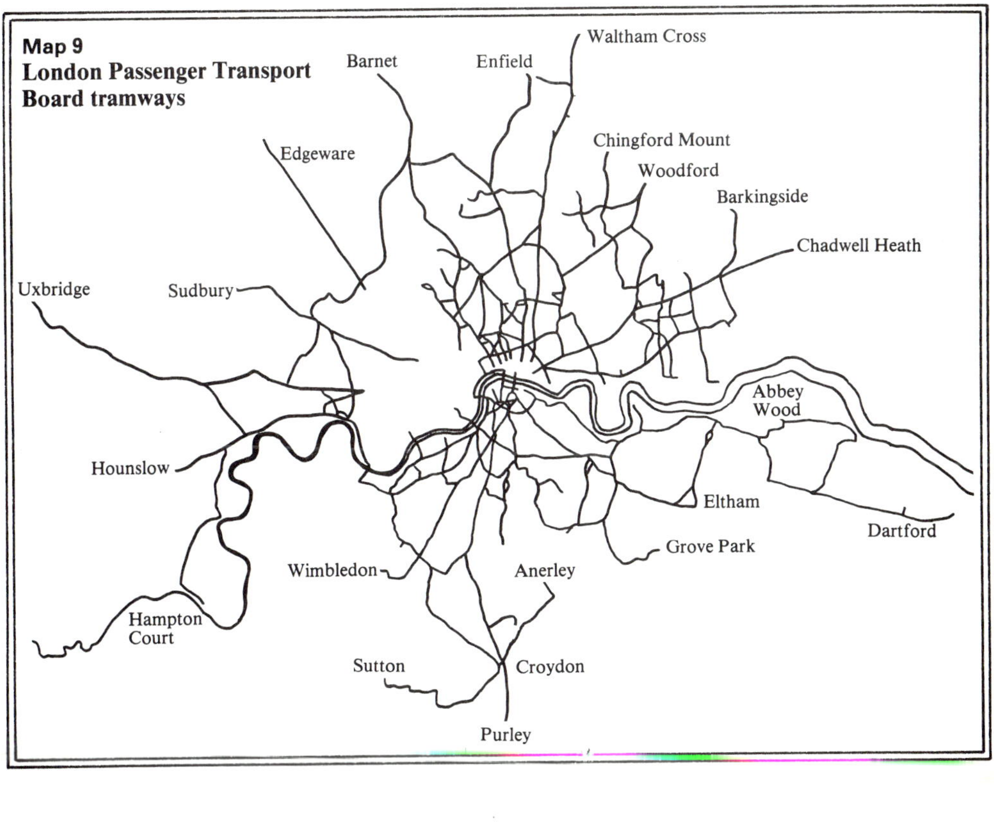

Map 9
London Passenger Transport Board tramways

earlier chapters many of these were taken to Brixton Hill depot for final scrapping. I have always thought that this depot would make an excellent model layout. It was the only ex-LCC depot that did not have a traverser and there was a change pit at the entrance to the depot, which was equipped only for overhead operation. The single access track fanned out in the depot to give seven long storage roads. I estimate that it could have taken around 50 four-wheel tramcars. During these early years of the LPTB it was used to store old Bexley, Croydon, Erith and LCC tramcars. Since the cars from the small systems were not equipped with plough carriers they must have been towed to Brixton Hill depot. Presumably this was undertaken late at night or on Sundays. Once at the depot they could be driven under their own power. On a model layout this would provide opportunity to operate cars from many systems with different liveries and designs. The whole depot could be modelled in 4 mm scale within a space of 2 ft 0 in × 6 ft 0 in including all the approach tracks. This would be a practical proposition and would prove an unusual model.

Once the initial activity was completed, the longer term aims of the LPTB became clear. The domination of the bus operators was reflected in the plans. There was to be no place for the tramcar in the public transport of London. The trolleybus developments pioneered by the LUT were to continue, and plans were authorised for the replacement of more tramway routes by the trolleybus. It is, perhaps, slightly ironic to remember that the original name given to the trolleybus was the 'trackless tram'. Under such a scheme there was no place for the purchase, let alone the development, of new tramcars. Thus the promise heralded by the prototype car LCC No 1 was not to see fulfilment. However, in a way the LPTB did construct one tramcar. Early in 1933 LCC car No 1370 (an E/1 Class car) was involved in an accident which severely damaged it. It arrived at Charlton repair works at the time that the

ME/3 Class car number 1446 had just completed its rebuilding into a bogie car. It had been unlicenced for a number of years while in store. With the prospect of number 1370 being off the road for a long time, opportunity was taken to use the unexpired portion of the Metropolitan Stage Carriage Licence. But this required the ME/3 car to be renumbered 1370(ii). Hence the strange, out of sequence, numbering of this car.

The old 1370(i) needed a new upper-deck. Opportunity was taken to give the lower-deck flush panelling and E/3 type ventilators. The new upper-deck and roof owed much to the influence of car number 1. The result was a far more modern and sleek vehicle. By the time the work was complete the LPTB was in ownership. As it needed a new number the car re-entered service as number 2 (designated E/1 or in some quarters E/1x). The modelling of this car is described in detail at the end of this chapter.

In August 1935 it was announced that there would be a programme of re-building for many of the existing tramcars. They were to be given flush panelled sides and far more modern ends with the destination and route number boxes recessed in the front panelling. The whole interior was also up-graded. The process was officially known as the 'rehabilitation programme' and those cars so treated were known as 'rehabs'. This has been recognised in some quarters by the designation of a suffix 'r' to the class classification (for example E/1 would become E/1r). The plan, when announced, was for up to 250 tramcars to be so treated. As it turned out just 154 cars were actually rehabilitated. Most of the rehabs were E/1 cars but some HR/2 and Croydon tramcars were included. The programme was completed by 1937. The design of the 'rehabs' is shown in Diagram 27 (rear endpaper).

The basis of LPTB policy regarding tramcars was becoming clearer. They were aiming for a fleet of tramcars that had no peculiarities regarding maintenance or repair. As far as possible the tramcars had to have uniform

Left *Rehabilitated E/1 Class No 985 at a change pit. Note the destination boxes inset in the end panels and the E/3 type ventilators for the lower saloon* (S. Eades).

Below *Model of standard E/1 Class in London Transport livery. This was constructed from the BEC Kit* (model and photo, D. Orchard).

(or at least common to a large number) equipment. If the basic equipment was much the same as other cars then the tramcar (like ex LCC No 1) had a chance of not being scrapped immediately. Where the equipment differed then the tram was scrapped or sold when opportunity arose. Thus all the experimental MET tramcars leading to the Feltham design were withdrawn from service by 1936 with the exception of 2167 (ex-MET No 330) which had more conventional equipment than the others and survived to 1949.

In 1935 the conversion to trolleybus operation made a start. Some of the remaining ex-LUT lines were replaced by trolleybus operation. The conversion programme continued, mainly north of the Thames but with the occasional route south of the river. To give an idea of the pace of the conversion programme it is useful to look at the route mileage. At the formation of the LPTB there were 328 miles of tramway and 17 miles of trolleybus. By 1937 the tramway routes were down to 266 miles with the trolleybus up to 122 miles. By the following year the trolleybus had more route miles than the trams, with trams at 175 to the 198 of the trolleybus. In 1939 trams were down to 135 miles and trolleybuses up to 236 miles. However, the programme was soon to slow down due to the outbreak of hostilities.

When war was declared the LPTB had 1,255 tramcars. The first outward effect on the trams was the masking of headlamps. An exercise that reduced the light visible to enemy aircraft and no doubt made the driver thankful that he had rails to guide him. Interior lighting was also reduced by removing half the lamps and hooding the remainder. To assist other road users the fenders of the tramcars were painted white. When the bombing of the capital began in 1940 the trams were fitted with anti-splinter mesh over the windows. This was stuck to the glass and made it impossible for the passengers to see where the tramcar was. It did not take long before a small diamond shape clear section was left in the centre of each window allowing the passengers to see whether they had arrived at their stop on the route. Throughout this time the tramway crews had to cope with difficult circumstances. When a section of track was bombed the breakdown crews would work continuously to repair the damage. In the meantime the service would be worked to either side of the crater and passengers had to change cars. In some cases tramcars returning to the depot would take long diversions using interconnecting tracks to by-pass obstructions.

Some of the worst damage was caused when bombing came close to, or even into the depots. Most of the tramcars would have their windows blown out and many were damaged beyond repair. There was one incident when a depot was hit just before the rush hour. In order to provide a sort of service the least damaged cars were quickly cleaned out and pressed into service. One of them had every window blown out. At the first stop a passenger commented on the lack of windows to the conductor who replied that, owing to the hostilities they were running a skeleton service!

In the early days of the war tramcars were being damaged faster than they could be repaired. Purley depot was used as a storage area for bomb damaged tramcars. Some vehicles that had been placed in store waiting for the demolition torch were given a reprieve and brought back into service. Tram crews developed unofficial bell codes when caught up in a bombing raid. There was one code for stop and another to make a run for it. Service cars that were caught by bursting baskets of incendiary bombs would have their roofs cleared by the driver and conductor knocking the bombs off using the trolley poles. At one stage the busy embankment tracks were kept in operation by a temporary bridge over a bomb crater. The major Blitz lasted from 1940 to 1941. From then on there were occasional bombing raids but the tramways were left relatively unscathed. The development of the flying bombs (V1s) and rockets (V2s) brought an increase in the damage but by no means to the level of the earlier Blitz. There is a story that after the development of the flying bomb many passengers would choose to travel on older tramcars where possible in order not to hear the noise of any flying bomb which was drowned out by the rattle of the tramcar.

The effect of this period on the tramway can be readily assessed when it is realised that every tramcar in the fleet of around 1,000 vehicles was damaged on at least one occasion. 73 tramcars were totally destroyed, 41 E/1, 17 HR/2, the only HR/1, 8 E/3, 2 Felthams, 2 ex-Walthamstow, 1 ex-Croydon and 1 ex-West Ham. Of these, all but five were destroyed by direct enemy action.

Throughout the wartime period the rationalization programme continued and by the end of hostilities in 1945 the fleet comprised of the prototype car No 1, the E/1x No 2, the ex-East Ham bogie cars, the E/1, HR/2, E/3, ME/3 Classes, the ex-Croydon bogie cars, the ex-West Ham bogie cars, the ex-Walthamstow bogie cars, the Feltham cars and a works fleet of three rail-grinders, six stores vans, two wheel vans and twenty snowbrooms. Thus, apart from the works cars, the fleet had a uniformity of appearance to the average passenger. There was the standard London tramcar the E/1 and its various derivatives, or the streamlined Feltham. By this time all the passenger vehicles were fitted with windscreens.

The end of the war brought a change to the organisation of transport in London. In 1948 the London Passenger Transport Board was replaced by the London Transport Executive (LTE). The trams had become nationalised, although this brought no change of attitude towards them. The conversion programme was resurrected. This time there would be no move to continued use of electric power with the trolleybus. The trams were to give way to the bus. The LTE were keen to conclude the programme and it was only the post-war difficulties in obtaining new buses that stopped them abandoning the tram immediately. A statement was issued early in the life of the LTE announcing that the lack of new buses would mean that the trams would continue for at least five years. However, even this short reprieve was actually to be cut by a year. In 1950 the final two year replacement programme was announced. Such was the desire to be rid of the tram that even then the end came three months earlier than scheduled. During the last week of operation the tramcars ran with large notices in place of the usual advertisements. These stated 'Last Tram Week — On The 5th July We Say Goodbye To London'. And so the last service tram, No 1951 (an E/3 Class car) arrived at New Cross in the early hours of July 6, 1952. A large crowd of onlookers cheered the car. The public service given to London by tramcars over a period of 91 years had come to an end.

On many routes the track was lifted during road repairs. I remember seeing the gangs raising and cutting the rail ready for it to be taken away. The

Left *The preserved HR/2 car No 1858 at the East Anglia Transport Museum. The car was being prepared for repainting when this photo was taken* (D. Voice).

Below *Model of the HR/2 Class car constructed from the Varney kit. It is believed that only one production run was ever produced of this kit* (model and photo, D. Voice).

Right *LPTB No 2 seen at Greens End, Woolwich* (W.J. Haynes).

wooden setts were taken out and piled to one side. In the evenings the local residents would appear with barrows, pushchairs, prams or anything on wheels. The old setts would be loaded up and carried back for firewood. The blocks were soaked in tar and the top surface was liberally coated with road chippings. They used to burn with a distinctive smell and the occasional explosion. However, with the shortages at the time they were very welcome and to a young schoolboy like myself it added excitement to the living room fire.

For the modeller the post-war period is both interesting and frustrating. Apart from the rehabilitation programme and the fitting of windscreens (vestibules) to all service cars, there were all kinds of repairs and changes carried out. In the modeller's eyes the most important modifications (apart from the rehabilitation programme) were the removal of waist rails, the simpler and cleaner looking single advertisement guide strip replacing the older triple box and, of course, a whole variety of destination and route

number boxes. Wartime damage led to more variations appearing. When these are added to the increasing number of minor scratches and dents from the busier roads after the war, it is even more important to work from photographs. To be truly accurate it is necessary to have different photographs showing each side of the chosen vehicle as close in date as possible. Although I have to admit I have yet to see a model deliberately built with a dented dash panel! Yet photographs of the last tram week show that hardly any tramcar was unscathed. When modelling it has always been my preference to complete the models as if they had just been delivered from the paint shop after a major overhaul. Perhaps I will have a go at the tram modeller's equivalent of the railway modeller's weathering. Although even at the end, the London tram fleet was never allowed to get into the state of some present day trains or buses.

Although the last tram in London ran over 30 years ago there are still remnants of the system to be seen. That unique feature the Kingsway Subway was too valuable to lose. Half of it is now the Strand Underpass and used by motor vehicles; the remainder is the London Flood Control Centre. As a result the ramp leading to the northern entrance has never been changed. Today the conduit tracks are still in the stone setts and the whole ramp looks only a little more dusty than it did in the days when the tramcars ran. Many of the old tram depots are still recognisable. There is also a surprising amount of tramway related architecture and equipment stored on the streets of London. Indeed the gathering of information on what remains is, in itself, a fascinating way of discovering more about London's tramways.

Thankfully the tramcars themselves did not disappear entirely. There are today five London tramcars still in the metropolis. Three were saved directly for preservation and were brought together first at Clapham Transport

Museum. They later appeared in the London Transport Collection at Syon Park and they can now be seen at the new premises at Covent Garden. These tramcars are Feltham No 2099 (preserved in MET livery as No 355), E/1 No 1025 and ex-West Ham four-wheel car No 290 (the latter cars being in London Transport livery). The London Transport Collection also have a double-deck horse car that is currently on show while awaiting restoration, and a single bogie truck from an HR/2 tramcar.

The fifth tramcar is to be found at Bonwell Street Depot (actually in Digby Street, Bethnal Green). This consists of the lower-deck of E/1 Class car No 1622 and the upper-deck from another E/1 Class tramcar. These will be united under an ambitious restoration programme to produce the only example of a preserved rehabilitated London tramcar. This work is being

Above *The second No 1370. This is the rebuilt M Class car No 1446, lengthened into a bogie car and classified ME/3. This shows the car as it appeared straight from the works in 1933, carrying the LCC livery and coat of arms, but the legal lettering shows the owner to be LPTB (R. Elliott).*

Left *Still to be seen today is this stretch of conduit track leading to the Kingsway subway north end, now used as the London flood control centre (D. Voice).*

undertaken by volunteers of the London County Council Tramways Trust (a society dedicated to the restoration of London tramcars). They have already proven their expertise at such work with LCC B4 Class No 106. It is difficult to realise that this superbly presented tramcar was bought for preservation as a snowbroom (No 022). The restoration of No 106 was also carried out at Bonwell Street depot. The work was carried out by a small, dedicated team of volunteers in their spare time. When complete it was taken to the National Tramway Museum at Crich. The LCC Tramways Trust also have a longer term project to restore one of the LCC Trailer Cars. It is hoped to use the surviving body of T86 with the running gear from T131 to bring a trailer car back to life. However, extensive work on this project will not be possible until the current restoration programme on number 1622 has been completed.

By coincidence I happened to be at the National Tramway Museum on the first full day of public service of the LCC tramcar No 106. I must say I hesitated to board the car as the floors were so highly painted it seemed

Above *7mm scale models of London Transport Feltham (on the left) and ex-LCC No 1* (model and photo, D. Orchard).

Below *The skirt of Ex-LCC No 1 at the National Tramway Museum, Crich, showing the cut-out added when the car was at Leeds, but carrying the London Transport livery and name* (D. Voice).

wrong to walk on them. But I did mount the car and climbed the stairs to have a ride that will be in my memories forever. The tramcar rode beautifully and with a breeze in my hair and the sun shining down one could wish for nothing better. The National Tramway Museum has two more London tramcars and part of a third. The rightly famous LCC No 1 (restored in London Transport livery) is on display in one of the exhibition bays. Access is encouraged to the platform and stairs allowing viewing of the lower and upper saloons. One is reminded of its time in Leeds as it still carries that fleet number (301) inside the end of the upper-deck. Alongside No 1 is a display case, the front of which uses the side of London Street Tramways horse tramcar No 39. The experimental centre entrance Feltham car (MET No 331, LT No 2168, Sunderland No 100) is also to be found at the National Tramway Museum. There is still much work to be done on this tramcar and it is scheduled to be in the next phase of restoration at the museum. Of course, working on a prototype car is greatly different from building a model. It is quite practical to build a model of any of these preserved tramcars in one's spare time over a month or so at modest cost. The restoration of LCC 106 (the smallest of all the preserved electric London Tramcars) took an estimated 30,000 hours of volunteer time spread over ten years. The cost of the work was £15,000 (the volunteer labour was, of course, provided free). The London County Council Tramways Trust estimate that £30,000 will be needed to complete the 1622 project.

Further afield the lower saloon of MET tramcar No 94 has been used as the basis for the newest vehicle to join the Seaton Tramway fleet in South Devon. Originally a Type A tramcar it has now been rebuilt into a single deck clerestory roofed car of great character and charm. It is currently providing a further period of public service long after being withdrawn from the streets of London. The last preserved London tramcar to be found in Great Britain is the HR/2 Class No 1858. This car was purchased for preservation when the London system stopped working. It is unusual because it spent many years in a wire mesh 'cage' at Chessington Zoo. It is now part of the public service vehicle collection at the East Anglia Transport Museum at Carlton Colville near Lowestoft. On the international scene one Feltham was taken to America. Ex-MET 341 (LT 2085, Leeds 526) can be seen at the Seashore Electric Railway Museum in Maine, USA.

I must put in a word of caution regarding the use of preserved vehicles for modelling purposes. It is always necessary to check against photographs of the appropriate vehicle in the period being modelled. LCC 1 at the National Tramway Museum is displayed in London Transport livery. However, it still retains the modifications along the bottom edge of the sides that were introduced when the tramcar was at Leeds. If a model is made to the exact condition that the tramcar is in at Crich then the model can only represent the preserved tramcar. It would not be appropriate to use it on a London layout. The other example that could mislead modellers is that of LCC 106. Quite deliberately this tram has been rebuilt in the design of the B Class cars modified for the Plumstead to Woolwich route. There were eight cars so modified and No 106 was not amongst them. However in order to enable the preserved tramcar to be operated it was necessary for it to be fitted with a trolley pole. The more familiar condition of the open-top period of B Class tramcars was for conduit-only operation. The other aspect that needs to be carefully checked is the advertisements. Often preserved tramcars today gather much needed funds from letting out their advertising space. One example, which is not a London tramcar, is Bolton 66 which carries British Telecom advertisements while running in Blackpool.

Although it is over thirty years since the trams ran in the streets of London there are real possibilities that they will be seen again. The new trams will not be like the E/1s or Felthams but will have similarities to the 'Supertrams' now operating on the Tyne and Wear Metro. This type of transport is now called 'light rail' and London Transport started serious investigation in 1979. With the escalating costs of Underground extensions, less expensive options were worth considering. Light rail can be equally effective, even if it is less conventional in this country. By 1981 the ideas had concentrated on a public service to the India and Millwall Docks areas in the Isle of Dogs. In October 1982 government approval was announced with proposals for two routes, both ending in the Docks area. The first was to run east-west from Tower Hill and the second north-south from Mile End. The latter caught the public imagination as it was envisaged that the first half mile would be actual street tramway. All the remaining route mileage would be on reserved track. We are following these developments with great interest and look forward to a successful completion of the Docklands Light Rail project. At the time of writing the bill was on its way through Parliament. The Mile End terminus is now in question as the new prefered option is Stratford, which would not need street track.

Works car number 012, an ex-LCC wheel carrier (courtesy I. Hodgson).

Table 18: Renumbering scheme for London Passenger Transport Board

Number	Class/type	Previous owner	Year last car in service	Disposal
1	Exp.	LCC	1951	Sold to Leeds
2	E/1x	LPTB	1952	Scrapped
5-32	—	Ilford	1938	Scrapped
33-40	—	Ilford	1938	Sold to Sunderland
41-44	—	Ilford	1937	Scrapped
48-80	—	East Ham	1935	Scrapped
81-100	EH(E/1 type)	East Ham	1952	Scrapped
101-159	HR2	LCC	1952	Scrapped
160	E/3	LCC	1952	Scrapped
161-210	E/3	Leyton	1952	Scrapped
211-294	—	West Ham	1938	Scrapped
295-344	E/1 style	West Ham	1952	Scrapped
345-349	W/1	Croydon	1935	Scrapped
365-374	B/2	Croydon	1935	Scrapped
375-399	E/1	Croydon	1952	Scrapped
402-551	E	LCC	1938	Scrapped
552-601	E/1	LCC	1952	Scrapped
602-751	E	LCC	1938	Scrapped
752-1426	E/1 (&ME/3)	LCC	1952	Scrapped
1427-1476	M (&ME/3)	LCC	1951	Scrapped
1477-1676	E/1	LCC	1952	Scrapped
1677-1726	M	LCC	1940	Scrapped
1727-1851	E/1	LCC	1952	Scrapped
1852	HR1	LCC	1940	Scrapped
1853-1903	HR2	LCC	1952	3 to Leeds, rest scrapped
1904-2003	E/3	LCC	1952	Scrapped
2004-2041	—	Walthamstow	1937	Scrapped
2042-2061	E/1 style	Walthamstow	1952	Scrapped
2066-2119	Feltham	MET	1951	Sold to Leeds
2120-2165	Feltham	LUT	1951	Sold to Leeds
2166	Exp.	MET	1936	Scrapped
2167	Exp.	MET	1949	Scrapped
2168	Exp.	MET	1937	Sold to Sunderland
2169-2254	H	MET	1938	Scrapped
2255	Exp.	MET	1936	Scrapped
2256-2260	F	MET	1938	Scrapped
2261-2281	G	MET	1938	Scrapped
2282-2301	C/1	MET	1937	Scrapped
2302-2316	E	MET	1938	Scrapped
2317	Exp.	LUT	1935	Scrapped
2318-2357	T	LUT	1936	Scrapped
2358-2402	U	LUT	1936	Scrapped
2403-2405	U2	LUT	1936	Scrapped
2406-2410	WT	LUT	1936	Scrapped
2411	XU	LUT	1936	Scrapped
2412-2466	A	MET	1936	Scrapped

Number	Class/type	Previous owner	Year last car in service	Disposal
2467-2482	B2	MET	1936	Scrapped
2483-2497	C/2	MET	1937	Scrapped
2498-2521	B	MET	1936	Scrapped
2522-2529	W	LUT	1936	Scrapped
Suffix C	B	Bexley	1933	Scrapped
Suffix E	W/1	Croydon	1933	Scrapped
Suffix D	—	Erith	1934	Scrapped
Suffix S	J	Southmet	1935	Scrapped
Suffix S	K	Southmet	1934	Scrapped
Suffix S	L	Southmet	1934	Scrapped
Suffix S	O	Southmet	1934	Scrapped
Suffix S	M	Southmet	1936	Scrapped
01-054	Works	LCC	1952	Scrapped
055	Works	West Ham	1938	Scrapped
056	Works	Croydon	1937	Scrapped
057	Works	Ilford	1937	Scrapped
02-014	Works	MET	1938	Scrapped
001-006	Works	LUT	1938	Scrapped
1A	Works	West Ham	1934	Scrapped
19S	Works	Southmet	1934	Scrapped
20D	Works	Erith	1933	Scrapped
63K	Works	Walthamstow	1935	Scrapped
148	Works	LUT	1936	Scrapped

Livery

1933 Initially cars were left in their previous owners' livery. The old fleet names were painted out in the appropriate colour and paper stickers with the LPTB name and address were applied. Some livery experiments were carried out including a blue on three cars (including ex-Leyton E/3 number 192).

1933-34 There were two versions of the LPTB 'standard' livery. At Hendon they used red and broken white. The trucks, fenders, undergear, wire mesh, handrails and trolley standards were black. Yellow lining was used on the red (dashes only) with the white unlined. Charlton used the red with a rich cream. Again, yellow lining on the red dashes and no lining on the cream, but there was a black line between the red and cream colours. Fenders, handrails, interior of dash and controllers were black. Trucks and undergear were light grey for a short while then black was used. In both cases the letters and numbers were gold and the roofs silver or white.

1935-39 Red and rich cream. Yellow lining was used on the dashes with no lining on the cream and a black line between the red and cream areas. Fenders, handrails, interior of dash, trucks, undergear, wire mesh, trolley standards and controllers black. Letters and numbers plain gold. Roofs were silver or white.

1939-45 As before except fenders were now white, headlamp masks black and roofs brown oxide.

1945-52 As before except fenders again black and roofs brown oxide, later becoming dark grey.

LPTB tramcar Number 2, Class E/1x

We have already seen that LCC E/1 tramcar No 1370 was involved in an accident in 1933. It went into the repair shop for a complete re-building and returned to duty as LPTB No 2. The design of the rebuilt tramcar was very

Above *Model of the standard Feltham car made from the BEC Kit* (model I. Hodgson, photo D. Voice).

Below *Construction of LPTB No 2 starts with the modifications to the BEC Kit E Class car. The upper-deck is cut away and the panel below the lower saloon windows covered with plastic card* (D. Voice).

pleasing. The upper-deck was very similar to car No 1 while the lower-deck incorporated improvements from the E/3 design. In case you may get confused I should note here that the number 1370 did not disappear. The LCC took it upon themselves to re-number M Class car No 1446 to 1370 after converting it from its four-wheel condition into the bogie Class ME/3. As previously explained the re-numbering was carried out to save money on the Metropolitan Stage Licence. It could be quite perplexing when it is remembered that the two other M Class cars (Nos 1441 and 1444) retained their original numbers after their conversion.

I had in my range of kits, and odd bits and pieces, a second-hand BEC E/1. The model had been poorly constructed and rather badly treated before I had acquired it. Indeed the bogies did not work and the whole car needed re-building. It seemed like an ideal way to start my model of No 2. I took the model to pieces and removed the paint with strong stripper. This restored the castings back to their original form and the softness of the metal allowed me to restore the shape where they had become distorted. Of course, if a new BEC Kit is used (No 12) then this work is not necessary. Number 2 had been

rebuilt from a standard E/1 Class tramcar. The lower-deck, although modified, was in essence to the original design. But the upper-deck was quite different. I decided to use the lower half of the BEC Kit and scratchbuild the upper-deck. Taking the kit I cut the upper-deck from the sides. The cut was made along a line 4 mm above the moulding at the top of the lower-deck quarter lights. The upper-deck end castings were cut at the same time. The lower part of the model was assembled in the usual way until the construction resembled an open-top car. At this stage it was still unpainted as other modifications had to be made to the castings. The side panels below the lower saloon windows were quite flush on No 2. There was no waist rail or any curve to the panel, so I cut and filed the moulded waist rail from the kit sides. I had felt that the smooth panelling needed to be emphasised as much as possible. So I glued a piece of 15 thou plastic card (87 mm × 11 mm) over the complete panel.

Then I looked at the problem of the upper-deck. I decided that the scratch-built part would be made using the same techniques that I described in Chapter 1. These can be used to build a complete tramcar. For example if you wanted to build No 1 then the whole model will need to be scratchbuilt. By using these techniques the model can be built with surprising ease. There is a photo of a model of No 1 built by David Orchard. He pioneered this technique for tramways modelling and No 1 was the model he used to prove the versatility and simplicity of the method. However, back to No 2. Since the

Above *The prototype No 2 seen at Denmark Hill (W. J. Haynes).*

Right *Making the upper-deck, with the panelling and side window uprights in place. The end window uprights are being fixed in place (D. Voice).*

new upper-deck had to fit the kit-built lower-deck the technique had to be modified slightly. My first move was to construct the main panel. I took a strip of 15 thou brass ½ in wide (available from the standard range of brass strip that is now held by many specialist model shops). This was bent to fit around the top of the built-up kit. I had decided that the joint would be in the centre of one side. This is my normal practice as it keeps the joint away from stresses and it is easy to put strengthening plates across the joints. I achieved the curves at the ends by bending the strip with my fingers and adding the final touches with a pair of long nosed pliers, the business end wrapped in cloth to prevent marking the brass. When the ends fitted nicely I was able to mark the centre where the joint was to be and then cut the strip to length. The edges were filed to a perfect fit and I soldered the ends together using a strengthening backing strip. This joint I filed and sanded smooth. I marked out the position of the destination and route number slots on the car's ends. I found it useful to use a piece of dowelling as a support. I drilled out most of the slots and finished them to size with small square Swiss file. This was not the easiest of jobs but I could not work out any other way of ensuring that these prominent features could be made in exactly the right place. I felt sure that if they had not been central the model would be completely spoiled.

I sketched out the position of the five side uprights in relation to the lower saloon windows (Diagram 28). I marked the position of the lower saloon uprights on the inner edge of the brass strip using a felt tip pen. I laid the strip in place on the sketch using the marks to correctly align it. The uprights, 2 mm wide brass strip, were cut over length and soldered inside the upper saloon panel. This was repeated for the other side. Next I turned to the two wide uprights for the centre window of each end. These uprights were cut well over length from 2½ mm wide brass strip. I soldered them in place using the route number slot as a guide. The inside edge of each upright was just outside the edge of the slot. The final twelve uprights forming the small windows on the curved ends were cut from 2 mm wide brass strip. I used photographs as a guide and soldered them in position by eye for the first set of three uprights. I was then able to use a steel rule to ensure that the other nine uprights matched the first set.

The upper window frame horizontal strip was rather complex and I ended up fabricating it from five strips of brass. First I used a long strip of 2 mm wide brass and bent it to match the main upper-deck panel. Again, this was cut to give a joint in the centre of one side. Using the sketch as a guide, I soldered this upper strip in the correct position on the filed upright on each

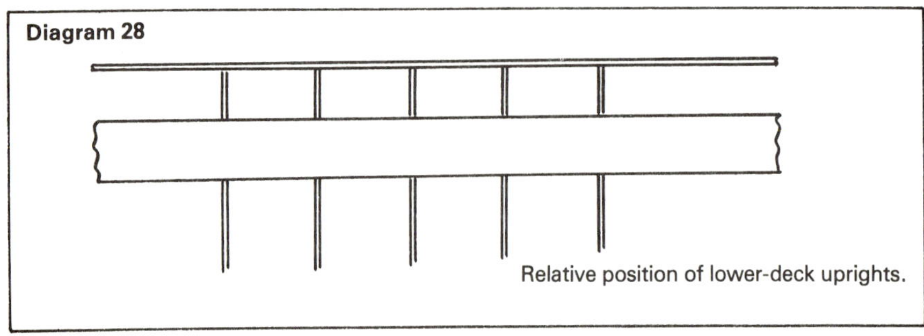

Diagram 28

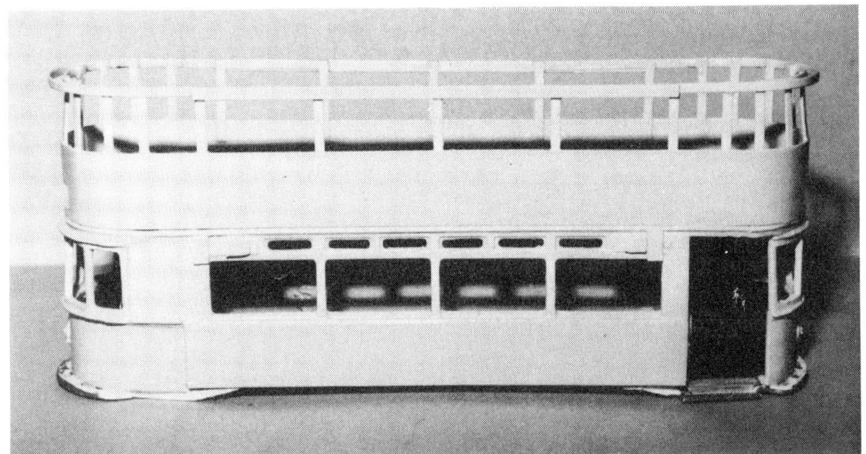

Above *The first coat of paint onto the body. Note the ventilators fitted to the lower saloon end quarter-lights* (D. Voice).

Right *Fixing the wind-screen in place. The peg holds the glazing while the glue sets overnight* (D. Voice).

Below left Diagram 28: *Sketch of position of five upper-deck uprights and horizontal brass strips in relation to lower-deck window uprights. Used to solder strips in place.*

side. I then cut the uprights to length. Two strips of 2½ mm wide brass were cut to fit over the four side windows. I soldered one each side over the 2 mm strip. I had to take care not to break the joints between the thinner strip and the uprights. Finally I cut two pieces of 2 mm wide brass, once for each end. These pieces were curved fit inside the first horizontal strip (see the photograph). Before the last curved strips were soldered in place the remaining uprights were bent inwards to clear the inner strip. Then they too were soldered in place and the uprights eased back until they could be soldered to the new strip. Each one was checked by eye against photographs of No 2. Any error was corrected by unsoldering the appropriate joint and re-positioning the uprights. I was very careful to get the inward slope of the uprights as close to the prototype angle as was practical. When I was happy with the result I cut the uprights to length and carefully filed off any sharp edges before glueing the upper-deck to the lower saloon.

I returned to the lower saloon and constructed the ventilators over the end quarter lights. These were built using 15 thou and 40 thou plastic card, as shown in Diagram 29. You can see by the photographs that I left the masks on the headlamps (as supplied in the kit). This was because I wanted to model the tramcar in its post-war condition. The main body of the tram was now complete and I gave it a couple of coats of matt white inside and out, a couple of coats of cream (Humbrol HR114), followed by a coat of gloss varnish. Using my usual masking techniques I painted the red panels, first with two coats of matt paint and then one of gloss (Humbrol 19). The lower saloon bulkheads were all red except for the doors which were picked out in dark brown (Humbrol HR142) and the used ticket box which was black. The platform floor was dark grey (Humbrol matt 67). The upper-deck floor was cut from 15 thou plastic card and stuck in place. Its upper surface was painted dark grey.

The only lining on this car was on the lower dashes. For this I used yellow self-adhesive tape in the way described in previous chapters. The London Transport fleet name and number were taken from BEC transfers. The whole outside was then given a coat of gloss varnish. I glazed the windows with acetate sheet. The lower saloon was quite straightforward but the windscreens were a little more awkward. I cut a strip 11 mm wide and over length for each end. They were long enough to be glued securely in place to the panel at the end of the windscreen. I used a good quantity of glue knowing that it would be hidden when the stairs were fitted. A smear of glue on the upright next to the entrance and the glazing strip was sprung into place. A wooden peg, borrowed from my wife, held it in position overnight. The next morning the excess was cut off using a very sharp craft knife. The upper saloon was glazed using two strips of acetate 21 mm wide. These were butt jointed behind the centre pillar of each side. I used the full depth of the inside of the main panel to glue the acetate in place. I particularly made sure that the glazing strip was well tucked into the curve of each end and covered the destination and route number slots. On the prototype the destination and route number blinds were set back behind the slots and presented a flat surface. This seemed difficult to achieve on the model, so I decided to fit the destination and route number directly on to the curved glazing. I chose the destination (via Blackfriars, Embankment) from the set for South East London produced by Tramalan. I cut them over size and glued them behind the glazing. The route number '36' came from my box of destinations and route numbers and I am not sure of the source. Inside the ends of the upper-deck I covered the backs of the paper destinations and route numbers with pieces of card painted cream. I then cut the panels at the top of the stairwell from 15 thou plastic card, painted them dark brown and glued them in place. The upper-deck seating was cut from BEC seating strip. They were painted a dull mid-blue and glued in place. As is my preference, model passengers were added. The stairs were painted red with dark grey treads and risers. They were then glued in place.

My second hand kit had damaged bogies so I had to build chassis in the way described in Chapters 2 and 7. If you are using a new kit then this complication is not necessary. I added passengers to the lower saloon. The side frames of the bogies were painted matt and then gloss black. Controllers and hand brakes (bent from brass wire) were added. The kit lifeguards, life-trays and dog gates were fitted and painted black. The final part to be made was the roof. No 2 had a distinctive domed roof. This I made from 5 mm thick balsa. A piece of firm, close grained balsa was selected. It was cut to the correct width and the ends curved to match the model. The roof curvature on the sides and ends was sanded to shape using a solid sanding block first and then the foam type. The balsa was sealed using sander/sealer (with some talcum powder mixed in). Three thick coats were applied, smoothing between each coat and finally working to a glass like finish. I painted the roof dark grey. Two trolley planks were cut from 15 thou plastic card 42 mm long and 5 mm wide. These were painted dark grey and then drilled in the centre. They were glued to the roof 5 mm apart. The roof was given two coats of gloss varnish. I cut a false roof from some card, about 1½ mm thick, to fit inside the upper-deck. The bottom of it was painted white and the edge dark grey. I wedged it inside the top of the upper-deck and spread glue over it. The roof was placed on top in the correct position. When the glue had set I removed the roof. Holes were drilled for the fine tubing which was to take the twin trolley poles. The pieces of tube were glued in place, and the top touched-in with dark grey paint. Trolley retaining hooks were bent from nickel silver wire (see Diagram 30). They were glued in place and tested with the trolley poles that I had made while waiting for the paint to dry on the main body. All was well so I glued the roof in place. Finally the driver and conductor were added with the central handrails at the entrances. I had not put any advertisements on the model at this stage. Number 2 did carry a large advertisement on each side of the upper-deck panelling and a small advertisement on the end of the dash panel beside the lower saloon. However, I did not have transfers which were appropriate to the post war London scene. I was so pleased with the way the model had turned out that I preferred to wait until I obtained suitable transfers from Mabex.

Number 2 was a unique vehicle in the London Transport fleet. However, there were other rehabilitated tramcars that were given domed type roofs and other features similar to No 2. Most of the rehabilitated tramcars can be built

Diagram 29: *Fabrication of lower-deck ventilator from plastic card. This is the front nearside. The rear nearside is slightly different, consult photographs for detail.*

Diagram 30: *Trolley retaining hooks, bent from nickel silver wire. Glue under the roof, cutting the card false roof as necessary.*

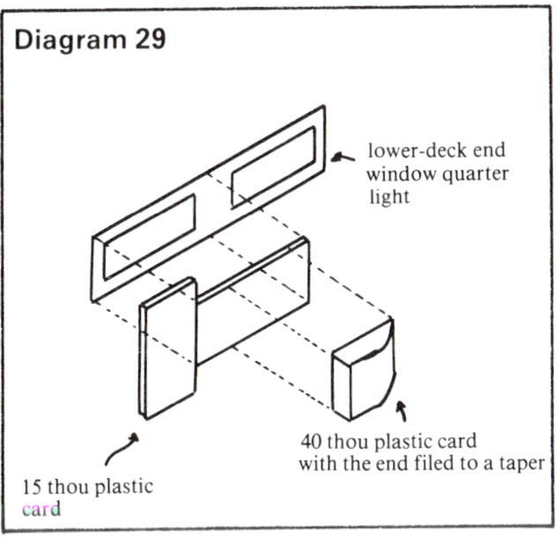

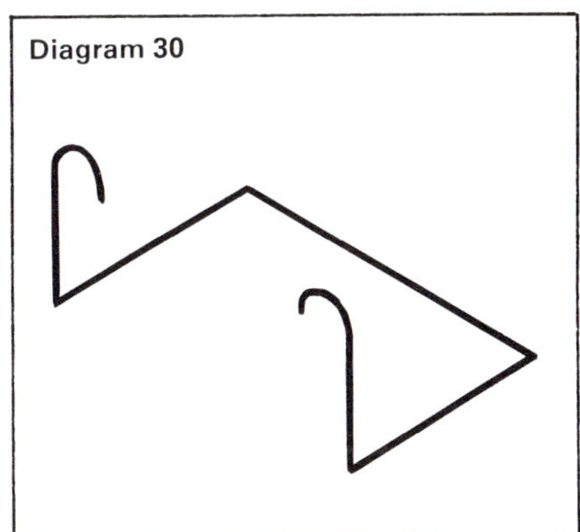

The completed model with Mabex advertisements of the appropriate period (model and photo, D. Voice).

by modifying BEC Kit No 12 using very similar methods. One advantage of the standard rehabilitated tramcar is that the original white metal roof from the kit can be used. Indeed for many of these cars it would only be necessary to provide the smooth panels by adding an extra skin of 15 thou plastic card over the white metal parts. On the upper deck this would have to include the necessary slots for the indicator and route number blinds. In all cases the small ventilators on the end quarter lights will be necessary. Although the London Tramcar may have appeared to be standard there is enough variety to keep a modeller happy for a lifetime.

Appendix 1

Sources for the modeller of London's tramways Societies

Societies

Tramway modelling

The Tramway and Light Railway Society The Society caters nationally for people who are interested in modelling tramways or who have a desire to find out more about tramways from historic, research and general viewpoints. There is a large model tramway layout to the scale of ¾ in to 1 ft. There are other active groups who model in smaller scales and a particularly large and enthusiastic following in 4 mm to 1 ft scale, with its own modelling secretary. The society publishes literature and photographs to help the modeller. There is a regular magazine which always has a column devoted to 4 mm and allied scales. Meetings are held in London and the various area centres. Further information is available from: The Tramway and Light Railway Society, 6 The Woodlands, Brightlingsea, Colchester, Essex.

Other tramway societies

The Light Rail Transit Association This society promotes the retention and development of tramways. It is an international body, well known for its support of LRT (light rail transit) and upgraded tramways. Members receive *Modern Tramway* by post each month and can buy major new LRTA books at reduced rates. Regular meetings are held in many centres and the LRTA arranges study tours. Further information from: Light Rail Transit Association, 6 Hermitage Woods Crescent, St John's, Woking, Surrey.

The Tramway Museum Society This society runs Britains National Tramway Museum at Crich, Derbyshire, where there are some 40 trams (horse, steam and electric) dating from 1873to 1953. Most are restored and are operated to give rides to visitors. An Edwardian street scene is being built around the tramway. The society also collects archival material — photos, documents and small items of historical interest for research and eventual display. The museum depends upon volunteer working members but it welcomes anyone to membership, whether they can help actively or not. Membership gives free access to the museum and free riding on the trams, with reciprocal arrangements at some other museums. Further information from: The Tramway Museum Society, 49 Allman Road, Erdington, Birmingham.

London County Council Tramways Trust This society was originally formed for the purpose of restoring LCC Class B tramcar number 106, which is now successfully completed and is operating at the National Tramway Museum, Crich, Derbyshire. Work has now commenced on the next project, the restoration of London Transport E/1 tramcar number 1622. The work is carried out at Bonwell Street Depot, Digby Street, Bethnal Green, London E2. Further information from: Jeffrey Mackenzie, 25 Welland House, Ryehill Estate, Peckham Rye, London, SE15 3JG.

Tramcar kits of London's trams

BEC Kits, PO Box 19, Farnham, Surrey, GU10 2AH. A large range of white-metal kits of London trams. All in 4 mm scale and having ready-to-run mechanisms. Available from specialist model shops or direct from the manu-facturer. The complete range of individual items is only available directly from BEC Kits.

Keil Kraft Ltd Plastic kit of West Ham 4 wheel car No 102 (LT No 290). Although this model is to 1:72 scale it can be used by 4 mm modellers to make the 17 ft long saloon type of car. It is available from model shops.

ABS, Streetscene series: There is the George Train original 1861 horse tramcar available as a kit. For details contact Wrightlines, 141 Portland Road, Bournemouth, BH9 1NG.

R. Meadowcroft Models, 277 Keighley Road, Colne, Lancs, BB8 7HD. They produce an etched brass kit of the LCC single-deck F and G Classes. Also useful is the range of stamped brass body parts which can be used for various London tramcars, see the description of the LUT Palace car.

Other tramcar kits

Hadfields Plastics Distributors Tower Models, 44 Cookson Street, Blackpool, Lancs, FY1 3ED. Plastic kits of Blackpool trams, suitable for modification to London tramcars as described in the text.

Merseyside Tramway Preservation Society, 87 Woodsorrel Road, Liverpool 15. There is a totally enclosed four-wheel car of the Priestly Standard design and the Bellamy roof adaptation kit.

E.W. Tennant, 77 High Street, Halesowen, West Midlands, B63 3BQ. Manufacturers of a single-deck tram kit, the Black Country Tividale car.

R. Collins, 7 Earby Grove, Blackley, Manchester, M9 1LL. A variety of Blackpool tramcar kits and a chassis in kit form to make a bogie mechanism with central motor and flexible drives.

Anbrico Scale Models, Perseverance Street, Pudsey, West Yorkshire. Whitemetal kits to 4 mm scale. Some may be suitable for conversion to London trams.

Overhead system and tram parts

Tramalan Components The Tram Terminus, Colyton, Seaton, Devon. Particularly useful to the London modeller is the range of destination blinds North, South East and South London.

R. Meadowcroft Models, 277 Keighley Road, Colne, Lancs, BB8 7HD. In addition to the range of tram parts and overhead system they also produce a range of bogie and four-wheel ready-to-run mechanisms.

'O' and 'OO' gauge drawings and 'O' gauge tram parts

Terry Russell, Chaceside, St Leonards Park, Horsham, West Sussex. There is a complete range of 'O' Gauge tram parts, ready-to-run chassis and overhead. Of particular interest are the London tram drawings included in the catalogue. These are listed below. (Note that those marked with an asterisk are available in 4 mm scale.)

*TC1   LCC 'Bluebird' No 1
*TC2   London Transport E/3-HR2
*TC3   London Transport E/1 rehabilitated car
*TC5   London Transport Feltham
*TC10 MET Type E single deck
 TC11 LUT Type T
*TC14 LUT Stores Van No 4
*TC18 LUT Type W
*TC40 London Transport E/1, double trolley
*TC41 LCC E/1 unvestibuled, single trolley
*TC42 MET Prototype Feltham No 320
*TC43 MET Prototype Feltham No 330
*TC56 LCC Class M
 TC64 London Transport Ex-West Ham No 64 (LT No 272)
*TC65 LCC Class A
*TC66 LCC Class B open top
*TC67 LCC Class C enclosed top
*TC68 LCC Class D
*TC69 LCC Class F
*TC70 LCC Trailer Car No T10
 TC71 LUT Type U2
 TC72 LUT Type S2
 TC73 Southmet Type K
*TC74 LCC Class B No 106
 TC75 London Transport E/1 rehabilitated car No 1622

Advertisements and destination blinds

BEC Kits, PO Box 19, Farnham, Surrey, GU10 2AH. They will supply any of their destination and advertisement transfers as separate items.
Tramalan Components, The Tram Terminus, Colyton, Seaton, Devon. There is a range of scale destination blinds taken from actual London tram blinds.
Mabex, 15 Coastguard Square, Barden Road, Eastbourne, East Sussex, BN22 7EE. There is a large range of advertisements, destination blinds, crests, letters, numbers and fleet names suitable for tramway modelling.

Track

Hartel (Conrad) tramway track. This is the only ready-to-run scale tramway track available. It is made in West Germany and distributed in this country by either Bob's Models, 520 Coventry Road, Small Heath, Birmingham, B10 0UN or M.G. Sharps, 712 Attercliffe Road, Sheffield, S9 3RP.
PC Models, 2 Marsh Lane, Birmingham, B23 6NX. Manufacturers of 4 mm fine scale tramway track system. They produce grooved rail and parts for

points and crossovers. The track must be made up, but can be constructed to any gauge and radius of curve. It is the nearest to exact scale tram rail ever produced.

Tramalan Components, The Tram Terminus, Colyton, Seaton, Devon. There is a system of converting model railway track to street tramway by laying flexible cobble strip.

Where to see preserved tramcars
Horse trams
London street tramways One side restored and displayed at the National Tramway Museum, Crich.

London Tramways Company Preserved and displayed, awaiting restoration, at the London Transport Collection, Covent Garden.

Electric trams
London County Council No 106 Restored and running at the National Tramway Museum, Crich.

Metropolitan Electric Tramways No 331 Preserved and displayed, awaiting restoration, at the National Tramway Museum, Crich.

Metropolitan Electric Tramways No 355 Restored and displayed at the London Transport Collection, Covent Garden.

London Transport No 1 Preserved, repainted and displayed at the National Tramway Museum, Crich.

London Transport No 290 Restored and displayed at the London Transport Collection, Covent Garden.

London Transport No 1025 Restored and displayed at the London Transport Collection, Covent Garden.

London Transport No 1622 Under active restoration by London County Council Tramways Trust, Bonwell Street Depot, Bethnal Green.

London Transport No 1858 Restored and running at East Anglia Transport Museum, Carlton Colville. This tramcar may run in Blackpool during the centenary of their tramways in 1985.

Photographs of London trams
W.J. Haynes: 18 Lamberts Field, off Rye Close, Bourton on the Water, Cheltenham, Glos, GL54 2EH. This specialist transport photographer offers a large and comprehensive range of photographs of trams, trolleybuses, buses and coaches from systems all over the country. The London tramway system is particularly well covered.

Mumbles Railway Company: 46 Townhill Road, Sketty, Swansea, SA2 0UR (postal only). Specialist transport postcard publisher and distributor with an extensive range of coloured postcards of British and European tramcars. Of particular interest are the colour cards of LCC and London Transport trams.

Appendix 2

List of books about London's tramways

Note: Those marked with an asterisk were in print or under preparation at the time of writing.

Books including details of specific systems

Barking Urban District Council *The Tramways of East London,* by 'Rodinglea', pub TLRS & LRTL; **Tramways in Metropolitan Essex Vol 2,* by V.E. Burrows, pub Author.

Bexley Urban District Council *The Tramways of Woolwich & South East London,* by 'Southeastern', pub LRTL & TLRS.

Croydon Corporation **The Tramways of Croydon (Revised Edition),* by G.E. Baddley, pub LRTA & TLRS; *The Tramways of South London and Croydon 1899-1949,* by K.G. Harrie, pub Author.

Dartford Urban District Council *The Tramways of Woolwich & South East London,* by 'Southeastern', pub LRTL & TLRS.

East Ham Corporation *The Tramways of East London,* by 'Rodinglea', pub TLRS & LRTL; **Tramways in Metropolitan Essex Vol 2,* by V.E. Burrows, pub Author.

Erith Urban District Council *The Tramways of Woolwich & South East London,* by 'Southeastern', pub LRTL & TLRS.

Gravesend and Northfleet Electric Tramways *The Tramways of Kent Vol 1,* by 'Invicta', pub LRTL & TLRS.

Ilford Corporation *The Tramways of East London,* by 'Rodinglea', pub TLRS & LRTL; **Trams and Trolleybuses in Ilford,* by L.A. Thomson, pub Ilford and District Historical Society; **Tramways in Metropolitan Essex Vol 2,* by V.E. Burrows, pub Author.

Leyton Corporation *The Tramways of East London,* by 'Rodinglea', pub TLRS & LRTL.

London County Council **London County Council Tramways Handbook,* by 'Kennington', pub TLRS; *The Tramways of Woolwich & South East London,* by 'Southeastern', pub LRTL & TLRS; *London County Council Tramways, the Pullman Review,* reprinted LRTL; *Trams in Wandsworth and Battersea,* by C. Dunbar, pub LRTL; **London's Tramway Subway,* by C. Dunbar, pub LRTL; **LCCT 106,* by E.R. Oakley, pub London County Council Tramways Trust; *Tramways in Metropolitan Essex Vol 1,* by V.E. Burrows, pub Advertiser Press; *Trams in Eltham 1910-1952,* by J. Kennett, pub The Eltham Society; **The Wheels Used to Talk to Us,* by T. Cooper,

pub Tallis; *The Tramways of South London and Croydon 1899-1949*, by K.G. Harrie, pub Author; *The LCC Trailers,* by M.J.D. Willsher, pub LRTA; *LCC History in three volumes,* by E.R. Oakley, under preparation.
London Transport *London Transport Tramways Handbook,* by D.W. Willoughby & E.R. Oakley, pub by the Authors; *London Tramway Memories*, by H. Ellis, pub LRTL; *ABC of London Transport Trams and Trolleybuses*, by S.L. Poole, pub Ian Allan; *Trams in Wandsworth and Battersea*, by C. Dunbar, pub LRTL; *London's Tramway Subway,* by C. Dunbar, pub LRTL; *Trams in Eltham 1910-1952,* by J. Kennett, pub The Eltham Society; *The Wheels Used to Talk to Us*, by T. Cooper, pub Tallis; *The Tramways of South London and Croydon 1899-1949*, by K.G. Harrie, pub Author; *London Trams in Camera*, by J. Thompson, pub Ian Allan; *Special, London's Non-Standard Trams and Track 1946-1952,* by D. Thompson, pub Sheaf Publishing; *The Felthams*, by K.C. Blacker, pub Dryhurst Publications; *The Felthams of North London's Tramways 1938-1952,* by J. Barrie, pub LRTL.
London United Tramways, *London United Tramways,* by G. Wilson, pub George Allen & Unwin; *London United Tramways,* by B. Connelly, pub TLRS; *The Felthams,* by K.C. Blacker, pub Dryhurst Publications; *The Feltham Car,* reprinted LRTL.
Metropolitan Electric Tramways *The Metropolitan Electric Tramways,* by T. A. Gibbs, pub TLRS; *The Felthams,* by K.C. Blacker, pub Dryhurst Publications; *The Feltham Car*, reprinted LRTL; *The Metropolitan Electric Tramways, Vol 1,* by C.S. Smeeton, pub LRTA and TLRS; *The Metropolitan Electric Tramways, Vol 2,* by C.S. Smeeton, under preparation.
South Metropolitan Electric Tramways *The Tramways of Croydon (Revised Edition),* by G.E. Baddley, pub LRTA & TLRS; *The Tramways of South London and Croydon 1899-1949,* by K.G. Harrie, pub Author.
Walthamstow Corporation *The Tramways of East London,* by 'Rodinglea', pub TLRS & LRTL.
West Ham Corporation *The Tramways of East London,* by 'Rodinglea', pub TLRS & LRTL; *Tramways in Metropolitan Essex Vol 2,* V.E. Burrows, pub Author.
Works Cars, all systems *London's Elusive Trams,* by C. Withey, *Scale Trains* December 1982 and April 1984.

General & pictorial books about London's tramways

The London Tramcar, by R.W. Kidner, pub Oakwood Press; *London Tramway Pictorial,* by D.W. Willoughby & E.R. Oakley, pub Authors; *Trams in South East London,* by D.W. Willoughby & E.R. Oakley, pub Authors; *Trams in South West London,* by D.W. Willoughby & E.R. Oakley, pub Authors; *Trams in West London,* by D.W. Willoughby & E.R. Oakley, pub Authors; *Trams in East London,* by D.W. Willoughby & E.R. Oakley, pub Authors; *Trams in Inner North London,* by D.W. Willoughby & E.R. Oakley, pub Authors; *Trams in Outer North London,* by D.W. Willoughby & E.R. Oakley, pub Authors; *Trams of Bygone London,* by M. Dryhurst, pub Dryhurst Publications; *Around London by Tram,* by T. Cooper & J. Gentry, pub Sheaf Publishing.

Books which include reference to London's tramways

Horse tramways *The British Horse Tram Era (With Special Reference to the Metropolis),* by E.R. Oakley, pub TLRS.

Steam tramways *The British Steam Tram,* by J.S. Webb, pub TLRS; *The History of The Steam Tram 1873-1947,* by H.A. Whitcombe, pub Oakwood Press.

Electric tramways *London Bus and Tram Album,* by V.H. Darling, pub Ian Allan; *London Bus and Tram Album 2nd Series*, by M. Dryhurst, pub Ian Allan; *London on Wheels, Public Transport in London in the Nineteenth Century*, pub British Transport Commission; *A History of London Transport Vol 1,* by T.C. Barker & M. Robbins, pub George Allen and Unwin; *A History of London Transport Vol 2,* by T.C. Barker & M. Robbins, pub George Allen and Unwin; *Roads and Rails of London 1900-1933,* by C.F. Klapper, pub Ian Allan; *London's Trams and Trolleybuses,* by J.R. Day, pub London Transport; *Great British Tramway Networks,* by Bett and Gilham, pub LRTL; *Trams and Trolleybuses of 1950's,* by J. Thompson, pub Ian Allan; *British Trams in Camera*, by J. Thompson, pub Ian Allan; *The Southerden Tramway Scene 1925-1935,* by V.E. Burrows, pub Glasney Press; *British Electric Tramways*, E. Jackson-Stevens, pub David & Charles; *British Trams,* by L.F. Folkard, pub Bradford Barton; *Tramway Memories,* by J. Joyce, pub Ian Allan; *Tramway Heyday,* by J. Joyce, pub Ian Allan; *The Golden Age of Tramways,* by C.F. Klapper, pub Routledge and Kegan Paul; *Tramcar Treasury*, by D. Gill, pub George Allen and Unwin; *The British Tram,* by F.E. Wilson, pub Model and Allied Publications Ltd; *Trams in Colour Since 1945,* by J. Joyce, pub Blandford; *The Brush Electrical Engineering Co. Ltd. and It's Tramcars,* by J.H. Price, pub TLRS; *Hurst Nelson Tramcars,* by J.H. Price, pub Nemo Publications; *British Electric Car Co. Ltd,* by J.H. Price, pub Nemo Publications; *Mountain and Gibson,* by J.H. Price, pub Nemo Publications; *Ally Pally, The Alexandra Palace — Its Transport and Its Troubles,* by C.T. Goode, pub Forge Books.

Books on tramway modelling

How to go Tram and Tramway Modelling, by David Voice, pub Patrick Stephens Ltd.

Useful magazines

The Bulletin, pub The Tramway and Light Railway Society; *Tramway Review,* pub The Light Rail Transit Association; *Modern Tramway,* pub The Light Rail Transit Association; *The Journal,* pub The Tramway Museum Society.

Index

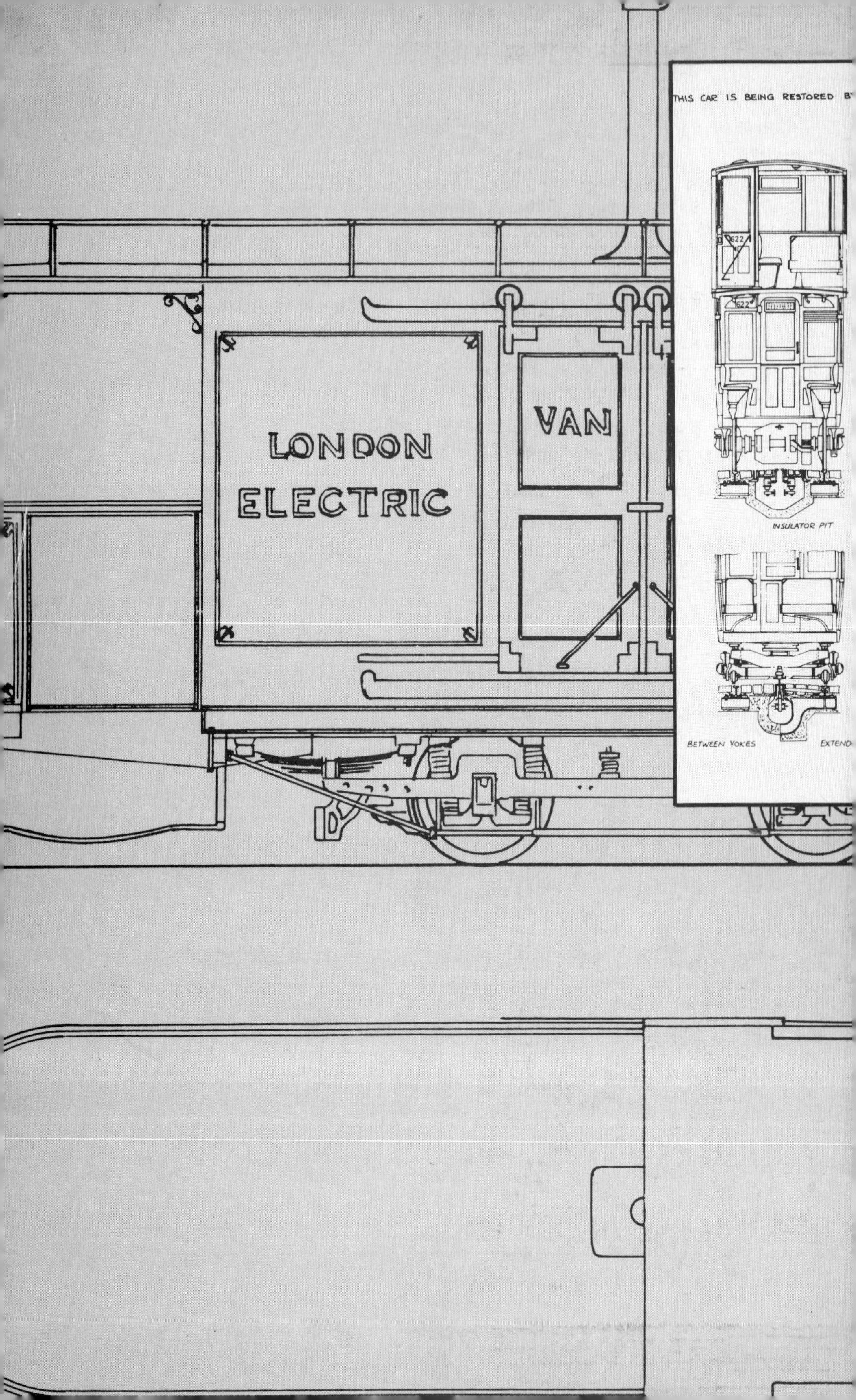

LONDON
ELECTRIC
VAN
THIS CAR IS BEING RESTORED B
622
622
INSULATOR PIT
BETWEEN YOKES
EXTEND